# THE NEW BOOK
# OF
# CHRISTIAN PRAYERS

# THE NEW BOOK
# OF
# CHRISTIAN PRAYERS

*Compiled by*

**Tony Castle**

CROSSROAD • NEW YORK

1986

The Crossroad Publishing Company
370 Lexington Avenue, New York, N.Y. 10017

Copyright © 1986 by Tony Castle

Printed in the United States of America

**Library of Congress Cataloging-in-Publication Data**

The New book of Christian prayers.

   Includes indexes
   1. Prayers. I. Castle, Tony.
BV245.N49 1986     242'.8     86-11581
ISBN 0-8245-0781-9

# CONTENTS

# INTERCESSORY PRAYERS

# OCCASIONAL PRAYERS

# INTRODUCTION

Our relationship with the Risen Christ, like any relationship, cannot develop and deepen without regular communication; to grow in prayer is to grow in the Christian life. This book was compiled to be a stimulant to and a resource for prayer.

For nearly two millennia, Christians have formulated and recorded prayers for use in public and private worship. Christianity is essentially a community Faith, as the early Christians appreciated immediately after Pentecost Day (Acts 2:42–7), and many of the prayers which have come down to us were originally gathered together for use in public worship. With the passing of time the appreciation grew that the Christian family included not only the living members of the Church but also those who had gone before. In using the prayers of our Christian heritage – those of the early Christians, the Medievals, the Reformers or the Victorians – the teaching we have received of the Communion of Saints (Heb 12:1) becomes a living reality. Solidarity with the Christians of the past, raising our minds and hearts to God in their words, must enrich our common bond in the love of God.

While the ideal, in private prayer, is to express ourselves in our own words, or the words of Scripture, there are occasions, for example in times of tiredness, sickness, grief or depression, when the desire and need to pray is not matched by the ability. Then the prayers of others, praying from a like situation, are quite literally, a God-send.

Essentially, this book is intended to be a practical support to those who wish to pray, but, like a kaleidoscope reflecting the changing pattern of prayer over the centuries, it provides an opportunity to learn a little of those who first prayed these prayers. The extensive indices give not only the authors' names and dates but also a little information about their lives and historical setting. Every century is represented, each major Christian tradition and each continent. There are prayers of saints and sinners, poets and playwrights, pastors and politicians, mums and mystics (the two are not mutually exclusive) – all of them sharing with us their struggle to give expression to their living relationship with God.

While the prayers are arranged thematically, it is of interest to compare the prayers from the different ages of Church history; the prayers of the early Christians, with their unmistakable Jewish roots, with those of the martyrs seeding the Church: the more developed theology of the Fathers' prayers with the devotional approach of the Medievals or the fresh vitality of the Reformers: the stylised, structured, Victorian prayers with the liberated expressions of the Moderns.

By the very nature of prayer, no compilation of prayers can be complete and suffers from the limitation of being one person's selection. An effort has been made to include most of the famous and familiar prayers, with others of interest and appeal. However, if your favourite prayer is not included, I beg your pardon and hope that you will find new favourites from amongst the hundreds in this book. I am grateful to Mrs Sheila Marchant and Mrs Jaquie Galley for typing the manuscript.

Tony Castle

# ACKNOWLEDGMENTS

The editor wishes to express his gratitude to the following for granting permission to reproduce material of which they are the publisher, author or copyright holder. An asterisk indicates that the prayer has been adapted.

The British Broadcasting Corporation for prayers from *New Every Morning*.

Darton, Longman and Todd Ltd. for two prayers by Metropolitan Anthony Bloom from *Living Prayer*, published and copyright 1980, by Darton, Longman and Todd Ltd.

Oxford University Press for prayers by John Baillie from *A Diary of Private Prayer*. William Heinemann Ltd. for two prayers by Malcom Boyd from his book, *Are You Running With Me, Jesus?*

Augsburg Publishing House of Minneapolis for two prayers by J. Barrie Shepherd from *Diary of Daily Prayer*.

The Lutheran Publishing House of Adelaide, Australia, for the prayers of Bruce Prewer first published in *Australian Prayers* and *Australian Psalms*: the prayers of Terry Falla from *Be Our Freedom, Lord*.

The Presbyterian Publishing House of Atlanta, Georgia, for the prayers of William Kadel from *Prayers For Every Need*.

St. Paul Publications for three prayers from *To Him Be Praise* edited by Costante Berselli.

Faber and Faber Publishers for three prayers by Dag Hammarskjold from *Markings* translated by W. H. Auden and Leif Sjoberg; also an extract, *Choruses From the Rock* by T. S. Eliot from *Collected Poems 1909–1962* by T. S. Eliot.

The Longman Group for a number of early Christian prayers from the compilation, by M. Hamman, called *Early Christian Prayers*; also a prayer by Eric Milner-White, from *A Cambridge Bede Book*.

Messrs. A. R. Mowbray for prayers from *The Prayer Manual*, compiled by Frederick B. Macnutt: also a prayer by Richard Harries and 'Lord Jesus Christ' from *Praise in all our days*, a Taize prayer; also the prayer, 'O God the Father of all' by Mother Teresa and Brother Roger, taken from *The Wonder of Love* and published by A. R. Mowbray with the approval of Taize.

The Society for Promoting Christian Knowledge for an extract from *My God, My Glory* by Eric Milner-White; extracts from *One Man's Prayer* by George Appleton; a prayer by Amy Carmichael from *Edges of His Ways*; prayers by Canon Frank Colquhoun from *Family Prayers*, copyright Frank Colquhoun, published by Triangle/S.P.C.K. 1984.

The Grail for the use of the prayer that bears their name.

The Very Rev. Canon Charles Walker for the use of the prayer of the Jesus Caritas Fraternity.

Christian Aid for two prayers from *Caring For God's World* (1971) by Geoffrey Hyder and Tony Hodgson.

The Abbey Trustees of Downside Abbey for the use of the prayers of Hubert van Zeller O.S.B.

Marshall Pickering for the prayers of Flora Larsson from *Just a Moment, Lord*.

Mr Edward England of Edward England Books for the prayers of Leslie Weatherhead from *A Private House of Prayer*, published by Arthur James Ltd.

The Mothers' Union for a prayer from their M.U. prayer book.

The Rev. John R. W. Stott for a prayer first published in *Prayers for use at the Alternative Services* by A. R. Mowbray.

The Very Rev. Alan Warren for one of his prayers.

Hodder and Stoughton Ltd. for five prayers by Jamie Wallace from *A Month of Sundays*; also five prayers by Monsignor Michael Buckley, first published in *The Treasury of the Holy Spirit*: eight prayers by Canon Frank Colquhoun from *Parish Prayers* (1967); four from *New Parish Prayers*; four prayers from *Contemporary Parish Prayers*; one prayer by Leonard Barnett from *A New Prayer Diary*.

William Collins, Publishers, for the prayers of William Barclay from *A Plain Man's Book of Prayers*; two prayers of Mother Teresa from *A Gift of God* and material from *Le Milieu Divin* by Teilhard de Chardin.

Fontana Paperbacks for the use of an extract from *Treat Me Cool, Lord* by Carl Burke.

Curtis Brown Ltd. of New York for one prayer by Thomas Merton from *Thoughts in Solitude*.

S.C.M. Press for the prayers of Rex Chapman taken from *A Kind of Praying*, *Out of the Whirlwind* and *Book of Prayer for Students*; the prayers of Caryl Micklem from *Contemporary Prayers for Modern Worship*; the prayers of Dietrich Bonhoeffer from *Letters and Papers from Prison*.

Sheed and Ward Ltd. for the prayers of Caryll Houselander.

Gill and Macmillan Ltd. of Dublin for the prayers of Michel Quoist from *Prayers of Life*.

The Reverend Dick Williams for contacting and obtaining approval from contributors to his *More Prayers for Today's Church*, published by Kingsway Publications Ltd.

Macmillan of London and Basingstoke for prayers by Carmen Bernos de Gasztold from *Prayers from the Ark*.

The Reverend Llewellyn Cumings for one of his prayers published in *Family Prayers* published by Triangle/S.P.C.K.

The Reverend Basil Naylor for the use of several of his prayers.

The Episcopal Church of the U.S.A. for prayers from their prayer book.

The Iona Community for one of their prayers.

Prayers by Huub Oosterhuis are reprinted from *Your Word Is Near*, copyright by the Missionary Society of St. Paul the Apostle in the State of New York; used by permission of Paulist Press; first published in the Dutch language by Uitgeverij Ambo, copyright 1966.

Seabury Press for two prayers by Alan Paton taken from *Instrument of Thy Peace*.

Doubleday and Co. Inc. for a prayer by Henri Nouwen from *The Difficulties of Praying*.

Forward Movement Publications for two prayers by Monica Furlong.

Griffin House Press for a prayer by Jean Vanier from *Tears of Silence*.

Mayhew-McCrimmon Ltd. for the prayers of Michael Hollings and Etta Gullick (separately and together) from *The One who Listens* and *The Shade of His Hand*.

While every effort has been made to trace copyright holders, and ascribe prayers correctly, if there should be any error or omission, the publishers will be happy to rectify this at the first opportunity.

# I  RELATIONSHIP WITH GOD

## IN TRINITY OF PERSONS

1 O Lord God, almighty, immortal, invisible, the mysteries of whose being are unsearchable; accept, we beseech thee, our praises for the revelation which thou hast made of thyself, Father, Son, and Holy Spirit, three persons and one God; and mercifully grant that, ever holding fast this faith, we may magnify thy glorious name; who livest and reignest, one God, world without end. Amen

*John Dowden*

2 Blessing and honour, thanksgiving and praise
more than we can utter be unto thee,
O most adorable Trinity, Father, Son and Holy Ghost,
by all angels, all men, all creatures
for ever and ever Amen and Amen.
To God the Father, who first loved us,
and made us accepted in the Beloved;
To God the Son who loved us,
and washed us from our sins in his own blood;
To God the Holy Ghost,
who sheds the love of God abroad in our hearts
be all love and all glory for time and for eternity. Amen

*Thomas Ken*

3 You, O eternal Trinity, are a deep sea, into which the more I enter the more I find, and the more I find the more I seek. The soul cannot be satiated in your abyss, for she continually hungers after you, the eternal Trinity, desiring to see you with the light of your light. As the heart desires the springs of living water, so my soul desires to leave the prison of this dark body and see you in truth.

O abyss, O eternal Godhead, O sea profound, what more

could you give me than yourself? You are the fire that ever
burns without being consumed; you consume in your heat all
the soul's self-love; you are the fire which takes away cold;
with your light you illuminate me so that I may know all your
truth. Clothe me, clothe me with yourself, eternal truth, so
that I may run this mortal life with true obedience, and with
the light of your most holy faith.

*St Catherine of Siena*

4 I am bending my knee
In the eye of the Father who created me,
In the eye of the Son who purchased me,
In the eye of the Spirit who cleansed me,
In friendship and affection.
Through Thine own Anointed One, O God,
Bestow upon us fullness in our need,
Love towards God,
The affection of God,
The smile of God,
The wisdom of God,
The grace of God,
The fear of God,
And the will of God,
To do on the world of the Three,
As angels and saints
Do in heaven;
Each shade and light,
Each day and night,
Each time in kindness,
Give Thou us Thy Spirit.

*Gaelic Prayer*

5 O Lord Almighty, Father unbegotten, upon us miserable
    sinners,
Have mercy.
O Lord, who hast redeemed the work of Thy hands by Thine
    only Son,
Have mercy upon us.
O Lord, Adonai, blot out our offences, and upon Thy people
Have mercy.
O Christ, Brightness of the Father's glory, and the express
    image of His person,
Have mercy upon us.

O Christ, who didst save the world at the command of the
   Father,
Have mercy upon us.
O Christ, Saviour of men, eternal Life of Angels,
Have mercy upon us.
O Lord, Spirit, the Comforter, Dispenser of pardon,
Have mercy upon us.
O Lord, Fountain of mercy and of sevenfold grace,
Have mercy upon us.
O Lord, most pitiful Forgiver, proceeding from Both,
O most bountiful Giver of gifts, Teacher, Quickener, of Thy
   goodness
Have mercy upon us.

*Sarum Missal*


6 Almighty God in Trinity
   From all my heart be thanks to thee
   For thy good deed, that thou me wrought,
   And with thy precious blood me bought,
   And for all good thou lends to me,
   O Lord God, blessed may thou be!
   All honour, joy and all loving
   Be to thy name without ending. Amen

*Richard Rolle*


7 Batter my heart, three-person'd God, for you
   As yet but knock, breathe, shine, and seek to mend.
   That I may rise and stand, o'erthrow me, and bend
   Your force to break, blow, burn, and make me new.
   I, like an usurp'd town, to another due
   Labour to admit you, but O, to no end!
   Reason, your viceroy in me, me should defend,
   But is captiv'd and proves weak or untrue.

   Yet dearly I love you, and would be loved fain,
   But am betrothed unto your enemy;
   Divorce me, untie, or break that knot again,
   Take me to you, imprison me, for I
   Except you enthral me, never shall be free,
   Nor ever chaste, except you ravish me.

*John Donne*

**8** Let thy mighty outstretched arm, O Lord God, be our defence; thy mercy and loving kindness in Jesus Christ, thy dear Son, our salvation; thy all true word our instruction; the grace of thy life-giving Spirit our comfort and consolation, unto the end and in the end; through the same Jesus Christ our Lord.

*Knox's Book of Common Order*

**9** Almighty God, you have revealed to your Church your eternal Being of glorious majesty and perfect love as one God in Trinity of Persons: give us grace to continue steadfast in the confession of this faith, and constant in our worship of you, Father, Son, and Holy Spirit; for you live and reign, one God, now and for ever.

*Episcopal Church, USA*

# GOD THE FATHER

**10** O thou whose pow'r o'er moving worlds presides,
Whose voice created, and whose wisdom guides,
On darkling man in pure effulgence shine,
And clear the clouded mind with light divine.
'Tis thine alone to calm the pious breast
With silent confidence and holy rest:
From thee, great God, we spring, to thee we tend,
Path, motive, guide, original, and end.

*Boethius*

**11** God is what thought cannot better; God is whom thought cannot reach; God no thinking can even conceive. Without God, men can have no being, no reason, no knowledge, no good desire, naught. Thou, O God, art what thou art, transcending all.

*Eric Milner-White*

**12** Thou mastering me
God! giver of breath and bread;
World's strand, sway of the sea;
Lord of living and dead;
Thou hast bound bones and veins in me,

Fastened me flesh,
And after it almost unmade, what with dread,
Thy doing; and dost thou touch me afresh?
Over again I feel thy finger and find thee.

*Gerard Manley Hopkins*

13 O Supreme and Unapproachable Light! O Whole and Blessed
Truth, how far thou art from me, who am so near to thee! How
far art thou removed from my vision, though I am so near to
thine! Everywhere thou art wholly present, and I see thee not.
In thee I move, and in thee I have my being, and cannot come
to thee; thou art within me, and about me, and I feel thee
not.

*St Anselm*

14 O Thou who art unchangeable, whom nothing changes! Thou
who art unchangeable in love, precisely for our welfare not
submitting to any change: may we too will our welfare,
submitting ourselves to the discipline of Thy unchangeableness, so that we may, in unconditional obedience, find our rest
in Thy unchangeableness.

*Søren Kierkegaard*

15 O eternal and most gracious God, the God of security, and the
enemy of security too, who wouldst have us always sure of thy
love, and yet wouldst have us always doing something for it,
let me always so apprehend thee, as present with me, and
yet to follow after thee, as though I had not apprehended
thee.

*John Donne*

16 Lord, what am I, that, with unceasing care,
Thou didst seek after me – that Thou didst wait,
Wet with unhealthy dews, before my gate,
And pass the gloomy nights of winter there?
How oft my guardian angel gently cried,
'Soul, from thy casement look, and thou shalt see
How He persists to watch and wait for thee!'
And oh! how often to that voice of sorrow
'Tomorrow we will open,' I replied,
And when the morrow came, I answered still 'Tomorrow!'

*Henry Longfellow*

**17** O God, Thou art Life, Wisdom, Truth, Bounty, and Blessedness, the Eternal, the only true Good. My God and my Lord,
Thou art my hope and my heart's joy.

I confess, with thanksgiving, that Thou hast made me in
Thine image, that I may direct all my thoughts to Thee, and
love Thee.

Lord, make me to know Thee aright, that I may more and
more love, enjoy, and possess Thee. And since, in the life
here below, I cannot fully attain this blessedness, let it at least
grow in me day by day, until it all be fulfilled at last in the life
to come.

Here be the knowledge of Thee increased, and there let it
be perfected. Here let my love of Thee grow, and there let it
ripen; that my joy being here great in hope, may there in
fruition be made perfect.

*St Anselm*

**18** My God, my God, let me for once look on thee
As though nought else existed, we alone!
And as creation crumbles, my soul's spark
Expands till I can say – Even for myself
I need thee and I feel thee and I love thee.

*Robert Browning*

**19** Lord, teach me to seek thee,
and reveal thyself to me
when I seek thee.
For I cannot seek thee
except thou teach me,
nor find thee
except thou reveal thyself.
Let me seek thee in longing,
let me long for thee in seeking:
let me find thee in love
and love thee in finding.

*St Anselm*

**20** Eternal God, who are the light of the minds that know you,
the joy of the hearts that love you, and the strength of the wills
that serve you; grant us so to know you, that we may truly love
you, and so to love you that we may fully serve you, whom to
serve is perfect freedom, in Jesus Christ our Lord.

*St Augustine of Hippo*

**21** Give me, O Lord, a steadfast heart which no unworthy thought can drag downwards; an unconquered heart which no tribulation can wear out; an upright heart which no unworthy purpose may tempt aside. Bestow upon me also, O Lord my God, understanding to know thee, diligence to seek thee, wisdom to find thee, and a faithfulness that may finally embrace thee; through Jesus Christ, our Lord.

*St Thomas Aquinas*

**22** Lord of all power and might, who art the author and giver of all good things: graft in our hearts the love of thy name, increase in us true religion, nourish us with all goodness, and of thy great mercy keep us in the same; through Jesus Christ our Lord.

*Book of Common Prayer*

**23** Most loving Father, who hast taught us to dread nothing save the loss of Thee, preserve me from faithless fears and worldly anxieties, from corrupting passions and unhallowed love of earthly treasures; and grant that no clouds of this mortal life may hide me from the light of that love which is immortal and which Thou hast manifested unto us in Thy Son, Jesus Christ our Lord.

*William Bright*

**24** Grant, Lord, that we may hold to you without parting, worship you without wearying, serve you without failing; faithfully seek you, happily find you, and for ever possess you, the only God, blessed, now and for ever.

*St Anselm*

**25** Speak, gracious Lord, oh speak; thy servant hears:
For I'm thy servant and I'll still be so:
Speak words of comfort in my willing ears;
And since my tongue is in thy praises slow,
And since that thine all rhetoric exceeds;
Speak thou in words, but let me speak in deeds!

*Alexander Pope*

**26** Our Father in heaven, deliver us, we pray thee, from all manner of evil, whether it touch our body or soul, our property or good name, and at last, when the hour of death shall come, grant us a blessed end and graciously take us from this vale of sorrow to thyself in heaven, through Jesus Christ, thy Son, our Lord. Amen

*Martin Luther*

27 I bless thee, my Father and my Friend, for all that thou hast given me, and for all that thou hast taken from me; for all my trials and sorrows, as well as for all my joys. Thou hast mercifully led me through this wilderness, and hast borne with my many shortcomings and evil-doings. Thou art indeed most gracious and glorious, a Father of mercies, and a God of love. Rouse this sluggish heart of mine, and fill it with gratitude. And be with me, Lord, for the time to come. I know not what is before me, but thou knowest. Choose thou my portion for me. Lead me by thine own hand; and keep me close to thee, day by day, and night by night. My Father, I wish to love and obey thee. Take my heart, for I cannot give it to thee; and put away everything that hinders me from being altogether thine. Amen

*Ashton Oxenden*

28 Write Thy blessed name, O Lord, upon my heart, there to remain so indelibly engraved, that no prosperity, no adversity shall ever move me from Thy love. Be Thou to me a strong tower of defence, a comforter in tribulation, a deliverer in distress, a very present help in trouble, and a guide to heaven through the many temptations and dangers of this life.

*Thomas à Kempis*

29 Father! what hast Thou grown to now?
A joy all joys above,
Something more sacred than a fear,
More tender than a love!
With gentle swiftness lead me on,
Dear God! to see Thy face;
And meanwhile in my narrow heart
Oh make Thyself more space!

*Frederick Faber*

30 Grant me to recognise in other men, Lord God,
the radiance of your own face.

*Teilhard de Chardin*

31 Father in heaven, when the thought of you wakes in our hearts, let it not wake like a frightened bird that flies about in

dismay, but like a child waking from its sleep with a heavenly smile.

*Søren Kierkegaard*

**32** Lord, God almighty, Father of Jesus Christ, your beloved Child, through whom we have come to know you, God of the angels and powers, God of all creation, God of the race that lives in your presence, the race of the just.

I bless you because you have thought me worthy of this day and hour and worthy to be numbered among the martyrs and to drink the chalice of your Christ so as to rise and live for ever, body and soul, in the immortality of the Holy Spirit.

May I be numbered among the martyrs in your presence, a satisfying and acceptable sacrifice. You have made my life a preparation for this; you showed me that this was to be and now you have brought it about, like the faithful and true God that you are. I praise you and give you glory, through the eternal high priest, Jesus Christ your beloved Son. Through Him and with Him and with the Holy Spirit may glory be given to you now through all ages. Amen

*Polycarp of Smyrna*
*(his final prayer)*

**33** Most worthy art thou, O good and gracious God, of all praise, even for thine own sake which exceedeth all things in holiness. By thee only are we hallowed and made holy. As our duty continually bids us, we praise thee for our glorious redemption, purchased for us in thy dearly beloved Son, Jesus Christ. Give us, therefore, the Holy Spirit to govern us. And grant that all things that breathe with life may praise thee, through the same Jesus Christ, our Lord, who reigneth with thee and the Holy Ghost, one God for ever and ever.

*The Iona Books*

**34** You are a father and a mother to me, a brother, a friend; you manage my house for me;
you are all that is, and all that is is in you; you are that which exists, and nothing else exists, save only you.
You too, brothers, should take refuge with him. When you have learned that you exist in him alone, the things of which you are told that 'no eye has seen, no ear has heard, no human heart conceived' them, will be yours.
We ask you for what you promised to give us, Jesus undefiled.
We praise you and thank you; we give you glory, men though

we are and weak; we acknowledge that you alone are God and
that there is no other for all eternity. Amen

*Acts of Peter*

**35** Almighty God, unto whom all hearts are open, all desires
known, and from whom no secrets are hid; cleanse the
thoughts of our hearts by the inspiration of thy Holy Spirit,
that we may perfectly love thee, and worthily magnify thy holy
name, through Jesus Christ our Lord. Amen

*Gregorian Sacramentary*

**36** O gracious and holy Father, give us wisdom to perceive thee,
diligence to seek thee, patience to wait for thee, eyes to
behold thee, a heart to meditate upon thee, and a life to
proclaim thee; through the power of the Spirit of Jesus Christ
our Lord.

*St Benedict of Nursia*

**37** O God, the Father of our Saviour Jesus Christ, Whose name is
great, Whose nature is blissful, Whose goodness is inexhaustible, God and Ruler of all things, Who art blessed forever;
before Whom stand thousands and thousands, and ten
thousand times ten thousand, the hosts of holy angels and
archangels; sanctify, O Lord, our souls and bodies and spirits,
search our consciences, and cast out of us every evil thought,
every base desire, all envy and pride, all wrath and anger, and
all that is contrary to Thy holy will. And grant us, O Lord,
Lover of men, with a pure heart and contrite soul, to call upon
Thee, our holy God and Father Who art in heaven.

*Liturgy of St James*

**38** May he who created everything
keep the number of his chosen people, throughout the
    world,
up to the strength he determined
through his dear servant, Jesus Christ.
Through him he called us from darkness to light,
from ignorance to knowledge of the glory of his name.

We have confidence in you:
you were at the beginning of creation;
you have opened our inward eyes
to give us knowledge of you,
who alone are the Most High, in highest heaven,
the Holy One, at ease among the holy.

We implore you, Lord, to help and defend us.
Deliver the oppressed, pity the insignificant,
raise the fallen, show yourself to the needy,
heal the sick,
bring back those of your people who have gone astray,
feed the hungry, lift up the weak,
take off the prisoners' chains.
May every nation come to know
that you alone are God,
that Jesus Christ is your servant,
that we are your people, the sheep of your pasture.
Do not count all your servants' sins,
but cleanse us with the cleanness of your truth
and guide our steps towards holiness,
so that we may do what is just and pleasing
to you and those placed over us.
Let us see your face, Lord,
and we shall peacefully pursue what is good,
protected by your strong hand,
kept from all sin by your mighty arm,
preserved from those who hate us without cause.

Give concord and peace
to us and to all living on the earth,
as you gave them to our fathers
when they prayed to you, believing truly,
ready to obey the All Powerful, the All Holy.

To those who rule and lead us on the earth
you, Lord,
have given them authority and kingship.
Grant them, Lord,
the health, peace, concord and stability
to use aright
the sovereignty you have bestowed on them.
Lord, may all they do conform
to what is good and pleasing to you,
that using with reverence, peacefully, gently,
the power you have given them,
they may find favour with you.

You alone have the means to do this for us,
and we thank you for it through Jesus Christ,
the High Priest, our souls' defender.

Glory and splendour be yours through him,
now and in every generation,
age after age. Amen

*Clement of Rome**

**39** Be thou my vision, O Lord of my heart,
Be all else but naught to me, save that thou art;
Be thou my best thought in the day and the night,
Both waking and sleeping, thy presence my light.
Be thou my wisdom, be thou my true word,
Be thou ever with me, and I with thee, Lord;
Be thou my great Father, and I thy true son;
Be thou in me dwelling, and I with thee one.
Be thou my breastplate, my sword for the fight;
Be thou my whole armour, be thou my true might;
Be thou my soul's shelter, be thou my strong tower;
O raise thou me heavenward, great power of my power.
Riches I heed not, nor man's empty praise;
Be thou mine inheritance now and always;
Be thou and thou only the first in my heart;
O sovereign of heaven, my treasure thou art.
High king of heaven, thou heaven's bright sun
O grant me its joys after vict'ry is won;
Great heart of my own heart, whatever befall,
Still be thou my vision, O ruler of all.

*Celtic Prayer*
*(translated by Mary Byrne (1880–1931)*
*versified by Eleanor Hull (1860–1935) )*

**40** We thank you, holy Father, for your holy name, which you
have made to dwell in our hearts, and for the knowledge, faith
and immortality which you have made known to us through
your servant Jesus: to you be glory for ever.

*Didache*

**41** O God, watch over me always, in my work, in my words, in
the thoughts of my heart.
O God, have pity on me, in this world and in the world to
come.
O God, have pity on me, for I have sinned against you like
the mortal that I am; but, kind and gentle Master, forgive
me.
O God, may I not be afraid or disturbed when the time
comes for my soul to leave my body.

O God, do not be angry then and rebuke me, do not give
vent to wrath and punish me.

O God, do not show me the anger that my sins and misdeeds
deserve.

O God, do not hide your face from me when I come before
you, do not turn away from me when you pronounce your
sentence on our lives – the lives we have lived openly and
the lives that have been ours in secret.

O God, your Word was made flesh for me; for me he was
crucified, died, was buried and on the third day rose again.
Bind me to you, and let no evil spirit lord it over me and
snatch me out of your hands.

O God, do not let me give way to disloyalty. May the Enemy
find nothing in me that he can call his own.

O God, sharpen my will. May it be like a sword and cut all
sinful thoughts out of my mind.

O God, as you calmed the sea with a word, so drive out the
evil passions from my sinful nature. May sin die down and
disappear from all my members.

O God, grant that my heart may always be pure and my faith
orthodox for ever, yes for ever. Amen

*Rabbula of Edessa*

**42** Give, O Father,
perfection to beginners,
intelligence to the little ones,
aid to those who are running their course,
sorrow to the negligent,
fervour of spirit to the lukewarm,
to the perfect a good ending.

*St Irenaeus of Lyons*

**43** I appeal to you, Lord, God of Abraham, God of Isaac, God of
Jacob and Israel, you the Father of our Lord Jesus Christ.
Infinitely merciful as you are, it is your will that we should
learn to know you. You made heaven and earth, you rule
supreme over all. You are the true, the only God; there is no
other god above you. Through our Lord Jesus Christ and the
gifts of the Holy Spirit, grant that all may come to know you,
because you alone are God; let them draw strength from you;
keep them from all teaching that is heretical, irreligious or
godless.

*St Irenaeus of Lyons*

**44** O Lord, how wonderful in depth and height,
But most in man, how wonderful Thou art!
With what a love, what soft persuasive might
Victorious o'er the stubborn fleshly heart;
Thy tale complete, of saints Thou dost provide
To fill the throne which angels lost through pride!

*John Henry Newman*

**45** God, this word we call you by
is almost dead and meaningless,
transient and empty
like all the words men use.
We ask you
to renew its force and meaning,
to make it once again
a name that brings your promise to us.
Make it a living word
which tells us
that you will be for us
as you have always been –
trustworthy and hidden
and very close to us,
Our God, now and for ever.

*Huub Oosterhuis*

**46** O my God, shall I one day see thee? What sight can compare
to that great sight? Shall I see the source of that grace which
enlightens me, strengthens me, and consoles me? As I came
from thee, as I am made through thee, so, O my God, may I at
last return to thee, and be with thee for ever and ever.

*John Henry Newman*

**47** May the defence of the Most High be above and beneath,
around and within us, in our going out and in our coming in, in
our rising up and in our going down, all our days and all our
nights, until the dawn when the Son of Righteousness shall
arise with healing in His wings for the people of the world,
through Jesus Christ our Lord.

*Prayer of the Parachute Regiment*

**48** Father, forgive the cold love of the years,
While here in the silence we bow,
Perish our cowardice! Perish our fears!
Kindle us, kindle us now.

Lord, we believe, we accept, we adore.
Less than the least though we be.
Fire of love, burn in us, burn evermore
Till we burn out for Thee.

*Amy Carmichael*

**49** Good and great God! How should I fear
To come to Thee, if Christ be not there!
Could I but think, He would not be
Present, to plead my cause for me;
To Hell I'd rather run, than I
Would see Thy face, and He not by.

*Robert Herrick*

# FATHER CREATOR

**50** Now we must praise the Ruler of Heaven,
The might of the Lord and His purpose of mind,
The work of the Glorious Father; for He,
God Eternal, established each wonder,
He, Holy Creator, first fashioned the heavens
As a roof for the children of earth.
And then our Guardian, the Everlasting Lord,
Adorned this middle-earth for men.
Praise the Almighty King of Heaven.

*Caedmon*

**51** O God of mountains, stars, and boundless spaces!
O God of Freedom and of joyous hearts!
When Thy Face looketh forth from all men's faces,
There will be room enough in crowded marts:
Brood Thou around me, and the noise is o'er;
Thy universe my closet with shut door.

*George Macdonald*

**52** Lord, purge our eyes to see
Within the seed a tree,
Within the glowing egg a bird,
Within the shroud a butterfly.
Till, taught by such we see
Beyond all creatures, Thee
And hearken to Thy tender word
And hear its 'Fear not; it is I'.

*Christina Rossetti*

**53** Teach me, Father, how to go
Softly as the grasses grow;
Hush my soul to meet the shock
Of the wild world as a rock;
But my spirit, propt with power,
Make as simple as a flower.
Let the dry heart fill its cup,
Like a poppy looking up;
Let life lightly wear her crown,
Like a poppy looking down,
When its heart is filled with dew,
And its life begins anew.

Teach me, Father, how to be
Kind and patient as a tree.
Joyfully the crickets croon
Under shady oak at noon;
Beetle, on his mission bent,
Tarries in that cooling tent.
Let me, also, cheer a spot,
Hidden field or garden grot –
Place where passing souls can rest
On the way and be their best.

*Edwin Markham*


**54** O Thou, who fillest heaven and earth, ever acting, ever at rest, who art present everywhere and everywhere art wholly present, who art not absent even when far off, who with thy whole being fillest yet transcendest all things, who teachest the hearts of the faithful without the din of words; teach us, we pray Thee, through Jesus Christ our Lord.

*St Augustine of Hippo*


**55** Lord
isn't your creation wasteful?
Fruits never equal
the seedlings' abundance.
Springs scatter water.
The sun gives out
enormous light.
May your bounty teach me
greatness of heart.
May your magnificence
stop me being mean.

Seeing you a prodigal
and open-handed giver
let me give unstintingly
like a king's son
like God's own.

*Helder Camara*

**56** Almighty God, Lord of Heaven and earth, in whom we live
and move and have our being; who doest good unto all men,
making thy sun to rise on the evil and on the good, and sending
rain on the just and on the unjust: Favourably behold us thy
servants, who call upon thy name, and send us thy blessing
from heaven, in giving us fruitful seasons, and satisfying us
with food and gladness, that both our hearts and mouths may
be continually filled with thy praise, and we may ever give
thanks to thee in thy holy Church; through Jesus Christ our
Lord.

*John Cosin*

**57** Thou takest the pen – and the lines dance.
Thou takest the flute – and the notes shimmer.
Thou takest the brush – and the colours sing.
So all things have meaning and beauty in that space beyond
time
where Thou art. How, then, can I hold back anything from
Thee?

*Dag Hammarskjöld*

**58** Lord, may we love and respect all your creation, all the earth
and every grain of sand in it. May we love every leaf, every ray
of your light.
    May we love the animals: you have given them the rudi-
ments of thought and joy untroubled. Let us not trouble them;
let us not harass them, let us not deprive them of their
happiness, let us not work against your intentions.
    For we acknowledge that to withhold any measure of love
from anything in your universe is to withhold that same
measure from you.

*F. Dostoevsky*
*(adapted from The Brothers Karamazov)*

**59** Sweet sovereign Lord of this so pined-for Spring,
How breathe the homage of but one poor heart
With such small compass of Thy everything?

Ev'n though I knew this were my life's last hour,
It yet would lie, past hope, beyond my power
One instant of my gratitude to prove,
My praise, my love.

That 'Everything'! – when this, my human dust,
Whereto return I must,
Were scant to bring to bloom a single flower!

*Walter de la Mare*

**60** *Prayer of the Butterfly*
Lord!
Where was I?
Oh yes! This flower, this sun,
thank you! Your world is beautiful!
This scent of roses . . .
Where was I?
A drop of dew
rolls to sparkle in a lily's heart.
I have to go . . .
Where? I do not know!
The wind has painted fancies
on my wings.
Fancies . . .
Where was I?
Oh yes! Lord,
I had something to tell you:
Amen.

*Carmen Bernos de Gasztold*

**61** *Prayer of the Tortoise*
I am coming.
One must take nature as she is!
It was not I who made her!
I do not mean to criticize
this house on my back –
It has its points –
but you must admit, Lord,
it is heavy to carry!
Still,
let us hope that this double enclosure,
my shell and my heart,
will never be quite shut to You.

*Carmen Bernos de Gasztold*

**62** *Prayer of the Elephant*
Dear God,
it is I, the elephant,
your creature,
who is talking to you.
I am so embarrassed by my great self,
and truly it is not my fault
if I spoil your jungle with my big feet.
Let me be careful and behave wisely,
always keeping my dignity and poise.
Give me such philosophic thoughts
that I can rejoice everywhere I go
in the lovable oddity of things.

*Carmen Bernos de Gasztold*

**63** *Prayer of the Ox*
Dear God, give me time,
Men are always so driven!
Make them understand that I can never hurry.
Give me time to eat.
Give me time to plod.
Give me time to sleep.
Give me time to think.

*Carmen Bernos de Gasztold*

**64** O Little Brother Bird, that brimmest with full heart, and having naught, possessest all, surely thou dost well to sing! For thou hast life without labour, and beauty without burden, and riches without care. When thou wakest, lo, it is dawn; and when thou comest to sleep it is eve. And when thy two wings lie folded about thy heart, lo, there is rest. Therefore sing, Brother, having this great wealth, that when thou singest thou givest thy riches to all.

*St Francis of Assisi*

**65** *The Robin's Song*
God bless the field and bless the furrow,
Stream and branch and rabbit burrow,
Hill and stone and flower and tree,
From Bristol town to Wetherby –
Bless the sun and bless the sleet,
Bless the lane and bless the street,
Bless the night and bless the day,
From Somerset and all the way
To the meadows of Cathay;

Bless the minnow, bless the whale,
Bless the rainbow and the hail,
Bless the nest and bless the leaf,
Bless the righteous and the thief,
Bless the wing and the fin,
Bless the air I travel in,
Bless the mill and bless the mouse,
Bless the miller's bricken house,
Bless the earth and bless the sea,
God bless you and God bless me.

*An old English rhyme*

**66** For all the first sweet flushings of the spring;
The greening earth, the tender heavenly blue;
The rich brown furrows gaping for the seed;
For all thy grace in bursting bud and leaf . . .
For hedgerows sweet with hawthorn and wild rose;
For meadows spread with gold and gemmed with stars,
For every tint of every tiniest flower,
For every daisy smiling to the sun;
For every bird that builds in joyous hope,
For every lamb that frisks beside its dam,
For every leaf that rustles in the wind,
For spiring poplar, and for spreading oak,
For queenly birch, and lofty swaying elm;
For the great cedar's benedictory grace,
For earth's ten thousand fragrant incenses,
Sweet altar-gifts from leaf and fruit and flower . . .
For ripening summer and the harvesting;
For all the rich autumnal glories spread –
The flaming pageant of the ripening woods,
The fiery gorse, the heather-purpled hills,
The rustling leaves that fly before the wind
and lie below the hedgerows whispering;
For meadows silver-white with hoary dew;
For sheer delight of tasting once again
That first crisp breath, of winter in the air;
The pictured pane; the new white world without;
The sparkling hedgerows' witchery of lace,
The soft white flakes that fold the sleeping earth;
The cold without, the cheerier warmth within . . .
For all the glowing heart of Christmas-tide,
We thank thee, Lord!

*John Oxenham*

**67** We thank Thee for the stars wherewith Thou hast spangled the raiment of darkness, giving beauty to the world when the sun withdraws his light. All this magnificence is but a little sparklet that has fallen from Thy presence, Thou Central Fire and Radiant Light of all! These are but reflections of Thy wisdom, Thy power, and Thy glory!

*Theodore Parker*

**68** If I have faltered more or less
In my great task of happiness;
If I have moved among my race
And shown no glorious morning face;
If beams from happy human eyes
Have moved me not; if morning skies,
Books, and my food, and summer rain
Knocked on my sullen heart in vain:
Lord, thy most pointed pleasure take
And stab my spirit broad awake.

*Robert Louis Stevenson*

**69** Almighty One, in the woods I am blessed. Happy everyone in the woods. Every tree speaks through Thee. O God! What glory in the woodland! On the heights is peace – peace to serve Him.

*Ludwig van Beethoven*

**70** Let my soul praise you that it may love you, let it praise you for your mercy and kindness. Without ceasing, your whole creation speaks your praise. Man speaks his praise, animals and lifeless things praise you through those who see and speak on their behalf. Your creation helps our souls rise up to you and wonder at your love. In that wonder we find strength and refreshment.

*St Augustine of Hippo*

**71** Maker of me, go on making me, and let me help Thee. Come, oh Father, here I am: let us go on. I know that my words are those of a child, but it is Thy child that prays to Thee. It is Thy dark I walk in, it is Thy hand I hold.

*George Macdonald*

**72** O God, we thank thee for this earth, our home; for the wide sky and the blessed sun, for the salt sea and the running water, for the everlasting hills and the never-resting winds, for trees and the common grass underfoot. We thank thee for our senses by which we hear the songs of birds, and see the splendour of the summer fields, and taste of the autumn fruits, and rejoice in the feel of the snow, and smell the breath of the spring. Grant us a heart wide open to all this beauty and save our souls from being so blind that we pass unseeing when even the common thornbush is aflame with thy glory; O God, our Creator, who livest and reignest for ever and ever.

*Walter Rauschenbusch*

**73** We thank you, Lord of all creation, for the wonder of the world in which we live, for the earth and all that springs from it, and for the mystery of life and growth. We pray that our gratitude may be shown by our care to conserve the powers of the soil, by our readiness to learn from scientific research, and by our concern for a fair distribution of the earth's resources. We ask these things in the name of Christ our Lord.

*Basil Naylor*

**74** Lord, we pray Thee that Thou wilt open our eyes to behold the heaven that lies about us, wherein they walk who, being born of the new life, serve Thee with the clearer vision and the greater joy.

*Robert Louis Stevenson*

**75** Almighty God, whose glory the heavens are telling, the earth thy power and the sea thy might, and whose greatness all feeling and thinking creatures everywhere herald; To thee belongeth glory, honour, might, greatness, and magnificence, now and for ever, to the ages of ages.

*Liturgy of St James*

## CHRIST THE SON OF GOD

**76** O Christ our God, the wisdom, power and glory of the Father, who didst visibly appear to all men as the Word made flesh, and having overcome the prince of darkness, didst return to thy throne on high; Grant to us thy supplicants, amid this dark world, the full outpouring of thy splendour, and appoint the holy angels to be our defenders, to guard our going out and coming in, till we take our place at thy right hand; where thou livest and reignest with the Father and the Holy Ghost, ever one God, world without end.

*Mozarabic Sacramentary* *

**77** O Blessed Jesus, who didst use Thine own most precious life for the redemption of Thy human brethren, giving no thought to ease or pleasure or worldly enrichment, but filling up all Thine hours and days with deeds of self-denying love, give me grace today to follow the road Thou didst first tread; and to Thy name be all the glory and the praise, even unto the end.

*John Baillie*

**78** Almighty God, our heavenly Father, Who hast given us in Thy Son Jesus Christ a fountain of life, which, springing up within us, can make all things new, we thank Thee for the deeper meaning which He gives to life – for the quickened sense of duty, the faith under sorrow, the immortal hopes, which we owe to Him. And we pray that His divine instructions may be so received by us with grateful hearts, that no resistance of ours may hinder his free working within us a miracle as when He changed the water into wine. In the power of His Spirit, may our griefs be transformed into consolations, – our infirmities into strength to do well, – our sins into repentance, – our fainting and halting spirits into a heavenly mind; and, finally, the doubts, the discouragements, the trials of this earthly life, into the full assurance and unclouded bliss of an eternal life with Thee, through the same Jesus Christ our Lord. Amen

*Henry W. Foote*

**79** Lord Jesus, who didst stretch out thine arms of love on the hard wood of the cross, that all men might come within the reach of thy saving embrace, clothe us in thy spirit, that we, stretching forth our hands in loving labour for others, may bring those who know thee not, to the knowledge and love of thee, who with the Father and the Holy Ghost livest and reignest one God.

*Charles H. Brent*

**80** O Christ, you take upon yourself all our burdens so that, freed of all that weighs us down, we can constantly begin anew to walk, with lightened step, from worry towards trusting, from the shadows towards the clear flowing waters, from our own will towards the vision of the coming Kingdom. And then we know, though we hardly dared hope so, that you offer to make every human being a reflection of your face.

*Roger Schutz*

81 Saviour, I know that none other
Stumbled before Thee as I stumbled,
Or did the deeds which I worked.
But this too I know,
That the greatness of my stumblings
And the multitude of my sins
Go not beyond the measure
Of the long-suffering of my God,
Beyond the height of his loving-kindness.
These things make me to venture;
These things give me wings, O my Christ.
Therefore giving thanks in mind,
Giving thanks in heart,
Giving thanks in the members
Of my soul and of my body,
I worship Thee, I magnify Thee,
I glorify Thee, my God
That art blessed
Now and for evermore.

*Simeon, the New Theologian*

82 O blessed Jesu Christ, who didst bid all who carry heavy burdens to come to thee, refresh us with thy presence and thy power. Quiet our understandings and give ease to our hearts, by bringing us close to things infinite and eternal. Open to us the mind of God, that in his light we may see light. And crown thy choice of us to be thy servants, by making us springs of strength and joy to all whom we serve.

*Evelyn Underhill*

83 O Jesus Christ, your life focuses the light of God upon us: it stabs the darkness of untruth and shows up in clear simplicity the sin, squalor and drabness which we have allowed to sully the world. Do not let us dim your light by ignorance or scorn of what you did on earth, but make our lives shine with your light and brighten the world we live in, to the glory of our heavenly father; for your name's sake.

*Christopher R. Campling*

**84** Lord Jesus Christ, I adore you,
   you wept over Lazarus and raised him from the dead;
   I beg that I may gain eternal life,
   and that you will cause to spring up within me
   your fountain of living water,
   gushing out for eternal life.

Lord Jesus Christ, I adore you,
transfixed to the cross,
wine and myrrh to quench your thirst:
I beg that your wound may be transformed
into a medicine for my soul.

Lord Jesus Christ, I adore you, laid in the tomb:
May your death be life to me.

*Gallican Formularies*

**85** Come, Lord, work upon us, set us on fire and clasp us close, be
fragrant to us, draw us to your loveliness, let us love, let us run
to you.

*St Augustine of Hippo*

**86** O most dear Lord and Saviour; sweet Jesu, I beseech thy
most courteous goodness and benign favour to be to me, most
wretched creature, my favourable Lord, keeper and defender; and in all necessities and needs to be my shield and
protection against all mine enemies bodily and ghostly.
   Merciful Jesu, I have none other trust, hope, nor succour,
but in thee alone, my dear Lord, sweet Jesu; the which of
thine infinite goodness made me of nought, like unto thy most
excellent image. And when I was lost by my first father
Adam's sin, with thy precious blood, dear Lord, thou re-
deemedst me, and since then, ever daily, most graciously,
with thy gifts of grace most lovingly thou feedest me.
   Grant me therefore, most gracious Lord and Saviour, to
dread thee and love thee above all things in this present life,
and after in joy and bliss without end.
   Sweet Jesu. Amen

*Richard Rolle*

**87** O good Shepherd, seek me out, and bring me home to Thy
fold again. Deal favourably with me according to Thy good
pleasure, till I may dwell in Thy house all the days of my life,
and praise Thee for ever and ever with them that are there.

*St Jerome*

**88** Lord Jesus Christ
who according to the will of the Father,
through the co-operation of the Holy Ghost,
hast by Thy death given life to the world:
Deliver me.

*St Margaret of Scotland*

**89** Jesu, Lord that madest me
And with thy blessed blood has bought,
Forgive that I have grievèd thee
With word, with will and eke with thought.

Jesu, in whom is all my trust,
That died upon the high rood-tree,
Withdraw my heart from fleshly lust,
And from all worldly vanity.

Jesu, for thy sore wounds' smart
Thy feet and hands that piercèd through,
Make me meek and low of heart,
And thee to love as I should do.

Jesu, most comfort for to see
For thy dear saints both all and one,
Comfort them that care-full be,
And help them that be woe-begone.

Jesu, keep thou them that be good,
Amend them that have grievèd thee,
And send them fruits of earthly food
As each man needeth in his degree.

Jesu, for all thy blessèd blood,
Bring, if thou wilt, those souls to bliss
From whom I have had any good,
And spare what they have done amiss.

*Richard de Castre*

**90** May the love of the Lord Jesus draw us to himself;
may the power of the Lord Jesus strengthen us in his service;
may the joy of the Lord Jesus fill our souls;
and may the blessing of God Almighty, the Father, the Son,
and the Holy Ghost, be with you and abide with you always.

*William Temple*

## For the Imitation of Christ

**91** Grant, O Lord, that this mind may be in us, which was also in Christ Jesus, who left the heaven of thy holiness and of thy glory that he might take upon him our sins and our sorrows, and seek and save that which was lost. Stir the hearts of thy people that they may multiply their labours in the cause of charity and love, that they may minister to the wants of others, and by their good works lead many to glorify our Father who is in heaven; through the same Jesus Christ our Lord.

*Charles J. Vaughan*

**92** O Saviour Christ, who dost lead them to immortal blessedness, who commit themselves to Thee: Grant that we, being weak, presume not to trust in ourselves, but may always have Thee before our eyes, to follow Thee, our guide; that Thou, who only knowest the way, mayst lead us to our heavenly desire. To thee with the Father and the Holy Ghost be glory for ever.

*Primer of 1559\**

**93** O Saviour, pour upon me thy spirit of meekness and love, annihilate the selfhood in me, be thou all my life. Guide thou my hand which trembles exceedingly upon the rock of ages.

*William Blake*

**94** Set before our minds and hearts, O heavenly Father, the example of our Lord Jesus Christ, who, when he was upon earth, found his refreshment in doing the will of him that sent him, and in finishing his work. When many are coming and going, and there is little leisure, give us grace to remember him who knew neither impatience of spirit nor confusion of work, but in the midst of all his labours held communion with thee, and even upon earth was still in heaven; where now he reigneth with thee and the Holy Spirit world without end.

*Charles J. Vaughan*

**95** Jesu, as thou me made and bought,
Be thou my love and all my thought;
And help that I be to thee brought;
Withouten thee may I do nought!

*Richard Rolle*

**96** O God of patience and consolation, grant we beseech thee
that with free hearts we may love and serve thee and our
brethren; and, having thus the mind of Christ, may begin
heaven on earth, and exercise ourselves therein till that day
when heaven, where love abideth, shall seem no strange
habitation to us; for Jesus Christ's sake.

*Christina Rossetti*

**97** Give me, O Christ, the courage of faith. Pierce the hidden
depths of my spirit like a two-edged sword. Give me your clear
light to guide my conscience. Give me that love which delights
me in the seclusion of my timid heart and without which I
cannot know you as the Lord of all things, of atoms and stars,
of human bodies and spiritual worlds. Then shall I be truly
blessed in you, then shall I have my heart's desire and the
purpose of my existence.

*Hugo Rahner*

**98** O Lord Jesus, forasmuch as Thy life was despised by the
world, grant us so to imitate Thee, though the world despise,
and with Thy image always before our eyes, to learn that only
the servants of the Cross can find the way of blessedness and of
true light. Hear us and save us, Lord Christ.

*Thomas à Kempis*

**99** If I were not yours, my Christ,
I would feel a finite creature,
I have been born and my life is dissolving away,
I eat, sleep, rest and walk,
sicken and am healed;
numberless are the desires and torments that assail me.
I enjoy the sunlight and the fruit of the earth;
but I die and my flesh will crumble into dust,
like that of the animals who have not sinned.
What more have I than they?
Nothing more, if not God.
If I were not yours, my Christ,
I would feel a dead creature.

*St Gregory of Nazianzus*

**100** Lord Jesus Christ, pierce my soul with your love so that I may
always long for you alone, who are the bread of angels and the
fulfilment of the soul's deepest desires. May my heart always
hunger and feed upon you, so that my soul may be filled with

the sweetness of your presence. May my soul thirst for you, who are the source of life, wisdom, knowledge, light and all the riches of God our Father. May I always seek and find you, think upon you, speak to you and do all things for the honour and glory of your holy name. Be always my only hope, my peace, my refuge and my help in whom my heart is rooted so that I may never be separated from you.

*St Bonaventure*

**101** Lord Jesus, let me know myself; let me know thee,
And desire nothing else but thee.
Let me love myself only if I love thee,
And do all things for thy sake.
Let me humble myself and exalt thee,
And think of nothing else but thee.
Let me die to myself and live in thee,
And take whatever happens as coming from thee.
Let me forsake myself and walk after thee,
And ever desire to follow thee.
Let me flee from myself and turn to thee,
So that I may merit to be defended by thee.
Let me fear for myself, let me fear thee,
And be among those that are chosen by thee.
Let me distrust myself and trust in thee,
And ever obey for the love of thee.
Let me cleave to nothing but thee,
And ever be poor because of thee.
Look upon me that I may love thee,
Call me, that I may see thee,
And forever possess thee, for all eternity.

*St Augustine of Hippo*

**102** May the strength of God guide me this day, and may his power preserve me.
May the wisdom of God instruct me; the eye of God watch over me; the ear of God hear me; the word of God give sweetness to my speech; the hand of God defend me; and may I follow the way of God.
Christ be with me, Christ before me,
Christ be after me, Christ within me,
Christ beneath me, Christ above me,
Christ at my right hand, Christ at my left,
Christ in the fort, Christ in the chariot,
Christ in the ship.

Christ in the heart of every man who thinks of me,
Christ in the mouth of every man who speaks to me.
Christ in every eye that sees me.
Christ in every ear that hears me.

*Attributed to St Patrick*

**103** I come to thee, O Lord, not only because I am unhappy
without thee; not only because I feel I need thee, but because
thy grace draws me on to seek thee for thy own sake, because
thou art so glorious and beautiful. I come in great fear, but in
greater love. Oh may I never lose, as years pass away, and the
heart shuts up, and all things are a burden, let me never lose
this youthful, eager, elastic love of thee. Make thy grace
supply the failure of nature. Do the more for me, the less I can
do for myself.

*John Henry Newman*

**104** To thee, then O Jesus, do I turn my true and last end. Thou
art the river of life which alone can satisfy my thirst. Without
thee all else is barren and void. Without all else thou alone art
enough for me. Thou art the Redeemer of those that are lost;
the sweet Consoler of the sorrowful; the Crown of Glory for
the victors; the recompense of the Blessed. One day I hope to
receive of thy fullness, and to sing the song of praise in my true
home. Give me only on earth some few drops of consolation,
and I will patiently wait thy coming that I may enter into the
joy of my Lord.

*St Bonaventure*

**105** O Lord Jesus, acknowledge what is thine in us, and take away
from us all that is not thine; for thy honour and glory. Amen
*St Bernardine*

**106** Sever me from myself that I may be grateful to you;
may I perish to myself that I may be safe in you;
may I die to myself that I may live in you;
may I wither to myself that I may blossom in you;
may I be emptied of myself that I may abound in you;
may I be nothing to myself that I may be all to you.

*Erasmus*

**107** You are our elder Brother; you have trodden our path before
us, O Christ Jesus, the path of every one of us; you have
forgiven all our sins; you inspire us each and all to give a

nobler, more convinced and more active example of Christian
life.

O Jesus, our true Bread, and the only substantial Food for
our souls, gather all the peoples around your table. Your altar
is divine reality on earth, the pledge of heavenly favour, the
assurance of a just understanding among peoples, and of
peaceful rivalry in the true progress of civilisation.

Nourished by you and with you, O Jesus, men will be
strong in faith, joyful in hope, and active in the many varied
expressions of charity.

Our wills will know how to overcome the snares of evil, the
temptations of selfishness, the listlessness of sloth. And the
eyes of men who love and fear the Lord will behold the vision
of the land of the living, of which the wayfaring Church
militant is the image, enabling the whole earth to hear the first
sweet and mysterious voices of the City of God.

O Jesus, feed us and guard us, and grant that we may see the
good things in the land of the living! Amen

*Pope John XXIII*

**108** I need Thee to teach me day by day, according to each day's
opportunities and needs. Give me, O my Lord, that purity of
conscience which alone can receive, which alone can improve
Thy inspirations.

My ears are dull, so that I cannot hear Thy voice. My eyes
are dim, so that I cannot see Thy tokens. Thou alone canst
quicken my hearing, and purge my sight, and cleanse and
renew my heart.

Teach me to sit at Thy feet, and to hear Thy word.

*John Henry Newman*

**109** O Holy and ever-blessed Jesus, who being the eternal Son of
God and most high in the glory of the Father, didst vouchsafe
in love for us sinners to be born of a pure virgin, and didst
humble thyself unto death, even the death of the cross:
Deepen within us, we beseech thee, a due sense of thy infinite
love; that adoring and believing in thee as our Lord and
Saviour, we may trust in thy infinite merits, imitate thy holy
example, obey thy commands, and finally enjoy thy promises;
who with the Father and the Holy Ghost livest and reignest,
one God, world without end.

*John Wesley*

**110** May he give us all the courage that we need to go the way he shepherds us, that when he calls we may go unfrightened. If he bids us come to him across the waters, that unfrightened we may go. And if he bids us climb the hill, may we not notice that it is a hill, mindful only of the happiness of his company. He made us for himself, that we should travel with him and see him at last in his unveiled beauty in the abiding city, where he is light and happiness and endless home.

*Bede Jarrett*

**111** O Lord Jesus Christ, who hast said that Thou art the way, the truth, and the life; Suffer us not at any time to stray from Thee, who art the way; nor to distrust Thy promises, who art the truth; nor to rest in any other thing than Thee, who art the life; beyond which there is nothing to be desired, neither in heaven, nor in earth; for Thy Name's sake.

*Book of Christian Prayers, 1578*

# HOLY SPIRIT, THE PARACLETE

## *For the gift of the Spirit*

**112** O heavenly Father, the author and fountain of all truth, the bottomless sea of all understanding, send, we beseech you, your Holy Spirit into our hearts and lighten our understanding with the beams of your heavenly grace. We ask this, O merciful Father, for your dear Son, Our Saviour, Jesus Christ's sake. Amen

*Nicholas Ridley*

**113** O Lord, give us the grace of Thy Spirit, early to seek out, and evermore earnestly to follow the work which Thou hast appointed for us to do. Amen

*Henry Alford*

**114** O Lord, grant that my heart may be truly cleansed and filled with Thy Holy Spirit, and that I may arise to serve Thee, and lie down to sleep in entire confidence in Thee, and submission to Thy will, ready for life or for death. Let me live for the day, not overcharged with worldly cares, but feeling that my treasure is not here, and desiring truly to be joined to Thee in Thy heavenly kingdom, and to those who are already gone to

Thee. O Lord, save me from sin, and guide me with Thy Spirit, and keep me in faithful obedience to Thee, through Jesus Christ Thy Son, our Lord. Amen

*Thomas Arnold*

**115** Pour on us, O Lord, the spirit of love and brotherly-kindness; so that, sprinkled by the dew of Thy benediction, we may be made glad by Thy glory and grace; through Christ our Lord.

*Sarum Breviary*

**116** Strengthen me, O God, by the grace of thy Holy Spirit. Grant me to be strengthened with might in the inner man, and to empty my heart of all useless care and anguish. O Lord, grant me heavenly wisdom, that I may learn above all things to seek and to find thee, above all things to relish and to love thee, and to think of all other things as being, what indeed they are, at the disposal of thy wisdom. Amen

*Thomas à Kempis*

**117** May thy servants, O God, be set on fire with Thy Spirit, strengthened by Thy power, illuminated by Thy splendour, filled with Thy grace, and go forward by Thine aid; and after having manfully finished our course, may we be enabled happily to enter into Thy kingdom.

*Gallican Sacramentary*

**118** Give me, O Lord, purity of lips, a clean and innocent heart; humility, fortitude, patience.

Give me the Spirit of wisdom and understanding, the Spirit of counsel and strength, the Spirit of knowledge and godliness, and of Thy fear.

Make me ever to seek Thy face with all my heart, all my soul, all my mind; grant me to have a contrite and humble heart in Thy Presence.

Most high, eternal and ineffable Wisdom, drive away from me the darkness of blindness and ignorance; most high and eternal Strength, deliver me; most high and eternal Light, illuminate me; most high and infinite Mercy, have mercy on me.

*Gallican Formularies*

**119** O Eternal Father, help me, I beseech Thee, to bring forth in my life the fruits of the Spirit; the fruit of Love, that I may love Thee above all things, and all others in Thee and for Thy sake;

---

the fruit of Joy, that I may find Thy service my delight; the fruit of Peace, that, pardoned and accepted through Thy mercy, I may repose in Thy love; the fruit of Long-suffering, that I may bear, with patient submission to Thy will, all crosses and afflictions; the fruit of Gentleness, that I may subdue all risings of temper, and take calmly and sweetly all trials and provocations; the fruit of Meekness, that I may forgive freely all who may hurt me either by word or deed, and endure with patience all that may be laid upon me; the fruit of Temperance, that I may restrain all my desires, bringing them into subjection in all things to Thy holy will. Amen

*Treasury of Devotion*

**120** Let our souls, we beseech Thee, Almighty God, achieve this their desire, to be kindled by Thy Spirit; that being filled as lamps by Thy divine gift, we may shine like blazing lights before the presence of Thy Son Christ at his coming.

*Gelasian Sacramentary*

**121** O God, who has taught us to keep all your commandments of loving you and our neighbour: Grant us the grace of your Holy Spirit, that we may be devoted to you with our whole heart, and united to each other with a pure affection; through Jesus Christ our Lord.

*Leonine Sacramentary*

**122** O Lord, my God, teach me to pray for the right blessings. Steer the vessel of my life towards yourself, the peaceful harbour for storm-tossed souls. Show me the course I should sail, renew a willing spirit within me. May your Spirit curb my wandering senses and help me to observe your laws. Gladden my heart with your glorious presence within. For yours is the glory and the praise of all the saints forever.

*St Basil the Great*

**123** O God, renew our spirits by your Holy Spirit, and draw our hearts to yourself, that our work may not be a burden, but a delight. Let us not serve as slaves, with the spirit of bondage, but with freedom and gladness as your sons, rejoicing in your will; for Jesus Christ's sake.

*Benjamin Jenks*

**124** O God, in Thee alone can our wearied spirits find full satisfaction and rest, and in Thy love is the highest joy. Lord, if we have Thee, we have enough; and we are happy if Thou wilt but give peace to our consciences, and make us know how gracious and merciful Thou art. Preserve in our hearts that peace which passeth all understanding; and make us better and holier in time to come. Strengthen those of us who are in any sorrow or perplexity by the inward comfort of Thy Holy Spirit, and bid us know that our light affliction, which is but for a moment, worketh for us a far more exceeding and eternal weight of glory. For there will come a time when Thou wilt bring us to the place of perfect rest, where we shall behold Thy face in righteousness, and be satisfied from Thy eternal fullness. Amen

*Melchior Ritter*

125 Your Spirit, O God, came to the disciples through Jesus Christ our Lord: bless your disciples today with the same gift from the same Master, that they may find fullness of life in him, and serve him with joy and power all the days of their life, for his truth and mercy's sake. Amen

*Dick Williams*

## *Come Holy Spirit*

126 Creator Spirit, who broodest everlastingly over the lands and waters of earth, enduing them with forms and colours which no human skill can copy, give me today, I beseech Thee, the mind and heart to rejoice in Thy creation.

*John Baillie*

127 O God the Holy Ghost who art Light unto Thine elect,
Evermore enlighten us.
Thou who art Fire of Love,
Evermore enkindle us.
Thou who art Lord and Giver of Life,
Evermore live in us.
Thou who bestowest sevenfold grace,
Evermore replenish us.
As the wind is Thy symbol,
So forward our goings.
As the dove,
So launch us heavenwards.
As water,
So purify our spirits.

As a cloud,
So abate our temptations.
As dew,
So revive our languor.
As fire,
So purge out our dross.

*Christina Rossetti*

128 O Spirit of God
who dost speak to spirits
created in thine own likeness;
penetrate into the depths of our spirits,
into the storehouse of memories,
remembered and forgotten,
into the depths of being,
the very springs of personality,
and cleanse and forgive,
making us whole and holy,
that we may be thine
and live in the new being
of Christ our Lord.

*George Appleton*

129 O Thou Divine Spirit that, in all events of life, art knocking at
the door of my heart, help me to respond to Thee. I would not
be driven blindly as the stars over their courses. I would not be
made to work out Thy will unwillingly, to fulfil Thy law
unintelligently, to obey Thy mandates unsympathetically. I
would take the events of my life as good and perfect gifts from
Thee; I would receive even the sorrows of life as disguised
gifts from Thee. I would have my heart open at all times to
receive Thee – at morning, noon and night; in spring, and
summer, and winter. Whether Thou comest to me in sunshine
or in rain, I would take Thee into my heart joyfully. Thou art
Thyself more than the sunshine; Thou art Thyself compen-
sation for the rain; it is Thee and not Thy gifts I crave; knock,
and I shall open unto Thee.

*George Matheson*

130 These are the gifts I ask
Of Thee, Spirit serene;
Strength for the daily task,
Courage to face the road,

Good cheer to help me bear the traveller's load;
And for the hours that come between,
An inward joy in all things heard and seen.

*Henry van Dyke*

131 O Holy Spirit of God,
who with Thy holy breath doth cleanse the
hearts and minds of men,
comforting them when they be in sorrow,
leading them when they be out of the way,
kindling them when they be cold,
knitting them together when they be at variance,
and enriching them with manifold gifts;
by whose working all things live:
We beseech Thee to maintain and daily to increase
the gifts which Thou hast vouchsafed to us,
that with Thy light before us and within us
we may pass through this world
without stumbling and without straying;
who livest and reignest with the Father and the Son,
everlastingly.

*Erasmus*

132 Creator Spirit, by whose aid
The world's foundations first were laid,
Come, visit every pious mind,
Come, pour thy joys on humankind;
From sin and sorrow set us free,
And make us temples worthy thee.

*Attributed to Emperor Charlemagne*

133 Lead, Kindly Light, amid the encircling gloom,
Lead Thou me on!
The night is dark, and I am far from home;
Lead Thou me on!
Keep Thou my feet; I do not ask to see
The distant scene; one step enough for me.

I was not ever thus, nor pray'd that Thou
Shouldst lead me on.
I loved to choose and see my path; but now
Lead Thou me on!
I loved the garish day, and, spite of fears,
Pride ruled my will: remember not past years.

So long Thy power hath blest me, sure it still
Will lead me on,
O'er moor and fen, o'er crag and torrent, till
The night is gone;
And with the morn those angel faces smile
Which I have loved long since, and lost awhile.

*John Henry Newman*

134 Breathe on me O Lord, with that breath which infuses energy
and kindles fervour. In asking for fervour, I ask for all that I
can need, and all that Thou canst give. In asking for fervour, I
am asking for faith, hope, and charity, in their most heavenly
exercise; I am asking for that loyal perception of duty which
follows on yearning affection; I am asking for sanctity, peace,
and joy, all at once. Nothing would be a trouble to me,
nothing a difficulty, had I but fervour of soul.

Lord, in asking for fervour, I am asking for Thyself, for
nothing short of Thee, O my God. Enter my heart, and fill it
with fervour by filling it with Thee.

*John Henry Newman*

135 Holy Spirit think through me till your ideas are my ideas.

*Amy Carmichael*

136 O Come, O Holy Spirit, come!
Come as holy fire and burn in us,
Come as holy wind and cleanse us,
Come as holy light and lead us,
Come as holy truth and teach us,
Come as holy forgiveness and free us,
Come as holy love and enfold us,
Come as holy power and enable us,
Come as holy life and dwell in us.
Convict us, convert us,
Consecrate us, until we are wholly Thine
for Thy using, through Jesus Christ our Lord.

*Adapted by Charles Francis Whiston*
*from an ancient prayer*

137 Come, Holy Spirit, and daily increase in these thy servants thy
manifold gifts of grace; the spirit of wisdom and understanding, the spirit of counsel and strength, the spirit of knowledge
and true godliness; and fill them with the spirit of thy holy
fear, now and evermore.

*Gelasian Sacramentary*

**138** Spirit of the Living Christ, come upon us in the glory of your risen power; Spirit of the Living Christ, come upon us in all the humility of your wondrous love; Spirit of the Living Christ, come upon us that new life may course within our veins, new love bind us together in one family, a new vision of the Kingdom of God spur us on to serve you with fearless passion.

*Iona Community*

## God the Paraclete

**139** Almighty and Holy Spirit, the Comforter, pure, living, true, – illuminate, govern, sanctify me, and confirm my heart and mind in the faith, and in all genuine consolation; preserve and rule over me that, dwelling in the house of the Lord all the days of my life, to behold the beauty of the Lord, I may be and remain forever in the temple of the Lord, and praise Him with a joyful spirit, and in union with all the heavenly church. Amen

*Philip Melancthon*

**140** Come, thou Father of the poor,
Come with treasures which endure,
Come thou light of all that live!
Thou of all consolers best.
Thou the soul's delightful guest,
Dost refreshing peace bestow.
Thou in toil art comfort sweet,
Pleasant coolness in the heat,
Solace in the midst of woe.
Light immortal, light divine,
Visit thou these hearts of thine,
And our inmost being fill.
If thou take thy grace away
Nothing pure in man will stay;
All his good is turned to ill.
Heal our wounds, our strength renew.
On our dryness pour thy dew,
Wash the stains of guilt away.
Bend the stubborn heart and will;
Melt the frozen, warm the chill;
Guide the steps that go astray.

Thou on us, who ever more
Thee confess and thee adore,
With thy sevenfold gifts descend:
Give us comfort when we die,
Give us life with thee on high;
Give us joys that never end.

*Attributed to Stephen Langton*
*Translated E. Caswall*

**141** Heavenly King, Paraclete, Spirit of Truth, present in all
places and filling all things, treasury of good and choir-master
of life: come and dwell within us, cleanse us from all stains and
save our souls.

*Liturgy of St John Chrysostom*

**142** In the hour of my distress,
When temptations me oppress,
And when I my sins confess;
Sweet Spirit comfort me!

When I lie within my bed,
Sick in heart, and sick in head,
And with doubts discomforted,
Sweet Spirit comfort me!

When the house doth sigh and weep,
And the world is drown'd in sleep,
Yet mine eyes the watch do keep;
Sweet Spirit comfort me!

When (God knows) I'm tossed about,
Either with despair, or doubt;
Yet before the glass be out,
Sweet Spirit comfort me!

When the judgment is reveal'd,
And that open'd which was seal'd,
When to Thee I have appeal'd;
Sweet Spirit comfort me!

*Robert Herrick*

**143** O King, enthroned on high,
Thou Comforter divine,
Blest Spirit of all truth, be nigh
And make us Thine.

Thou art the Source of life,
Thou art our treasure-store;
Give us Thy peace, and end our strife
For evermore.

Descend, O heavenly Dove,
Abide with us alway;
And in the fullness of Thy love
Cleanse us, we pray.

*Eighth-century prayer*
*Translated by John Brownlie, 1857–1925*

**144** O Thou almighty Will
Faint are Thy children, till
Thou come with power:
Strength of our good intents,
In our frail home, Defence,
Calm of Faith's confidence,
Come, in this hour!

O Thou most tender Love!
Deep in our spirits move:
Tarry, dear Guest!
Quench Thou our passion's fire,
Raise Thou each low desire,
Deeds of brave love inspire,
Quickener and Rest!

O Light serene and still!
Come, and our spirit fill,
Bring in the day:
Guide of our feeble sight,
Star of our darkest night,
Shine on the path of right,
Show us the way!

*King Robert I of France*

**145** O Holy Spirit, Love of God, infuse thy grace, and descend
plentifully into my heart; enlighten the dark corners of this
neglected dwelling, and scatter there thy cheerful beams;
dwell in that soul that longs to be thy temple; water that
barren soil, overrun with weeds and briars, and lost for want
of cultivating, and make it fruitful with thy dew from heaven.
Oh come, thou refreshment of them that languish and faint.
Come, thou star and guide of them that sail in the tempestuous sea of the world; thou only haven of the tossed and

shipwrecked. Come, thou glory and crown of the living, and only safeguard of the dying. Come, Holy Spirit, in much mercy, and make me fit to receive thee. Amen

*St Augustine of Hippo*

**146** O Holy Spirit, Who, in all ages hast comforted and strengthened martyrs and confessors; Who hast ever been the sustaining comfort and sweet refreshment of the sorrowful and the suffering; Who sheddest abroad love, joy, and peace, in the hearts of the faithful and obedient followers of Christ; grant that we may be filled with all the fullness of Thy gifts of grace; that, by Thy holy inspiration, we may think those things that be good, and, by Thy merciful guiding, may perform the same. Amen

*Treasury of Devotion*

# I BELIEVE

**147** I believe in God, the Father almighty, creator of heaven and earth, and in Jesus Christ, his only Son, our Lord, who was conceived by the Holy Spirit, born of the Virgin Mary, suffered under Pontius Pilate, was crucified, died, and was buried. He descended into hell. The third day he rose again from the dead. He ascended into heaven, sitteth at the right hand of God the almighty Father. From thence he shall come to judge the living and the dead. I believe in the Holy Spirit, the holy Catholic Church, the Communion of Saints, the forgiveness of sins, the resurrection of the body, and life everlasting. Amen

*Traditional Apostles' Creed*

**148** I believe in Jesus as a perfect revelation of God and the only sure Master for my life.

Because of Jesus, I believe in forgiveness – in the forgiveness of God to man, and from man to man, and from me to anyone who needs my forgiveness.

I believe that love is stronger than all other forces – that to love is better than to be angry, that it is better to give than to receive; better to serve than to be served; better to forget myself than to assert myself.

I believe that God's kingdom can come on earth, and that everything that is wrong in the life of the nation, or of the

Church, or in my life can be conquered by the power of
God.
    I believe that nothing that is wrong need be permanent.

*A. Herbert Gray*

**149** I believe that I cannot by my own reason or strength believe in
Jesus Christ my Lord, or come to him; but the Holy Ghost has
called me through the gospel, enlightened me by his gifts, and
sanctified and preserved me in the true faith; in like manner as
he calls, gathers, enlightens, and sanctifies the whole Christian Church on earth, and preserves it in union with Jesus
Christ in the true faith; in which Christian Church he daily
forgives abundantly all my sins, and the sins of all believers,
and will raise up me and all the dead at the last day, and will
grant everlasting life to me and to all who believe in Christ.
This is most certainly true. Amen

*Martin Luther*

**150** I believe in the love of God revealed in Jesus Christ.
I believe that behind the clouds of life shines the love of
    God.
I believe that God has a purpose for the world and a purpose
    for my life.
I believe that God wills the blessedness of all lives and of
    every single life.
I believe that Jesus Christ saves life from the power of sin
    and sorrow and death.
I believe in the life-giving power and grace of the Holy
    Spirit.
I believe that through faith and prayer and Sacrament I can
    live the life which is life indeed.
I believe that God calls my life to love and service.
I believe that through Christ life leads at last to the fullness of
    goodness, truth, and beauty.
I believe in the grace of our Lord Jesus Christ, and the love
    of God, and the fellowship of the Holy Spirit.

*Frederick B. Macnutt*

**151** We believe that God is spirit; and they that worship him
    must worship him in spirit and truth.
We believe that God is light: and if we walk in the light as he
    is in the light, we have fellowship one with another.
We believe that God is love: and that everyone that loveth is
    born of God and knoweth God.

We believe that Jesus is the son of God: and that God has given us eternal life, and this life is in his son.
We believe that if we confess our sins: he is faithful and just to forgive our sins.
We believe that he who doeth the will of God: shall abide for ever.

*H. Stobart*

**152** Lord, we believe in thee, help thou our unbelief; we love thee, yet not with perfect hearts as we would; we long for thee, yet not with our full strength; we trust in thee, yet not with our whole mind. Accept our faith, our love, our longing to know and serve thee, our trust in thy power to keep us. What is cold do thou kindle, what is lacking do thou supply; through Jesus Christ our Lord.

*Malcolm Spencer*

**153** Father in Heaven, give us faith for today. Thou art great and mighty; Thy power created the whole universe, and Thy wisdom created us in Thine image; Thy hands of divine providence still sustain all Thy creation. Yet, in a personal way, Thy power is with all who acknowledge Thee as Lord and who come before Thee by faith, through Jesus Christ. Grant us faith to believe in Thee; faith to live knowing that we are daily supported by Thy power; faith to trust in Thy constant care; faith to see, even in life's stresses, Thy hand of love; and faith to step forth to the tasks of life as seeing Thee walking beside us. We pray in the name of that One without whom faith would be meaningless, even Jesus our Lord. Amen

*William H. Kadel*

# DEPENDENCE UPON GOD

**154** O Omnipotent Good, who cares for each of us as if no one else existed and for all of us as if we were all but one! Blessed is the person who loves You. To You I entrust my whole being and all I have received from You. You made me for Yourself, and my heart is restless until it rests in You.

*St Augustine of Hippo*

**155** Grant, O God, that amidst all the discouragements, difficulties and dangers, distress and darkness of this mortal life, I may depend upon thy mercy, and on this build my hopes, as on a sure foundation. Let thine infinite mercy in Christ Jesus deliver me from despair, both now and at the hour of death.

*Thomas Wilson*

**156** In confidence of Thy goodness and great mercy, O Lord, I draw near unto Thee, as a sick person to the Healer, as one hungry and thirsty to the Fountain of life, a creature to the Creator, a desolate soul to my own tender Comforter. Behold, in Thee is all whatsoever I can or ought to desire; Thou art my Salvation and my Redemption, my Help and my Strength. Rejoice therefore this day the soul of Thy servant; for unto Thee, O Lord, have I lifted up my soul.

*Thomas à Kempis*

**157** O Lord, to be turned from you is to fall, to be turned to you is to rise, and to stand in you is to abide for ever; grant us in all our duties your help, in all our perplexities your guidance, in all our dangers your protection, and in all our sorrows your peace; through Jesus Christ our Lord.

*St Augustine of Hippo*

**158** O love triumphant over guilt and sin,
My soul is soiled, but Thou shalt enter in;
My feet must stumble if I walk alone,
Lonely my heart, till beating by Thine own,
My will is weakness till it rest in Thine,
Cut off, I wither, thirsting for the Vine,
My deeds are dry leaves on a sapless tree,
My life is lifeless till it live in Thee!

*Frederic Lawrence Knowles*

**159** O thou who hast willed to be called Love, give me love, that I may love thee more than I love myself, and care not at all what I do with myself, so long as I am doing what is pleasing in thy sight. Grant me, O Father, though I dare not always call myself thy child, at least to be thy faithful little servant and the sheep of thy pasture. Speak to thy servant's heart sometimes so that thy consolations may give joy to my soul. And teach me to speak to thee often in prayer. Take to thyself all my poverty and need, O Lord, my God and my Father. Have pity

on my weakness, O my strength; and may it be to thy great
glory that my feebleness continues to serve thee.

*William of Saint Thierry*

160 Almighty God, who knowest our necessities before we ask,
and our ignorance in asking: Set free thy servants from all
anxious thoughts for the morrow; give us contentment with
thy good gifts; and confirm our faith that according as we seek
thy kingdom, thou wilt not suffer us to lack any good thing;
through Jesus Christ our Lord.

*St Augustine of Hippo*

161 O Lord, never suffer us to think that we can stand by
ourselves, and not need thee.

*John Donne*

162 Suffer me never to think that I have knowledge enough to
need no teaching, wisdom enough to need no correction,
talents enough to need no grace, goodness enough to need no
progress, humility enough to need no repentance, devotion
enough to need no quickening, strength sufficient without thy
Spirit; lest, standing still, I fall back for evermore.

*Eric Milner-White*

163 O my God, I could not be at all, were You not in me: or should
I say I could not exist unless I were in you, 'of whom are all
things, by whom are all things, in whom are all things'?

*St Augustine of Hippo*

164 Saviour,
we thank you for showing us
in the perfection of your life
that by ourselves we can do nothing good or holy;
and since apart from you we can do nothing,
we praise and thank you for the promise
that in your love and power
we can do all things.
Take our sin away,
raise us with you to newness of life;
so that our lives,
taking all their goodness from You,
may give you all the glory
for ever and ever.

*Jamie Wallace*

# GOD'S WILL

**165** O my most dear Lord, I will have nothing in my memory but thee, my Lord and God, my very original, in whom I was from the beginning. Neither will I have anything in my understanding but thee only and all creatures in thee. Neither will I have in my will and desire any other thing but the execution and doing of thy most holy will.

*William Perin*

**166** O Heavenly Father, subdue in me whatever is contrary to
Thy holy will. Grant that I may ever study to know Thy
will, that I may know how to please Thee.
Grant, O God, that I may never run into those temptations,
which in my prayers I desire to avoid.
Lord, never permit my trials to be above my strength. Amen

*Thomas Wilson*

**167** Grant me, I beseech Thee, Almighty and most Merciful God, fervently to desire, wisely to search out, and perfectly to fulfil all that is well-pleasing unto Thee. Order Thou my worldly condition to the glory of Thy name; and, of all that Thou requirest me to do, grant me the knowledge, the desire and the ability, that I may so fulfil it as I ought, and may my path to Thee, I pray, be safe, straightforward and perfect to the end.

*St Thomas Aquinas*

**168** O Lord God Almighty, I charge Thee of Thy great mercy that Thou guide me to Thy will and to my soul's need better than I can myself, that above all things I may inwardly love Thee with a clear mind and clean body; for Thou art my Maker, my help and my hope.

*King Alfred*

**169** Grant me, O Lord, the single eye, that I may see the one thing needful, the thing that you want done. Don't let my vision be blurred by looking at too many things, or longing to please anyone but you. Give me simplicity of heart, quiet confidence in you, and eagerness to know and do your will.

*George Appleton*

**170** We let the world overcome us; we live too much in continual fear of the chances and changes of mortal life. We let things go too much their own way. We try too much to get what we can by our own selfish wits, without considering our neighbours. We follow too much the ways and fashions of the day, doing and saying and thinking anything that comes uppermost, just because there is so much around us. Free us from our selfish interests, and guide us, good Lord, to see your way, and to do your will.

*Charles Kingsley*

**171** May the will of God be wrought in all of us, and let him do unto each of us as seemeth best, and according to his perfect knowledge.

*St Kentigern*

**172** My Father, help me as a follower of Christ to say, 'Thy will be done.' Thou wouldest not have me accept Thy will because I must, but because I may. Thou wouldest have me take it, not with resignation, but with joy, not with the absence of mur-mur, but with the song of praise. How shall I reach this goal? I shall only reach it by feeling what the Psalmist felt – that Thy will comes from a 'good Spirit,' and goes towards a 'land of uprightness.' Teach me that Thy will is love; teach me that Thy love is wise. Guide me not blindfold, but with open eyes. Grant me the power to look both behind and before – behind to 'Thy good Spirit,' before to 'the land of uprightness.' Give me the blessedness of the man whose delight is in Thy law, who can tell of Thy statutes rejoicing the heart. I shall obey Thy will in perfect freedom when I can say, 'Thy Spirit is good'. Amen

*George Matheson*

**173** O Lord, you know what is best for me. Let this or that be done, as you please. Give what you will, how much you will and when you will.

*Thomas à Kempis*

**174** Most dear and tender Father, our defender and nourisher, fill us with your grace that we may cast aside our blindness and attraction to material things; and may instead put all our efforts into discovering your will and obeying your law. Let us work, like the birds and the flowers, for what gives you glory leaving all care in your hands. Amen

*Henry VIII's Primer*

**175** Renew my will from day to day,
Blend it with Thine, and take away
All that now makes it hard to say,
Thy will be done.

*Charlotte Elliott*

**176** O Lord, let me not henceforth desire health or life except to
spend them for you, with you and in you. You alone know
what is good for me; do therefore what seems best to you.
Give to me or take from me; conform my will to yours; and
grant that with humble and perfect submission and in holy
confidence I may receive the orders of your eternal providence, and may equally adore all that comes to me from you.

*Blaise Pascal*

**177** O Lord, make Thy way plain before me. Let Thy glory be my
end. Thy Word my rule, and then, Thy will be done.

*King Charles I*

**178** O God, by whom the meek are guided in judgment, grant us,
in all our doubts and uncertainties, the grace to ask what Thou
wouldst have us to do; that the spirit of wisdom may save us
from all false choices, and that in Thy light we may see light,
and in Thy straight path may not stumble, through Jesus
Christ our Lord.

*William Bright*

**179** Thy way, not mine, O Lord,
However dark it be;
Lead me by Thine own hand,
Choose out the path for me.
Smooth let it be or rough,
It will be still the best;
Winding or straight, it leads
Right onward to Thy rest.
Choose Thou for me my friends,
My sickness or my health;
Choose Thou my cares for me,
My poverty or wealth.
Not mine, not mine the choice
In things or great or small;
Be Thou my guide, my strength,
My wisdom, and my all.

*Horatius Bonar*

**180** O Lord God, when we pray unto thee, desiring well and meaning truly, if thou seest a better way to thy glory and our good, then be thy will done, and not ours: as with thy dear Son in the garden of Agony, even Jesus Christ our Lord.

*Eric Milner-White*

**181** Grant, gracious Father, that I may never dispute the reasonableness of thy will, but ever close with it, as the best that can happen. Prepare me always for what thy providence shall bring forth. Let me never murmur, be dejected, or impatient, under any of the troubles of this life, but ever find rest and comfort in this, this is the will of my Father, and of my God; grant this for Jesus Christ's sake. Amen

*Thomas Wilson*

**182** O my Lord, what a great comfort it is to me that thou didst not entrust the fulfilment of thy will to one so wretched as I! Blessed be thou for ever, let all things praise thee. May thy name be for ever glorified. I should indeed have to be good, Lord, if the fulfilment or non-fulfilment of thy will were in my hands. But as it is, though my will is not yet free from self-interest, I give it to thee freely.

*St Teresa of Avila*

**183** O my God, bestow upon us such confidence, such peace, such happiness in Thee, that Thy will may always be dearer to us than our own will, and Thy pleasure than our own pleasure. All that Thou givest is Thy free gift to us, all that Thou takest away Thy grace to us. Be Thou thanked for all, praised for all, loved for all; through Jesus Christ our Lord. Amen

*Christina Rossetti*

**184** O thou who art heroic love, keep alive in our hearts that adventurous spirit which makes men scorn the way of safety, so that thy will be done. For so only, O Lord, shall we be worthy of those courageous souls who in every age have ventured all in obedience to thy call, and for whom the trumpets have sounded on the other side; through Jesus Christ our Lord.

*John H. Oldham*

**185** Sweet Jesus, I thank thee with all my heart for that sweet-sounding prayer thou madest before thy sacred passion on the mountain of Olive. And, Lord, I thank thee, for there, indeed, thou didst teach us how to pray, when thou didst say: 'Father, not my will but thine be done'. Thy prayer, then, was not for thyself, rather for us, to teach us that when our will, as often it is, be found contrary to the Father in heaven, then are we to leave our will and pray that the will of the Father be done in us. Here and now, sweet Jesus, I beseech thee that I be ever ready to do thy will, not mine, for when my will accords with thine, that is joy to me. Grant me grace ever to seek out thy will, and so to come to thee.

*Richard Rolle*

186 Grant me, O Lord, to know what I ought to know, to love what I ought to love, to praise what delights Thee most, to value what is precious in Thy sight, to hate what is offensive to Thee.

Do not suffer me to judge according to the sight of my eyes, but to discern with a true judgment between things visible and spiritual, and above all things always to inquire what is the good pleasure of Thy will.

*Thomas à Kempis*

187 Jesu mine, grant me thy grace,
And for amendment might and space,
To keep thy word and do thy will,
To choose the good and leave the ill,
And that it so may be
Good Jesu, grant it me. Amen

*Richard Rolle*

188 O God, whose will it is that the gate of mercy should stand open to your people; look on us and have mercy upon us, we implore you. Grant that we, who by your grace are following your holy will, may continue along that same path all the days of our life, through Jesus Christ our Lord.

*Leonine Sacramentary*

189 O thou who hast taught us that we are most truly free when we lose our wills in thine: Help us to attain to this liberty by continual surrender unto thee; that walking in the way which thou hast prepared for us, we may find our life in doing thy will; through Jesus Christ our Lord.

*Gelasian Sacramentary*

**190** O God, whose will is done without our prayer, we pray that it may be done also by us. To this end do thou frustrate and bring to naught every evil counsel and purpose – such as the will of the devil, the world, and our own flesh – which would hinder the hallowing of thy name and prevent the coming of thy kingdom. Do thou strengthen and keep us steadfast in thy Word and in faith even unto the end. Let this thy good and gracious will be done. Amen

*Martin Luther*


**191** Lord, thou seest well that many there be that trust to my prayer, because of the graces thou showest me beyond my worth. Thou knowest well, Lord, that I am far from being what they deem me, but though my prayer be unworthy, do thou look at their humility and at their devotion, and whatever they desire to thy praise, grant it them of thy goodness. Grant to me, and to all others for whom we should pray, to love what is thy will.

*Richard Rolle*


**192** O Lord, if only my will may remain right and firm towards Thee, do with me whatsoever it shall please Thee. For it cannot be anything but good, whatsoever Thou shalt do with me. If it be Thy will I should be in darkness, be Thou blessed; and if it be Thy will I should be in light, be Thou again blessed. If Thou vouchsafe to comfort me, be Thou blessed; and, if Thou wilt have me afflicted, be Thou ever equally blessed. Amen

*Thomas à Kempis*


**193** O most merciful Lord, grant me your grace. May it work within me and help me to persevere to the end. Grant that I may always will what is most pleasing to you. Let your will be mine and my will yours. Grant that my heart may find complete peace in you, its true resting place. Amen

*Thomas à Kempis*


**194** O Lord Jesus Christ, who didst create me, redeem me, and foreordain me unto that which I now am: Thou knowest what Thou wilt do with me: deal with me according to Thy will and Thy mercy.

*King Henry VI*

**195** You have placed the honour of your will in my hands. Each word of your revelation says that you respect and trust me, that you give me dignity and responsibility. Teach me to understand that. Give me that holy maturity that is capable of receiving the light you grant and of assuming the responsibility that you entrust. Keep my heart awake that at all times it may be before you, and let what I do become one with the command and the obedience to which you have called me.

*Romano Guardini*

**196** Almighty God, in whom we live and move and have our being, you have made us for yourself, so that our hearts are restless until they rest in you; grant us purity of heart and strength of purpose, that no selfish passion may hinder us from knowing your will, no weakness from doing it; but that in your light we may see light clearly, and in your service find our perfect freedom; through Jesus Christ our Lord.

*St Augustine of Hippo*

**197** God Almighty, Eternal, Righteous, and Merciful, give to us poor sinners to do for Thy sake all that we know of Thy will, and to will always what pleases Thee, so that inwardly purified, enlightened, and kindled by the fire of the Holy Spirit, we may follow in the footprints of Thy well-beloved Son, our Lord Jesus Christ.

*St Francis of Assisi*

**198** Grant, O Lord God, that we may wait anxiously, as servants standing in the presence of their lord, for the least hint of thy will; that we may welcome all truth, under whatever outward forms it be uttered; that we may have grace to receive new thoughts with grace, recognising that thy ways are not as our ways nor thy thoughts as our thoughts; that we may bless every good deed, by whomsoever it may be done; that we may rise above all party strife and cries to the contemplation of the eternal Truth and Goodness, O God Almighty who never changest; through thy Son, our Saviour Jesus Christ. Amen

*Charles Kingsley*

**199** Grant us such grace that we may work Thy will,
And speak Thy words, and walk before Thy face,
Profound and calm like waters deep and still;
Grant us such grace.

*Christina Rossetti*

**200** O God, who hast commanded us to be perfect, as thou our Father in heaven art perfect: Put into our hearts, we pray thee, a continual desire to obey thy holy will. Teach us day by day what thou wouldest have us to do, and give us courage and strength to fulfil the same. May we never, from love of ease, decline the path which thou pointest out, nor, for fear of shame, turn away from it. We ask it for the honour of Jesus Christ our Saviour.

*Henry Alford*

**201** Dear Lord, quieten my spirit and fix my thoughts on thy will, that I may see what thou wouldst have done, and contemplate its doing without self-consciousness or inner excitement, without haste and without delay, without fear of other people's judgments or anxiety about success, knowing only that it is thy will and therefore must be done quietly, faithfully and lovingly, for in thy will alone is our peace.

*George Appleton*

**202** We beseech thee, O Lord, to enlighten our minds and to strengthen our wills, that we may know what we ought to do, and be enabled to do it, through the grace of thy most Holy Spirit, and for the merits of thy Son, Jesus Christ our Lord.

*William Bright*

**203** I do not know, O God, what may happen to me to-day, I only know that nothing will happen to me but what has been foreseen by you from all eternity, and that is sufficient, O my God, to keep me in peace. I adore your eternal designs. I submit to them with all my heart. I desire them all and accept them all. I make a sacrifice of everything. I unite this sacrifice to that of your dear Son, my Saviour, begging you by His infinite merits, for the patience in troubles, and the perfect submission which is due to you in all that you will and design for me.

*Madame Elizabeth of France*
*(whilst in prison awaiting execution)*

# SEEKING UNITY WITH GOD

**204** O Thou Who hast prepared a place for my soul,
Prepare my soul for that place:
Prepare it with holiness,
Prepare it with desire;
And even while it sojourneth upon earth
Let it dwell in heaven with Thee
Beholding the beauty of Thy countenance,
And the glory of Thy Saints,
Now and forever.

*Joseph Hall*

**205** O Lord God, grant us always, whatever the world may say, to
content ourselves with what thou wilt say, and to care only for
thine approval, which will outweigh all words.

*General Gordon*

**206** Our God, it is Thy will in us that willeth.
It is Thy desire in us that desireth.
It is Thy urge in us that would turn our nights,
which are Thine, into days, which are Thine also.
We cannot ask Thee for aught, for Thou knowest our
needs before they are born in us:
Thou art our need; and in giving us more of Thyself
Thou givest us all.

*Kahlil Gibran*

**207** Write deeply upon our minds, O Lord our God, the lessons of
thy holy Word, that only the pure in heart can see thee. Leave
us not in the bondage of any sinful inclination. May we neither
deceive ourselves with the thought that we have no sin, nor
idly acquiesce in aught of which our conscience accuses us.
Strengthen us by thy Holy Spirit to fight the good fight of faith,
and grant that no day may pass without its victory; through
Jesus Christ our Lord.

*Charles J. Vaughan*

**208** Holy the God who from my youth
has shown me life and light.
Stoop to me, make me strong,
that I may transmit that grace, as love bids,
to my brothers, your sons.

My spirit is the Holy Spirit's.
Therefore I believe and confess my faith,
which is the source of light and life to me.
Blessed Father,
man, your creature,
would have you make him holy like yourself,
for you have given him every means to become so.
Glory is yours, now and always,
age after age. Amen

*From a second-century papyrus*

**209** Give me, O Lord, a tender conscience; a conversation discreet and affable, modest and patient, liberal and obliging; a body chaste and healthful, competency of living according to my condition, contentedness in all estates, a resigned will and mortified affections: that I may be as Thou wouldest have me, and my portion may be in the lot of the righteous, in the brightness of Thy countenance, and the glories of eternity.

*Jeremy Taylor*

**210** O Lord seek us, O Lord find us
In Thy patient care,
Be Thy love before, behind us,
Round us everywhere.
Lest the god of this world blind us,
Lest he bait a snare,
Lest he forge a chain to bind us,
Lest he speak us fair,
Turn not from us, call to mind us,
Find, embrace us, hear.
Be Thy love before, behind us,
Round us everywhere.

*Christina Rossetti*

**211** Let us surrender the desire of earthly benefits for the true riches of grace. Let us, by means of our voluntary poverty, despise the world. Then will our lives be sweet and pleasing to the Lord. For our lives will breathe out the fragrance of Christ in the sight of God, if the dying of Christ is seen in our daily living and his life's example is made visible in our own. We shall, indeed, lay precious balm on the body of Christ, if in sincere faith and in obedience to his will, we give him our lives and our living.

*St Paulinus of Nola*

**212** O Lord, prepare my heart, I beseech Thee, to reverence
Thee, to adore Thee, to love Thee; to hate, for love of Thee,
all my sins, imperfections, shortcomings, whatever in me
displeaseth Thee; and to love all which Thou lovest, and
whom Thou lovest. Give me, Lord, fervour of love, shame for
my unthankfulness, sorrow for my sins, longing for Thy grace,
and to be wholly united with Thee. Let my very coldness call
for the glow of Thy love; let my emptiness and dryness, like a
barren and thirsty land, thirst for Thee, call on Thee to come
into my soul, Who refreshest those who are weary. Let my
heart ache to Thee and for Thee, Who stillest the aching of the
heart. Let my mute longings praise Thee, crave to Thee, Who
satisfiest the empty soul, that waits on Thee. Amen

*E. B. Pusey*

**213** Almighty Father, teach me to do everything with the utmost
sincerity. Save me from posing even to myself. Make my life
unaffected, simple and sincere. Cleanse me from selfishness;
let my gaze be outward rather than inward. Teach me to think
more of others than of myself. Forbid that my own interests
should be paramount. Pardon, I beseech Thee, all that is and
has been wrong in my life and character. Had I always sought
Thy will I should now have been strong in the Lord, instead of
being the weak, slothful, vacillating creature that I am. But it
is never too late. Help me to remedy the evil and henceforth to
build with honesty and prayer.

*Walter James*

**214** Guide me, teach me, strengthen me, till I become such a
person as thou wouldst have me be; pure and gentle, truthful
and high-minded, brave and able, courteous and generous,
dutiful and useful.

*Charles Kingsley*

**215** Give me grace, O my Father, to be utterly ashamed of my own
reluctance. Rouse me from sloth and coldness, and make me
desire thee with my whole heart. Teach me to love meditation, sacred reading, and prayer. Teach me to love that
which must engage my mind for all eternity.

*John Henry Newman*

**216** God, help me to be human. Help me to be able to appreciate
and bring out the best in everyone around me. You have
created man, so that he is capable to appreciate consciously all

the gifts that you have given him. Lord, help me to appreciate all that you have given me. Help me to be truly human.

*Teenagers' Prayer from Harare, Zimbabwe*

217 O God, in whose strong hands are the threads of every man's life, into Thy hands we would commit our lives with all their details and desires.

May we be able, in Thy strength, so to react to all those experiences which befall us, that we may wring from them victory in our souls and spiritual gain for the world.

May we love Thee enough to make all things work together for good.

*Leslie D. Weatherhead*

218 O Lord, I fling myself with all my weakness and misery into thy ever-open arms. I know that I am ignorant and much mistaken about myself. Thou, who seest in very truth, look mercifully on me. Lay thy healing hand upon my wounds. Pour the life-giving balm of thy love into my heart. Do for me what I have not the courage to do for myself. Save me in spite of myself. May I be thine; wholly thine, and, at all costs, thine. In humiliation, in poverty, in suffering, in self-abnegation, thine. Thine in the way thou knowest to be most fitting, in order that thou mightest be now and ever mine. Thou art my strength and my Redeemer. I am thy poor little creature, dependent on thy merciful charity alone. Amen

*Charles J. B. Besson*

219 Set me free, Lord, from faith and hope in lesser things.
Set me free from commitment to my own blueprints for my own future.
Set me free for faith and hope in you.
Set me free for commitment to your plans for my future.
Set me free to live and work and serve, building your future.
Set me free, Lord, to be a man.

*Rex Chapman*

220 Vouchsafe, O Lord, that I may be a Christian, without sin, without shame, and, should it please Thee, without pain, and a good answer at the dreadful and fearful judgment seat of Jesus Christ our Lord.

*Lancelot Andrewes*

221 Lead us into holiness, O God, by making our minds one with
you in peace. You have made us body and soul, each fitted to
its task. Let not our bodily desires war against our souls.
Deliver us from unhealthy enticements that we may come to
freedom and peace of mind; that we may not be overcome, fill
us with your own strength.

*Mozarabic Psalter*

222 Govern everything by your wisdom, O Lord, so that my soul
may always be serving you, in the way you will and not as I
choose. Let me die to myself so that I may serve you; let me
live to you, who are life itself. Amen

*St Teresa of Avila*

223 O Lord our God, safe under the shadow of your wings, let us
hope. You will support us both when we are little and when we
are old. When our strength is from you it is real strength, when
it springs from us it is weakness. Leaning upon you we can find
our way back to you, who are our refreshment and true
strength. Amen

*St Augustine of Hippo*

## SORROW FOR SIN, AND FORGIVENESS

224 O God, Who hast enkindled in the holy bosoms of all Thy
saints so great an ardour of faith, that they despised all bodily
pains, while hastening with all earnestness to Thee, the
Author of life; hear our prayers, and grant that the hateful
sweetness of sin may wax faint in us, and we may glow with the
infused warmth of love for Thee; through Thy mercy, O our
God, Who art blessed, and dost live, and govern all things,
world without end. Amen

*Mozarabic Sacramentary*

225 O my Creator!
Consume the thorns of all my offences.
Make clean my soul, make holy my mind,
Nail down my being in respect of your name,
Ever keep watch, guard and protect me
From every act and word that destroys the soul.
Make me holy, make me clean, set me in order.
Make me comely, give me understanding, give me light.

Make me a worthy temple of your Spirit,
No more a temple of sin,
But a child of light.
You alone are the shining brightness of souls,
And to you, as God and Master,
We give all glory every day of our lives.

*Simeon, the New Theologian*

**226** O Lord, the house of my soul is narrow;
enlarge it, that you may enter in.
It is in ruins, please repair it.
It is displeasing to you; I know and acknowledge it.
But to whom can I call for help, to clear and
repair it, but you?
Cleanse me from my secret faults, O Lord,
and spare your servant.

*St Augustine of Hippo*

**227** O Lord, who hast mercy upon all, take away from me my sins,
and mercifully kindle in me the fire of Thy Holy Spirit. Take
away from me the heart of stone, and give me a heart of flesh,
a heart to love and adore Thee, a heart to delight in Thee, to
follow and to enjoy Thee, for Christ's sake.

*St Ambrose of Milan*

**228** O God, deliver us from earthly desires, that no sin may reign
in us, but that we may with free spirits serve you, our only
Lord; through Jesus Christ. Amen

*Gelasian Sacramentary*

**229** Stir up your power, Lord, and with great might come among
us; and, because we are sorely hindered by our sins, let your
bountiful grace and mercy speedily help and deliver us;
through Jesus Christ our Lord.

*Gelasian Sacramentary*

**230** O Lord, because we often sin and have to ask for pardon, help
us to forgive as we would be forgiven; neither mentioning old
offences committed against us, nor dwelling upon them in
thought; but loving our brother freely as you freely love us; for
your name's sake.

*Christina Rossetti*

**231** O God, though our sins be seven, though our sins be seventy times seven, though our sins be more in number than the hairs of our head, yet give us grace in loving penitence to cast ourselves down into the depths of your Compassion.

*Christina Rossetti*

**232** Forgive me my sins, O Lord; forgive me the sins of my youth and the sins of my age, the sins of my soul and the sins of my body, my secret and my whispering sins, my presumptuous and my crying sins, the sins that I have done to please myself, and the sins that I have done to please others. Forgive me those sins which I know, and those which I know not; forgive them, O Lord, forgive them all of Thy great goodness.

*Lancelot Andrewes*

**233** Forgive us, O Lord,
For everything that has spoiled our home life:
For the moodiness and irritability which made us difficult to
   live with;
For the insensitiveness which made us careless of the feelings
   of others;
For selfishness which made life harder for others.

Forgive us, O Lord,
For everything that has spoiled our witness for Thee;
That so often men would never have known that we had
   been with Jesus and pledged ourselves to Him:
That we have so often denied with our lives that which we
   said with our lips;
For the difference between our creed and our conduct, our
   profession and our practice;
For any example which made it easier for men to criticise
   Thy Church or for another to sin.

When we think of ourselves and of the meanness and ugliness and weakness of our lives, we thank Thee for Jesus Christ our Saviour. Grant unto us a true penitence for our sins. Grant that at the foot of the Cross, we may find our burdens rolled away. And so strengthen us by Thy Spirit that in the days to come, we may live more nearly as we ought. Through Jesus Christ our Lord. Amen

*William Barclay*

**234** The hatred which divides nation from nation,
race from race, class from class,
Father, forgive.
The covetous desires of men and nations to
possess what is not their own,
Father, forgive.
The greed which exploits the labours of men,
and lays waste the earth,
Father, forgive.
Our envy of the welfare and happiness of others,
Father, forgive.
Our indifference to the plight of the homeless
and the refugee,
Father, forgive.
The lust which uses for ignoble ends the
bodies of men and women,
Father, forgive.
The pride which leads to trust in ourselves
and not in God,
Father, forgive.

*Coventry Cathedral Prayer, 1964*

**235** If my soul has turned perversely to the dark;
If I have left some brother wounded by the way;
If I have preferred my aims to Thine;
If I have been impatient and would not wait;
If I have marred the pattern drawn out for my life;
If I have cost tears to those I loved;
If my heart has murmured against Thy will,
O Lord, forgive.

*F. B. Meyer*

**236** Jesus, I wish you would let me wash your feet, since it was
through walking about in me that you soiled them. I wish you
would give me the task of wiping the stains from your feet,
because it was my behaviour that put them there. But where
can I get the running water I need to wash your feet? If I have
no water, at least I have tears: let me wash your feet with
them, and wash myself at the same time.

Teach me to sympathise with sinners from the depths of my
heart. That is the supreme virtue, for Scripture says: 'You
shall not gloat over Juda's sons on the day of their downfall;
you shall not boast to them on the day of their discomfiture.'

May I show compassion whenever anyone falls and his sin

comes to my notice. Instead of reproving him, proudly, may I grieve and lament with him. In weeping for others, may I weep for myself.

*St Ambrose of Milan**

**237** Help us, Lord, to see ourselves as you see us, and, in shame for what we are, to cast ourselves in trust upon your love; speak to us the word of pardon, for our trust is not in any virtue or wisdom of our own, but only in the mercy and love of God, which you have shown us in your life and death, our Lord and our God.

*William Temple**

**238** O Lord Jesus Christ, son of the living God, set Thine holy Passion, Cross and Death between Thy judgement and our souls, both now and in the hour of death. And vouchsafe, we beseech Thee, to grant unto the living mercy and grace, to the dead pardon and rest, to Thine holy Church peace and concord, and to us miserable sinners life and joy everlasting; who livest and reignest with the Father and the Holy Ghost, one God, world without end.

*Primer of 1559*

**239** O merciful God, full of compassion, longsuffering, and of great pity, who sparest when we deserve punishment. Make me earnestly to repent, and to be heartily sorry for all my misdoings; make the remembrance so burdensome and painful, that I may flee to thee with a troubled spirit and a contrite heart.

O merciful Lord, visit, comfort, and relieve me; cast me not out from thy presence, and take not thy Holy Spirit from me, but excite in me true repentance; give me in this world knowledge of thy truth, and confidence in thy mercy, and in the world to come life everlasting, for the sake of our Lord and Saviour, thy Son Jesus Christ. Amen

*Rev. Samuel Johnson*

**240** I have deceived myself, dear Christ, I confess it; I have fallen from the heights to the depths. O lift me up again, for well I know delusion came because I wanted it. If I presume again, I'll fall again, and fall to my undoing. Take me to you or I die. It cannot be that I alone shall find you hard and unresponsive.

*St Gregory of Nazianzus*

**241** O Searcher of hearts, You know us better than we know ourselves. You see the sins which our very sinfulness hides from our eyes. But our conscience does accuse us of failing; failing to watch against sin; failing to walk lovingly in one another's company; failing to offer ourselves completely, humbly to your will. Look upon our sorrow, lift us up from where we have fallen in our weakness. Let the dayspring still arise within our hearts bringing forgiveness, healing and strength. Amen

*James Martineau*

**242** Lord, I offer to you all the sins that I have committed from the moment when I could first offend you. Consume them, one and all in the fire of your love, and burn away all their stains. Cleanse my conscience and restore me to your grace and favour.

I also offer to you all that is good within me, though it is small and imperfect, that the good may become more perfect and I may become more and more acceptable to you. Weak and lazy as I am, bring me finally to everlasting union with you. Amen

*Thomas à Kempis*

**243** Lord Jesus, whereas I daily fall, and am ready to sin, vouchsafe me grace as often as I shall fall, to rise again; let me never presume, but always most meekly and humbly acknowledge my wretchedness and frailty, and repent with a firm purpose to amend; let me not despair because of my great frailty, but ever trust in thy most loving mercy and readiness to forgive.

*Robert Leighton*

**244** When I look back upon my life nigh spent,
Nigh spent, although the stream as yet flows on,
I more of follies than of sins repent,
Less of offence than Love's shortcomings moan,
With self, O Father, leave me not alone –
Leave not with the beguiler the beguiled;
Besmirched and ragged, Lord, take back thine own:
A fool I bring thee to be made a child.

*George Macdonald*

**245** O sweet Jesus, I grieve for my sins; vouchsafe to supply whatever is lacking to my true sorrow and to offer for me to

God the Father all the grief which thou hast endured because of my sins and those of the whole world.

*Mechthild of Magdeburg*

**246** O God! who humblest only that thou mayest lift up, who troublest only to calm, who dost shake only to stablish and settle, we bow to the sentence which condemns us. We accept it with penitence and tears. Hide nothing from us of our misery. Shed abroad in our souls thy pure and searching light, that we may see ourselves as we truly are! And at such a sight let there rise at once from us, a cry of surprise and anguish which shall rend the atmosphere of indifference around us, which shall reach thy ear and move thy fatherly compassion towards us, so that, renouncing henceforward all our self-esteem, humbled with a deep humility, believing with a simple faith, we may yield ourselves unreservedly to thy love, to be raised out of the depth of our misery by the depth of thy mercy.

*Adolphe Monod*

**247** Four things which are not in thy treasury,
I lay before thee, Lord, with this petition:
My nothingness, my wants,
my sins, and my contrition.

*Robert Southey*

**248** Almighty and everlasting God, who hatest nothing that thou hast made, and dost forgive the sins of all them that are penitent; Create and make in us new and contrite hearts, that we worthily lamenting our sins, and acknowledging our wretchedness, may obtain of thee, the God of all mercy, perfect remission and forgiveness; through Jesus Christ our Lord.

*Thomas Cranmer*

**249** O Lord Jesus Christ, look upon us with those eyes of yours, the eyes with which you looked upon Peter in the hall of judgement, that with Peter we may repent, and by your great love be forgiven and restored; for your mercy's sake.

*Lancelot Andrewes\**

**250** View me, Lord, a work of Thine:
Shall I then lie drown'd in night?
Might Thy grace in me but shine,
I should seem made all of light.

But my soul still surfeits so
On the poisoned baits of sin,
That I strange and ugly grow,
All is dark and foul within.

Cleanse me, Lord, that I may kneel
At Thine altar, pure and white:
They that once Thy mercies feel,
Gaze no more on earth's delight.

Worldly joys like shadows fade,
When the heav'nly light appears;
But the cov'nants Thou hast made,
Endless, know nor days, nor years.

In Thy word, Lord, is my trust,
To Thy mercies fast I fly;
Though I am but clay and dust,
Yet Thy grace can lift me high.

*Thomas Campion*

251 Forgive my sins, O Lord – forgive me the sins of my present
and the sins of my past, the sins of my soul and the sins of my
body; the sins which I have done to please myself, and the sins
which I have done to please others. Forgive me my wanton
and idle sins, forgive me my serious and deliberate sins,
forgive me those sins which I know and those sins which I
know not, the sins which I have laboured so hard to hide from
others that I have hid them from my own memory. Forgive
them, O Lord, forgive them all. Of thy great mercy let me be
absolved, and of thy bountiful goodness let me be delivered
from the bonds of all that by my frailty I have committed.
Grant this, O heavenly Father, for the sake of Jesus Christ,
our blessed Lord and Saviour. Amen

*Thomas Wilson*

252 Penetrate these murky corners where we hide memories, and
tendencies on which we do not care to look, but which we will
not yield freely up to you, that you may purify and transmute
them. The persistent buried grudge, the half-acknowledged
enmity which is still smouldering; the bitterness of that loss we
have not turned into sacrifice, the private comfort we cling to,
the secret fear of failure which saps our initiative and is really
inverted pride; the pessimism which is an insult to your joy.

Lord, we bring all these to you, and we review them with
shame and penitence in your steadfast light.

*Evelyn Underhill*

253 Superessential essence, nature uncreate,
   framer of the universe,
   I set thee, Lord, before me,
   and to thee I lift up my soul:
   I worship thee kneeling upon my knees,
   and I humble myself under thy mighty hand.
   I stretch forth my hands,
   my soul gaspeth unto thee as a thirsty land:
   I smite you my breast,
   and I say with the publican:
   God be merciful to me the mere sinner,
   the chief of sinners,
   To the sinner beyond the publican,
   be merciful as to the publican.

*Lancelot Andrewes*

254 Forgive them all, O Lord:
   our sins of omission and our sins of commission;
   the sins of our youth and the sins of our riper years;
   the sins of our souls and the sins of our bodies;
   our secret and our more open sins;
   our sins of ignorance and surprise,
   and our more deliberate and presumptuous sin;
   the sins we have done to please ourselves
   and the sins we have done to please others;
   the sins we know and remember,
   and the sins we have forgotten;
   the sins we have striven to hide from others
   and the sins by which we have made others offend;
   forgive them, O Lord, forgive them all for his sake,
   who died for our sins and rose for our justification,
   and now stands at thy right hand to make intercession for us,
   Jesus Christ our Lord.

*John Wesley*

255 O God, our Judge and Saviour, set before us the vision of thy
   purity and let us see our sins in the light of thy holiness. Pierce
   our self-contentment with the shafts of thy burning love, and
   let love consume in us all that hinders us from perfect service

of thy cause; for thy holiness is our judgment, so are thy
wounds our salvation.

*William Temple*

**256** Preserve me, Lord, from the sin which I fear so much:
contempt for your love. May I never sin against the Holy
Spirit who is love and union, harmony and peace. May I never
be separated from your Spirit, from the unity of your peace,
by committing the sin which can never be forgiven, neither
here nor in the world to come. Keep me, O Lord, among my
brothers and kinsfolk that I may proclaim your peace. Keep
me among those who preserve the unity of the Spirit in the
bond of peace.

*Baldwin of Canterbury (+1190)*

**257** You are rich in grace and mercy, you are willing to cleanse all
sinners from their guilt. Cleanse me, have pity on me. In your
mercy spare me, as you spared the publican and the sinful
woman. You take the sinfulness from sinners, O Christ, and
when we repent you make us welcome beside you. Redeemer
of the human race, in your mercy save me.

*Rabbula of Edessa*

**258** Almighty and merciful God, the fountain of all goodness, who
knowest the thoughts of our hearts: We confess that we have
sinned against thee, and done evil in thy sight. Wash us, we
beseech thee, from the stains of our past sins, and give us
grace and power to put away all hurtful things; that, being
delivered from the bondage of sin, we may bring forth fruits
worthy of repentance, and at last enter into thy promised joy;
through the mercy of thy blessed Son Jesus Christ our Lord.

*Alcuin*

**259** Remain, O Christ, in the hearts you have redeemed; You who
are perfect love, pour into our words sincere repentance.

We raise our prayer to you, O Jesus, with faith; pardon the
sin we have committed.

By the holy sign of the cross, by your tortured body, defend
us constantly as your sons.

*The Venerable Bede*

**260** Let us have clean hearts ready inside us for the Lord Jesus, so
that he will be glad to come in, gratefully accepting the

hospitality of those worlds, our hearts: he whose glory and power will endure throughout the ages. Amen

*Origen*

261 We give thee thanks, O heavenly Father, who hast delivered us from the power of darkness and translated us into the kingdom of thy Son; grant, we pray thee, that as by his death he has recalled us to life, so by his presence abiding in us he may raise us to joys eternal; through the same Jesus Christ our Lord.

*Mozarabic Sacramentary*

262 Almighty and most merciful God, we acknowledge and confess that we have sinned against thee in thought, and word, and deed; that we have not loved thee with all our heart and soul, with all our mind and strength; and that we have not loved our neighbour as ourselves. We beseech thee, O God, to be forgiving to what we have been, to help us to amend what we shall be, so that the love of goodness may ever be first in our hearts, and we may follow unto our life's end in the steps of Jesus Christ our Lord.

*John Hunter*

263 Almighty and most merciful Father, we have erred and strayed from thy ways like lost sheep. We have followed too much the devices and desires of our own hearts. We have offended against thy holy laws. We have left undone those things which we ought to have done; and we have done those things which we ought not to have done; and there is no health in us. But thou, O Lord, have mercy upon us, miserable offenders. Spare thou them, O God, which confess their faults. Restore thou them that are penitent; according to thy promises declared unto mankind in Christ Jesu our Lord. And grant, O most merciful Father, for his sake, that we may hereafter live a godly, righteous, and sober life, to the glory of thy holy Name.

*Book of Common Prayer, 1552*

264 Don't tire of Your world, Master.
Don't wash Your hands of Your children,
shaking us off as hopeless,
worthless.

Give us one more chance,
and yet another,
and another.

How Your heart must sorrow as You see our need;
our selfishness and sinfulness,
cruelty and degradation,
indifference to Your commands,
contempt of Your love.

If our hearts sicken over the daily news,
what must You feel?
You who hold the world in Your cupped hands,
bending over it lovingly;
listening, yearning,
challenging to better ways.

Yet spiteful arrows pierce Your heart daily;
Your malicious children spit up in Your face:
that kind face bent over them in tender compassion.
Father-God, forgive Your world:
go on forgiving Your children.
Don't leave us to our own devices,
to our self-made hell,
don't cast us away,
flinging us like unwanted playthings into the chill of
outer space.

We have no merits to plead;
our very wickedness must speak for us.
We need You.

O God, forgive Your world:
give us one more chance.

*Flora Larsson*

**265** Out of deep anguish I cry to you, Lord;
Lord, can you hear me?
To the groaning of my prayers
please carefully listen.
If you, Lord, keep a record of sins,
then none of us dare face you.
But in you we find forgiveness,
therefore we can adore you.
I wait, with all my soul I want,
and hope for the word I need.

With all my soul I long for my Lord,
more than night-watchmen waiting for dawn.
Like the weary looking for sunrise,
let all God's people wait in hope.
For with the Lord there is pure love,
with him is abundant liberty.
He alone can set us free
from all our sins.

*Bruce Prewer*
*(version of Psalm 130)*

# RECONCILIATION

**266** Father, who formed the family of man to live in harmony and peace: we acknowledge before you our divisions, quarrels, hatreds, injustices and greed.

May your Church demonstrate before the world the power of the gospel to destroy divisions, so that in Christ Jesus there may be no barriers of wealth or class, age or intellect, race or colour, but all may be equally your children, members one of another and heirs together of your everlasting kingdom.

*Timothy Dudley-Smith*

**267** Incarnate word of God, who in your flesh reconciled all men to the Father, and continue to reconcile all those who in heartfelt sorrow confess their sins, I thank you that your healing power has touched me, and cleansed me from the leprosy of sin. Mercifully direct all my thoughts, words and actions to the greater glory of the Father, and be my model and help for the rest of my life so that I may persevere in your service and love.

*Michael Buckley*

**268** Let us pray for those who have fallen away,
that they may recover their footing.
Let us pray for those standing firm,
that they may not be tempted to their downfall.
Let us pray for those of whose fall we have been told,
that they may admit the gravity of their sin
and realise that it calls for a serious remedy.

*Cyprian of Carthage*

**269** Let us pray to the Lord, entreating him with sighs and tears, as befits people in our position – placed as we are between the many, lamenting that they have fallen away, and the faithful remnant that fears it may do the same itself; between the weak, laid low in large numbers, and the few still standing firm.

Let us pray that peace may very soon be restored to us, help reach us in our dangers, and God's gracious promises to his servants find fulfilment. May we see the Church restored and our salvation secured; after the rain, fair weather; after the darkness, light; after these storms and tempests, a gentle calm.

Let us ask him to help us, because he loves us as a Father loves his children, and to give us the tokens of his divine power that are usual with him.

*Cyprian of Carthage*

**270** Peace to all men of evil will. Let vengeance cease and punishment and retribution. The crimes have gone beyond measure, our minds can no longer take them in. There are too many martyrs . . . Lord do not weigh their sufferings on your scales of justice, and let them not be written in their act of accusation and demand redress. Pay them otherwise. Credit the torturers, the informers and traitors with their courage and strength of spirit, their dignity and endurance, their smile, their love, their broken hearts which did not give in even in the face of death, even in times of greatest weakness . . . take all this into account Lord for the remission of the sins of their enemies, as the price of the triumph of justice. Take good and not evil into account. And let us remain in our enemies' thoughts not as their victims, not as a nightmare, but as those who helped them overcome their crimes. This is all we ask for them.

*Concentration camp prayer, recorded by Anthony Bloom*

**271** God our Father, we praise you for the gospel of reconciliation. We thank you for the work of the Holy Spirit drawing the scattered flock of Christ into a deeper unity. May this be a sign of hope to our divided world. Enable us, who bear your name, to be instruments of your peace and ever to believe that the peace for which we pray is possible; through Jesus Christ our Lord. Amen

*Kenneth Greet*

# GIFT OF ONE'S SELF

272  O Lord, I give myself to thee, I trust thee wholly. Thou art
wiser than I, more loving to me than I myself. Deign to fulfil
thy high purposes in me whatever they be; work in me and
through me. I am born to serve thee, to be thine, to be thy
instrument. Let me be thy blind instrument. I ask not to see, I
ask not to know, I ask simply to be used. Amen

*John Henry Newman*

273  Lord, I know not what I ought to ask of Thee; Thou only
knowest what I need; Thou lovest me better than I know how
to love myself. O Father! give to Thy child that which he
himself knows not how to ask. I dare not ask either for crosses
or consolations; I simply present myself before Thee, I open
my heart to Thee. Behold my needs which I know not myself;
see and do according to Thy tender mercy. Smite, or heal;
depress me, or raise me up; I adore all Thy purposes without knowing them; I am silent; I offer myself in sacrifice;
I yield myself to Thee; I would have no other desire than to
accomplish Thy will. Teach me to pray. Pray Thyself in me.
Amen

*François Fénelon*

274  O God, our heavenly Father, who so loved the world that thou
didst give thine only Son to die upon the cross: Pour thy love
into our hearts, we humbly beseech thee; that we loving thee
above all things, may give up ourselves, our time, our money,
our talents, to thy service; for the sake of him who loved us
and gave himself for us, Jesus Christ thy Son our Lord.

*John R. W. Stott*

275  Do thou strengthen and prepare my soul first of all, Good of
all good, my Jesus, and do thou arrange that I may do
something for thee, for no one could bear to receive as much
as I have done, and pay nothing in return. Cost what it may,
Lord, permit me not to come into thy presence with such
empty hands, since a man's reward must be in accordance with
his works. Here is my life; here is my honour and my will. I
have given it all to thee; I am thine; dispose of me according to
thy desire.

*St Theresa of Avila*

**276** Stir us up to offer Thee, O Lord, our bodies, our souls, our spirits, in all we love and all we learn, in all we plan and all we do, to offer our labours, our pleasures, our sorrows to Thee; to work through them for Thy Kingdom, to live as those who are not their own, but bought with Thy blood, fed with Thy body; Thine from our birth-hour, Thine now, and Thine for ever and ever.

*Charles Kingsley*

**277** O God, you made me for yourself, to show forth your goodness through me. Show forth, I humbly pray, the life-giving power of your nature, help me to such a true and lively faith, such a thirst after the life and spirit of your Son, Jesus, in my soul that all that is within me may be turned from every inward thought or outward action that is not you.

*William Law*

**278** Lord Jesus Christ, no matter where we are, far away or near at hand, off involved in the hurly-burly of life, immersed in human cares or joys, light-hearted or down in the dumps, draw us to yourself, draw us so that we become totally yours.

*Søren Kierkegaard*

**279** I vow and consecrate to God all that is in me: my memory and my actions to God the Father; my understanding and my words to God the Son; my will and my thoughts to God the Holy Ghost; my heart, my body, my tongue, my senses and all my sorrows to the sacred Humanity of Jesus Christ, 'who was contented to be betrayed into the hands of wicked men and to suffer the torment of the Cross'.

*Francis of Sales*

**280** What shall I render unto Him for all His benefits? I can only give my own self, all I have, and all I am. I desire to surrender myself wholly unto Thee, my God, to live more simply as one separated unto Thee, not finding my joy and comfort in the earthly blessings Thou so richly bestowest on me, but, while thankful for the gracious gifts, looking only to the Giver as the Source of my happiness and the Object of my life. I cannot shake off the habits of thought and feeling which many years have wrought in me; I can only ask of Thee to have mercy on me, poor and needy as I am, and subdue in me all that is perverse and wayward in my heart, and so fill me with Thy

pure and heavenly love, that all my narrowness and selfishness
may be done away in the wideness of Thy love. Amen

*Maria Hare*

281  Turn in, my Lord, turn in to me,
     My heart's a homely place;
     But thou canst make corruption flee,
     And fill it with thy grace:
     So furnishèd it will be brave,
     And a rich dwelling thou shalt have.

*Christopher Harvey*

282  Father,
     Well I know that, given one trusting heart,
     Silently, unnoticed, far away,
     Thy Kingdom comes:

     Well I know that men shall never guess
     Where was the solitary heart that trusted Thee:

     That heart shall dwell unknown,
     Remote and quiet and content in Thee:
     Yet none the less through it,
     Through that weak, solitary, foolish heart,
     Thy Will of love to save mankind
     Shall have been done:

     O Father, Father,
     Here is all my heart, my mind, my will,
     For Thee.

*John S. Hoyland*

283  O Lord, in the simplicity of my heart, I offer myself to thee
     today, to be thy servant for ever, to obey thee, and to be a
     sacrifice of perpetual praise. Amen

*Thomas à Kempis*

284  Lord, teach us to understand that your Son died to save us, not
     from suffering, but from ourselves; not from injustice, far less
     from justice, but from being unjust. He died that we might
     live – but live as he lives, by dying as he died who died to
     himself.

*George Macdonald*

**285** Lord, bestow on me two gifts,
  – to forget myself
  – never to forget thee.
  Keep me from self-love, self-pity, self-will
  in every guise and disguise
  nor ever let me measure myself by myself.
  Save me from self,
  my tempter, seducer, jailer;
  corrupting desire at the spring,
  closing the avenues of grace,
  leading me down the streets of death.
  Rather, let my soul devote to thee
  its aspirations, affections, resolutions.
  Let my mind look unto thee
  in all its searchings, shinings, certitudes.
  Let my body work for thee
  with its full health and abilities.
  Let thy love pass
  into the depth of my heart,
  into the heart of my prayer,
  into the heart of my whole being;
  So that I desert myself
  and dwell and move in thee
  in peace, now and evermore.

*Eric Milner-White*

**286** Almighty and eternal God, so draw our hearts to thee, so
guide our minds, so fill our imaginations, so control our wills,
that we may be wholly thine, utterly dedicated unto thee; and
then use us, we pray thee, as thou wilt, but always to thy glory
and the welfare of thy people; through our Lord and Saviour
Jesus Christ.

*William Temple*

**287** O Lord my God,
  Rescue me from myself, and give me to thee;
  take away from me everything which draws me from thee;
  give me all those things which lead me to thee;
  for Jesus Christ's sake.

*Precationes Piae, 1564*

**288** O eternal God, who has made all things for man, and man for
thy glory: sanctify our bodies and souls, our thoughts and our
intentions, our words and actions. Let our body be a servant

of our mind, and both body and spirit servants of Jesus Christ;
that doing all things for thy glory here, we may be partakers
of thy glory hereafter; through the same Jesus Christ our
Lord.

*Jeremy Taylor*

**289** Living or dying, Lord, I would be Thine; keep me Thine own
for ever, and draw me day by day nearer to Thyself, until I be
wholly filled with Thy love, and fitted to behold Thee, face to
face.

*E. B. Pusey*

**290** To Thee, O Jesu, I direct my eyes;
To Thee my hands, to Thee my humble knees;
To Thee my heart shall offer sacrifice;
To Thee my thoughts, who my thoughts only sees;
To Thee my self – my self and all I give;
To Thee I die; to Thee I only live.

*Attributed to Sir Walter Raleigh*

**291** My Lord and my God,
take me from all that keeps me from you.
My Lord and my God,
grant me all that leads me to you.
My Lord and my God,
take me from myself and give me completely to you.

*Nicholas of Flüe*

**292** Lord, sweet Jesus, this life is full of temptations and enemies,
and help there is none save in thee, dear Jesus. Take me, then,
sweet Jesus, to be under thy rule and thy shepherding, and let
thy handiwork never be undone. Take me, therefore, wholly
to thy heart, that all my desiring be for thee who wholly
ransomed me, so that my heart may never turn from thee
for any temptation, but ever cleave fast to thee, for to love
thee, sweet Jesus, is my most need, my most need, my most
speed.

*Richard Rolle*

**293** Help me, O God, to put off all pretence and to find my true
self.
Help me, O God, to discard all false pictures of you,
whatever cost to my comfort.

Help me, O God, to let go all my problems, and fix my mind
  on you.
Help me, O God, to see my own sins, never to judge my
  neighbour and may the glory be all yours.
Into your hands I commend my spirit,
Your will, not mine, be done.

*Anthony Bloom*

294 Lord, I believe, but would believe more firmly; O Lord, I
  love, but yet would love more warmly. I offer unto Thee my
  thoughts, that they may dwell on thee; my deeds, that they
  may be according to Thee; my sufferings, that they may be for
  Thee. Amen

*Treasury of Devotion*

295 O God, worthy of an infinite love, I have nothing which can
  adequately measure thy dignity but such is my desire towards
  thee, that if I had all that thou hast, I would gladly and
  thankfully resign all to thee.

*St Gertrude*

296 Lord Jesus,
  I give you my hands to do your work.
  I give you my feet to go your way.
  I give you my eyes to see as you do.
  I give you my tongue to speak your words.
  I give you my mind that you may think in me.
  I give you my spirit that you may pray in me.
  Above all, I give you my heart that you may love in me your
    Father and all mankind.
  I give you my whole self that you may grow in me, so that it
    is you, Lord Jesus
  Who live and work and pray in me.

*The Grail Prayer*

297 With all my heart and soul, O God, I thank Thee, that in all
  the changes and chances of this mortal life, I can look up to
  Thee, and cheerfully resign my will to Thine. I have trusted
  Thee, O Father, with myself; my soul is in Thy hand, which I
  truly believe Thou wilt preserve from all evil; my body, and all
  that belongs to it are of much less value. I do therefore, with
  as great security as satisfaction, trust all I have to Thee.
  Amen

*Thomas Wilson*

**298** O my God, thou hast wounded me with love,
Behold the wound that is still vibrating.
O my God, thou hast wounded me with love.
O my God, thy fear hath fallen upon me,
Behold the burn is there and throbs aloud.
O my God, thy fear hath fallen upon me.
O my God, I have known all that is vile,
And thy glory hath stationed itself in me,
O my God, I have known all that is vile.
Take my blood that I have not poured out,
Take my flesh unworthy of thy suffering,
Take my blood that I have not poured out.
Take my heart that has beaten for vain things,
To throb under the thorns of Calvary.
Take my heart that has beaten for vain things.
Ah, thou God of pardon and promises,
What is the pit of mine ingratitude!
Ah, thou God of pardon and promises.
God of terror and God of holiness,
Alas, my sinfulness is a black abyss,
God of terror and holiness.
Thou God of peace, of joy and delight,
All my tears, all my ignorances,
Thou God of peace, of joyous delight.
Thou, God, knowest all this, all this,
How poor I am, poorer than any man,
Thou, O God, knowest all this, all this.
And what I have, my God, I give to thee.

*Paul Verlaine*

**299** O Lord, help us to go out of ourselves, so that we may give ourselves over to Thee, with all our powers, with all that we are and all that we have.

*Jacob Boehme*

**300** Be thou a light unto my eyes, music to mine ears, sweetness to my taste, and full contentment to my heart. Be thou my sunshine in the day, my food at table, my repose in the night, my clothing in nakedness, and my succour in all necessities. Lord Jesu, I give thee my body, my soul, my substance, my fame, my friends, my liberty and my life. Dispose of me and all that is mine as it may seem best to thee and to the glory of thy blessed name.

*John Cosin*

**301**  We offer thee the material of our daily life, believing that thou
canst make it a stepping-stone to heaven.

Free us from fuss and worry and fret, with the thoughts of
thy eternal love.

Help us to laugh at our petty discontent and jealousies and
give us that divine discontent that reaches always for thee and
sees thy goodness everywhere.

Help us to live now in the kingdom prepared for those who
love thee.

*Elsie Chamberlain*

**302**  Lord, my thoughts turn in upon myself. Turn them upward to
thee and outward to thy other children, that I may forget
myself, and lose all fear and anxiety, all self-seeking and
self-consciousness, in worship of thee and in love of others. O
save me from myself to worship, love and serve in perfect
freedom.

*George Appleton*

**303**  O God, grant that at all times you may find me as you desire
me and where you would have me be, that you may lay hold on
me fully, both by the Within and the Without of myself, grant
that I may never break this double thread of my life.

*Teilhard de Chardin*

**304**  Take my life, and let it be
Consecrated, Lord, to Thee;
Take my moments and my days,
Let them flow in ceaseless praise.
Take my hands, and let them move
At the impulse of Thy love.
Take my feet, and let them be
Swift and beautiful for Thee.

Take my voice, and let me sing
Always, only, for my King;
Take my lips, and let them be
Filled with messages from Thee.
Take my silver and my gold;
Not a mite would I withhold.
Take my intellect, and use
Every power as Thou shalt choose.

Take my will, and make it Thine:
It shall be no longer mine.
Take my heart: it is Thine own:
It shall be Thy royal throne.
Take my love; my Lord, I pour
At Thy feet its treasure-store.
Take myself, and I will be
Ever, only, all for Thee.

*Frances R. Havergal*

305 Lord Jesus Christ,
take all my freedom,
my memory, my understanding, and my will.
All that I have and cherish,
you have given me.
I surrender it all to be guided by your will.
Your grace and your love are wealth enough for me.
Give me these, Lord Jesus,
and I ask for nothing more.

*Ignatius of Loyola*

# INDWELLING GOD

306 Help me, O Lord, to descend into the depths of my being,
below my conscious and sub-conscious life until I discover my
real self, that which is given me from thee, the divine likeness
in which I am made and into which I am to grow, the place
where your Spirit communes with mine, the spring from which
all my life rises.

*George Appleton*

307 Grant me, O Lord, the royalty of inward happiness and the
serenity which comes from living close to thee. Daily renew
the sense of joy, and let the eternal spirit of the Father dwell in
my soul and body, filling every corner of my heart with light
and grace, so that bearing about with me the infection of a
good courage, I may be a diffuser of life and may meet all ills
and crosses with gallant and high-hearted happiness, giving
thee thanks always for all things.

*Robert Louis Stevenson*

**308** O Thou that in our bosom's shrine
Dost dwell, unknown, because divine!
I thought to speak, I thought to say,
'The light is here,' 'Behold the way.'
'The voice was thus,' and 'Thus the word,'
And 'Thus I saw,' and 'That I heard' –
but from the lips that half essayed,
The imperfect utterance fell unmade.
Unseen, secure in that high shrine,
Acknowledged, present and divine,
I will not ask some upper air,
Some future day to place Thee there . . .
Do only Thou in that dim shrine,
Unknown or known, remain divine . . .
Be Thou but there! In soul and heart
I will not ask to feel Thou art.

*Arthur H. Clough*

**309** Work within me, within us, within the Church.
Be at the centre of our lives.
Mould us in your image.
Bring about our transformation.
Make us fruitful, Lord,
Now,
Here as well as there,
Me as well as the others.

*Rex Chapman*

**310** O God, our true Life, in Whom and by Whom all things live. I praise, and bless, and adore Thee, I worship Thee, I glorify Thee, I give thanks to Thee for Thy great glory. I humbly beseech Thee to abide with me, to reign in me, to make this heart of mine a holy temple, a fit habitation for Thy Divine Majesty. O Thou Maker and Preserver of all things, visible and invisible! Keep, I beseech Thee, the work of Thine own hands, who trusts in Thy mercy alone for safety and protection. Guard me with the power of Thy grace, here and in all places, now and at all times, for evermore. Amen

*St Augustine of Hippo*

**311** And if still I cannot find Thee, O God, then let me search my heart and know whether it is not rather I who am blind than Thou who art obscure, and I who am fleeing from Thee rather

than Thou from me; and let me confess these my sins before
Thee and seek Thy pardon in Jesus Christ my Lord.

*John Baillie*

312  It is not far to go
     for you are near.
     It is not far to go,
     for you are here.
     And not by travelling, Lord,
     men come to you,
     but by the way of love,
     and we love you.

*Amy Carmichael*

313  Most Holy Spirit, Comforter Divine,
     through thee the life of prayer is made complete,
     through thee the suffering pilgrimage is made joyful,
     through thee the darkness is made light:
     illumine thou my life, inspire my prayer,
     be thou the unity that makes me one,
     that I may be all prayer,
     one coinherence with my Source and End,
     one coinherence with the world of men and nature's order,
     one wholeness in myself;
     purged, restored, reunited in the life
     from which man fell
     and which the passion of the Lord restored
     a temple for thy majesty.

*Gilbert Shaw*

314  Teach us, our God and king,
     In all things thee to see,
     That what we do in anything
     We do it unto thee.

*George Herbert*

315  Open wide the window of our spirits and fill us full of light;
     open wide the door of our hearts, that we may receive and
     entertain Thee with all our powers of adoration and love.

*Christina Rossetti*

316  O Lord, I rejoice and am exceeding glad;
     Because of thy goodness,
     In creating the world.

But much more abundantly,
For the glory of my soul;
Which cut out of nothing thou hast builded
To be a temple unto God,
A living temple of thine omnipresence,
An understanding eye,
A temple of eternity,
A temple of thy wisdom, blessedness, and glory.
O ye powers of mine immortal Soul, bless ye the Lord,
praise him and magnify him for ever.
He hath made you greater,
More glorious, brighter,
Better than the heavens,
A meeter dwelling place for his eternal Godhead
Than the heaven of heavens.
The heaven of heavens,
And all the spaces above the heavens,
Are not able to contain him.
Being but dead and silent place,
They feel not themselves.
They know nothing,
See no immensity nor wideness at all.
But in thee, my soul, there is a perceptive power
To measure all spaces beyond the heavens
And those spaces
By him into thee
To feel and see the heaven of heavens
All things contained in them,
And his presence in thee.
Nor canst thou only feel his omnipresence in thee,
But adore his goodness,
Dread his power,
Reverence his majesty,
See his wisdom,
Rejoice in his bounty,
Conceive his eternity,
Praise his glory.
Which being things transcendent unto place,
Cannot by the heavens at all be apprehended.
With reverence, O God, and dread mixed with joy,
I come before thee.
To consider thy glory in the perfection of my soul
The workmanship of the Lord.

*Thomas Traherne*

**317** God be in my head
And in my understanding.
God be in mine eyes
And in my looking.
God be in my mouth
And in my speaking.
God be in my heart
And in my thinking.
God be at mine end
And at my departing.

*Sarum Primer*

**318** O eternal God, who has taught us by thy holy word that our bodies are the temples of thy Spirit, keep us we most humbly beseech thee temperate and holy in thought, word, and deed, that at the last we, with all the pure in heart, may see thee, and be made like unto thee in thy heavenly kingdom, through Christ our Lord.

*Brooke Foss Westcott*

**319** I adore Thee, Lord Jesus, dwelling in my heart. I beseech Thee abide in me, in all the tranquillity of Thy power, in all the perfection of Thy ways, in all the brightness of Thy presence and in all the holiness of Thy Spirit; that I may know the breadth and length and depth and height of Thy love; and do Thou trample down in me all power of evil in the might of Thy Spirit to the glory of God the Father.

*Jean-Jacques Olier\**

**320** My God, I heard this day,
That none doth build a stately habitation
But he that means to dwell therein.
What house more stately hath there been
Or can be than is man? To whose creation
All things are in decay.
Since then, my God, thou hast
So brave a palace built, O dwell in it,
That it may dwell with thee at last;
Till then afford us so much wit,
That, as the world serves us we may serve thee,
And both thy servants be.

*George Herbert*

**321**  Be born in us
Incarnate Love
take our flesh and blood and
give us Your humanity;
take our eyes and
give us Your vision;
take our minds and
give us Your pure thought;
take our feet and
set them in Your path;
take our hands and
fold them in Your prayer;
take our hearts and
give them Your will
to Love.

*Caryll Houselander*

**322**  O my God, since Thou art with me, and I must now, in obedience to Thy commands, apply my mind to these outward things, I beseech Thee to grant me the grace to continue in Thy presence; and to this end do Thou prosper me with Thy assistance, receive all my work and possess all my affections.

*Brother Lawrence*

**323**  O Lord, my God, Light of the blind and Strength of the weak; yea, also, Light of those that see, and Strength of the strong; hearken unto my soul, and hear it crying out of the depths.

O Lord, help us to turn and seek Thee; for Thou hast not forsaken Thy creatures as we have forsaken Thee, our Creator. Let us turn and seek Thee, for we know Thou art here in our hearts, when we confess to Thee, when we cast ourselves upon Thee, and weep in Thy bosom, after all our rugged ways; and Thou dost gently wipe away our tears, and we weep the more for joy; because Thou, Lord, who madest us, dost remake and comfort us.

Hear Lord, my prayer, and grant that I may most entirely love Thee, and do Thou rescue me, O Lord, from every temptation, even unto the end. Amen

*St Augustine of Hippo*

**324**  O Christ my Lord, I pray that you will turn my heart to you in the depths of my being, where with the noise of creatures silenced and the clamour of bothersome thoughts stilled, I shall stay with you, where I find you always present and where I love and worship you.

*Leonard Lessius*

# ABANDONMENT INTO GOD'S HANDS

**325** Teach us, O Father, to trust Thee with life and with death,
And (though this is harder by far)
With the life and the death of those that are dearer to us
than our life.

Teach us stillness and confident peace
In Thy perfect will,
Deep calm of soul, and content
In what Thou wilt do with these lives Thou hast given.

Teach us to wait and be still,
To rest in Thyself,
To hush this clamorous anxiety,
To lay in Thine arms all this wealth Thou hast given.

Thou lovest these souls that we love
With a love as far surpassing our own
As the glory of noon surpasses the gleam of a candle.

Therefore will we be still,
And trust in Thee.

*John S. Hoyland*

**326** Eternal Father, even as your divine Son, Our Lord Jesus Christ, offers himself to your majesty as holocaust and victim for the human race, even so do I offer myself body and soul to you; do with me what you will; to this end I accept all troubles, mortifications, afflictions, which it shall please you to send me this day. I accept all from your divine will; O my God, may my will ever be conformed to yours!

*Columba Marmion*

**327** Into thy hands, Almighty Father, who dost will peace and purpose loving-kindness, we commend our spirits: our minds to know thee, our hearts to love thee, our wills to serve thee, for we are thine. Into thy hands, Incarnate Saviour, who hast taught us that thou art the way, the truth and the life, receive us and draw us after thee, that we may follow thy steps;

enlighten and guide us, lest the night of sin and error overwhelm us; abide in us and quicken us by the power of thine
indwelling. Into thy hands, O Lord the Spirit, who createst
good and destroyest evil, take us and fashion us after thine
image: let thy comfort strengthen, thy grace renew, and thy
fire cleanse us. Soul and body, in life and in death, in this
world of shadows and in thy changeless world of light eternal,
now and for ever, Father, Son, and Holy Spirit, into thy
hands.

*Frederick B. Macnutt*

**328** O Lord God, make my religion to be my love, my deepest
love, my delight, the love of my life.

Let me never be content with giving thee less than my whole
heart; and that, with no motive which is not pure, no mind
which is not joyful.

Make all my days a looking up and a going forth to greet and
meet that majesty of love which has visited and redeemed thy
people: – the love that would save to the uttermost and is the
glory of thy glory, illimitable, inexhaustible, world without
end.

*Eric Milner-White*

**329** Father,
I abandon myself into your hands;
do with me what you will.
Whatever you may do I thank you:
I am ready for all, I accept all.

Let only your will be done in me,
and in all your creatures.
I wish no more than this, O Lord.

Into your hands I commend my soul:
I offer it to you
with all the love of my heart,
for I love you, Lord,
and so need to give myself,
to surrender myself into your hands,
without reserve,
and with boundless confidence,
for you are my Father.

*Charles de Foucauld*

**330** I am Thine; save me. Behold, O Lord, I am Thy servant and the son of Thine handmaid; an unprofitable servant, yet a servant; a lost son, yet a son. We are all Thy people. Carest Thou not that we perish? Yea, Thou carest.

*Lancelot Andrewes*

**331** Into your hands we commit our spirit.
Into your hands, the open and defenceless hands of love,
into your hands, the accepting and welcoming hands of love,
into your hands, the firm and reliable hands of love,
we commit our spirit.

*Rex Chapman*

**332** O God, Who seest all our weaknesses, and the troubles we labour under, have regard unto the prayers of Thy servant, who stands in need of Thy comfort, Thy direction, and Thy help. Thou alone knowest what is best for us; let me never dispute Thy wisdom or Thy goodness. Lord, so prepare my heart, that no affliction may ever so surprise as to overbear me. Dispose me at all times to a readiness to suffer what Thy Providence shall order or permit. Grant that I may never murmur at Thy appointments, nor be exasperated at the ministers of Thy Providence. Amen

*Thomas Wilson*

**333** I know, O Lord, Thou wilt do Thy part towards me, as I, through Thy grace, desire to do my part towards Thee. I know well Thou canst never forsake those who seek Thee, nor disappoint those who trust Thee. Yet I know too, the more I pray for Thy protection, the more surely and fully I shall have it. And therefore now I cry out to Thee, and entreat Thee, first that Thou wouldest keep me from myself, and from following any will but Thine. Next, I beg of Thee that, in Thine infinite compassion, Thou wouldest temper Thy will to me. Visit me not, O my loving Lord, if it be not wrong so to pray, visit me not with those trying visitations which saints alone can bear! Pity my weakness, and lead me heavenwards in a safe and tranquil course. Still I leave all in Thy hands, only, if Thou shalt bring heavier trials on me, give me more grace, flood me with the fulness of Thy strength and consolation. Amen

*John Henry Newman*

**334** My God, I want Thy guidance and direction in all I do. Let Thy wisdom counsel me, Thy hand lead me, and Thine arm support me. I put myself into Thy hands. Breathe into my soul holy and heavenly desires. Conform me to Thine own image. Make me like my Saviour. Enable me in some measure to live here on earth as He lived, and to act in all things as He would have acted. Amen

*Ashton Oxenden*

**335** O Lord Jesu, our only health and our everlasting life, I give myself wholly unto Thy will; being sure that the thing cannot perish which is committed unto Thy mercy.

Thou, merciful Lord, wast born for my sake: Thou didst suffer both hunger and thirst for my sake; Thou didst preach and teach, didst pray and fast, for my sake: and finally Thou gavest Thy most precious body to die and Thy blood to be shed on the cross, for my sake. Most merciful Saviour, let all these things profit me which Thou freely hast given me. O Lord, into Thy hands I commit my soul.

*Primer of 1559*

**336** God, of your goodness, give me yourself; for you are sufficient for me. I cannot properly ask anything less, to be worthy of you. If I were to ask less, I should always be in want. In you alone do I have all.

*Julian of Norwich*

**337** Deign, Lord,
to fulfil
your high purposes in me,
whatever they be.
Work in and through me.
I am born to serve you,
to be yours,
to be your instrument.
Let me be your blind instrument;
I ask not to see;
I ask not to know;
I ask simply to be used.

*John Henry Newman*

# THE WORK OF PRAYER

**338** My God and Father,
helpme to pray
as my first work,
mine unremitting work,
my highest, finest, and dearest work;
as the work I do for thee, and by thee,
and with thee,
for thy other children and for the whole world.
Infuse and influence it with thy blessed Spirit,
that it be not unwilling, nor unworthy, nor in vain;
that it be not occupied with my own concerns,
nor dwell in the interests dear to myself;
but seek thy purposes, thy glory only;
that it be holy and more holy to the Holiest,
and ever and all through thy Son,
my Saviour Jesus Christ.

*Eric Milner-White*

**339** Lord, we know not what we ought to ask of Thee;
Thou only knowest what we need; Thou lovest us better
than we know how to love ourselves.

O Father! give to us, Thy children, that which we ourselves
know not how to ask. We would have no other desire than to
accomplish Thy will.

Teach us to pray. Pray Thyself in us, for Christ's sake.

*François Fénelon*

**340** Still am I haunting
Thy door with my prayers;
Still they are panting
Up thy steep stairs!
Wouldst thou not rather
Come down to my heart,
And there, O my Father,
Be what thou art?

*George Macdonald*

**341** Lord, our God, great, eternal, wonderful in glory, Who
keepest covenant and promises for those that love Thee with
their whole heart; Who art the Life of all, the Help of those
that flee unto Thee, the Hope of those who cry unto Thee;

cleanse us from our sins, secret and open, and from every thought displeasing to Thy goodness, cleanse our bodies and souls, our hearts and consciences, that with a pure heart and a clear soul, with perfect love and calm hope, we may venture confidently and fearlessly to pray unto Thee. Amen

*Coptic Liturgy of St Basil*

342 My prayers, my God, flow from what I am not,
I think thy answers make me what I am.
Like weary waves thought flows upon thought,
But the still depth beneath is all thine own,
And there thou mov'st in paths to us unknown.
Out of strange strife thy peace is strangely wrought.
If the lion in us pray – thou answerest the lamb.

*George Macdonald*

343 Good God, say amen to my prayers, if it be thy gracious will; but if in anything I have asked or done amiss, pardon my infirmities, and answer my necessities, for Jesus and His mercies' sake. Amen

*Thomas Wilson*

344 Lord, what a change within us one short hour
Spent in thy presence will prevail to make,
What heavy burdens from our bosoms take,
What parched grounds refresh, as with a shower!
We kneel, and all around us seems to lower;
We rise, and all, the distant and the near,
Stands forth in sunny outline, brave and clear;
We kneel how weak, we rise how full of power.
Why therefore should we do ourselves this wrong
Or others – that we are not always strong,
That we are ever overborne with care,
That we should ever weak or heartless be,
Anxious or troubled, when with us is prayer,
And joy and strength and courage are with Thee?

*Richard Chenevix Trench*

345 O Lord our God! You know who we are; men with good consciences and with bad, persons who are content and those who are discontent, the certain and the uncertain, Christians by conviction and Christians by convention, those who believe, those who half-believe, those who disbelieve.
     And you know where we have come from: from the circle of

relatives, acquaintances and friends or from the greatest loneliness, from a life of quiet prosperity or from manifold confusion and distress, from family relationships that are well ordered or from those disordered or under stress, from the inner circle of the Christian community or from its outer edge.

But now we all stand before you, in all our differences, yet alike in that we are all in the wrong with you and with one another, that we must all one day die, that we would all be lost without your grace, but also in that your grace is promised and made available to us all in your dear Son Jesus Christ. We are here together in order to praise you through letting you speak to us. We beseech you to grant that this may take place in this hour, in the name of your Son our Lord.

*Karl Barth*

**346** O Lord take away all coldness, all wanderings of the thoughts, and fix our souls upon thee and thy love, O merciful Lord and Saviour, in this our hour of prayer.

*Edward W. Benson*

**347** Lift up our souls, O Lord, to the pure, serene light of thy presence; that there we may breathe freely, there repose in thy love, there may be at rest from ourselves, and from thence return, arrayed in thy peace, to do and bear what shall please thee; for thy holy name's sake.

*E. B. Pusey*

**348** Lord, lay the taste of prayer upon my tongue,
And let my lips speak banquets unto Thee;
Then may this richest feast, when once begun,
Keep me in hunger through eternity.

*Ralph W. Seager*

**349** Holy Jesus, give me the gift and spirit of prayer; Supply my ignorances, passionate desires and imperfect choices with your grace that my needs may be fulfilled.

*Jeremy Taylor*

**350** Look graciously upon us, O Holy Spirit, and give us, for our hallowing, thoughts which pass into prayer, prayers which pass into love, and love which passes into life with thee for ever.

*New Every Morning*

**351** Lord you know what I want, if it be your will that I have it, and if it be not your will, good Lord, do not be displeased, for I want nothing which you do not want.

*Julian of Norwich*

**352** He prayeth well who loveth well
Both man and bird and beast;
He prayeth best who loveth best
All things both great and small,
For the dear God who loveth us
He made and loveth all.

*William Blake*

**353** Ah Lord, my prayers are dead, my affections dead, and my heart is dead: but thou art a living God and I bear myself upon thee.

*William Bridge*

**354** Be present with us as we pray, O Lord, that our prayers may reach you the quicker; and may our Saviour, who is seated in your presence, continually accompany us through the dangers of this life; through the same Jesus Christ, our Lord.

*Leonine Sacramentary**

**355** Almighty God, who has given us the desire to join with one another in our common prayer. We remember your promise that when two or three are gathered together in your name you will grant our requests; hear our prayers and fulfil our desires, granting us, above all else, a knowledge of your truth in this world and everlasting life with you in the next.

*St John Chrysostom*

**356** O Almighty God, from whom every good prayer cometh, and who pourest out, on all who desire it, the spirit of grace and supplication: Deliver us, when we draw near to thee, from coldness of heart and wanderings of mind; that with steadfast thoughts and kindled affection we may worship thee in spirit and in truth; through Jesus Christ our Lord.

*William Bright*

**357** O my Lord, I am in a dry land, all dried up and cracked by the violence of the north wind and the cold; but as thou seest, I ask for nothing more; thou wilt send me both dew and warmth when it pleaseth thee.

*Jane de Chantal*

**358** Lord, since thou hast taken from all that I had of thee, yet of thy grace leave that gift which every dog has by nature, that of being true to thee in my distress, when I am deprived of any consolation. This I desire more fervently than all thy heavenly kingdom.

*Mechthild of Magdeburg*

**359** I'll hope no more
For things that will not come:
And, if they do, they prove but cumbersome;
Wealth brings much woe,
And, since it fortunes so,
'Tis better to be poor,
Than so abound,
As to be drown'd
Or overwhelm'd with store.

Pale care, avant!
I'll learn to be content
With that small stock Thy bounty gave or lent.
What may conduce
To my most healthful use,
Almighty God, me grant;
But that, or this,
That hurtful is
Deny Thy suppliant.

*Robert Herrick*

**360** Teach us, O Spirit of God, that silent language which says all things. Teach our souls to remain silent in thy presence: that we may adore thee in the depths of our being and await all things from thee, whilst asking of thee nothing but the accomplishment of thy will. Teach us to remain quiet under thy action and produce in our soul that deep and simple prayer which says nothing and expresses everything, which specifies nothing and expresses everything.

*John Nicholas Grou*

**361** Why, O Lord, is it so hard for me to keep my heart directed toward you? Why do the many little things I want to do, and the many people I know, keep crowding into my mind, even during the hours that I am totally free to be with you and you alone? Why does my mind wander off in so many directions, and why does my heart desire the things that lead me astray? Are you not enough for me? Do I keep doubting your love and

care, your mercy and grace? Do I keep wondering, in the
centre of my being, whether you will give me all I need if I just
keep my eyes on you?

Please accept my distractions, my fatigue, my irritations,
and my faithless wanderings. You know me more deeply and
fully than I know myself. You love me with a greater love than
I can love myself. You even offer me more than I can desire.
Look at me, see me in all my misery and inner confusion, and
let me sense your presence in the midst of my turmoil. All I
can do is show myself to you. Yet, I am afraid to do so. I am
afraid that you will reject me. But I know – with the knowledge of faith – that you desire to give me your love. The only
thing you ask of me is not to hide from you, not to run away in
despair, not to act as if you were a relentless despot.

Take my tired body, my confused mind, and my restless
soul into your arms and give me rest, simple quiet rest. Do I
ask too much too soon? I should not worry about that. You
will let me know. Come, Lord Jesus, come. Amen

*Henri Nouwen*

362 O Lord our God, grant us grace to desire thee with a whole
heart, so that desiring thee we may seek and find thee; and so
finding thee, may love thee; and loving thee, may hate those
sins which separate us from thee, for the sake of Jesus Christ.

*St Anselm*

363 O Lord, hear our prayers,
not according to the poverty of our asking
but according to the richness of your grace,
so that our lives may conform to those desires
which accord with your will;
through Jesus Christ our Lord.

*Reinhold Niebuhr*

## II  DEVOTIONAL PRAYERS

## MORNING PRAYERS

**364** O God, our Father, we thank you for waking us to see the light of this new day. Grant that we may waste none of its hours; soil none of its moments; neglect none of its opportunities; fail in none of its duties. And bring us to the evening time undefeated by any temptation, at peace with ourselves, and with you. This we ask for your love's sake.

*William Barclay**

**365** We give you heartfelt thanks, heavenly Father, for the rest of the past night, and for the gift of a new day with its opportunities of living to your glory. May we so pass its hours in the perfect freedom of your service that, when evening comes, we may again give you thanks; through Jesus Christ our Lord.

*Office of the Orthodox Church*

**366** The day returns and brings us the petty sound of irritating concerns and duties. Help us to perform them with laughter and kind faces. Let cheerfulness abound with industry. Give us to go happily on our business all this day, bring us to our beds weary and content and undishonoured, and grant us in the end the gift of sleep; for Jesus Christ's sake.

*Robert Louis Stevenson*

**367** O Lord my God,
teach my heart this day where and how to see you,
where and how to find you.

You have made me and remade me,
and you have bestowed on me
all the good things I possess,
and still I do not know you.
I have not yet done that
for which I was made.

Teach me to seek you,
for I cannot seek you
unless you teach me,
or find you
unless you show yourself to me.

Let me seek you in my desire,
Let me desire you in my seeking.
Let me find you by loving you,
Let me love you when I find you.

*St Anselm*

**368** Almighty and everlasting God, with whom nothing is obscure, nothing dark, send forth thy light into our hearts that we may perceive the brightness of thy law and, walking in thy way, may fall into no sin; through thy beloved Son and our beloved example, Jesus Christ.

*Gregorian Sacramentary*

**369** O Lord, we thank thee for this new day with its new strength and vigour, its new hopes and its new opportunities. Help us to meet its joys with praise, its difficulties with fortitude, its duties with fidelity. Grant us wisdom and clear vision. Direct our steps and guard us from error. And of thy great mercy deliver us from evil; through Jesus Christ our Lord.

*H. Bisseker*

**370** For morning light and the gift of a new day,
we praise you, our heavenly Father;
and with thankful hearts we now entrust ourselves
and those we love into your hands,
praying that you will help us,
guide us, and keep us
in all that lies before us this day;
for the sake of Jesus Christ our Lord.

*Frank Colquhoun*

**371** Lord Jesus Christ, who alone art Wisdom, Thou knowest what is best for us; mercifully grant that it may happen to us only as it is pleasing to Thee and as seems good in Thy sight this day; for Thy Name's sake. Amen

*King Henry VI*

**372** O God, who hast folded back the mantle of the night, to clothe us in the golden glory of the day, chase from our hearts all gloomy thoughts, and make us glad with the brightness of hope, that we may effectively aspire to unwon virtues; through Jesus Christ our Lord.

*Ancient Collect*

373 Almighty God, we bless and praise Thee that we have wakened to the light of another day; and now we will think of what a day should be.

Our days are Thine, let them be spent for Thee.

Our days are few, let them be spent with care.

There are dark days behind us, forgive their sinfulness; there may be dark days before us, strengthen us for their trials. We pray Thee to shine on this day, the day which we may call our own.

Lord, we go about our daily work; help us to take pleasure therein. Show us clearly what our duty is; help us to be faithful in doing it. Let all we do be well done, fit for Thine eye to see.

Give us strength to do, patience to bear, let our courage never fail.

When we cannot love our work, let us think of it as Thy task, and by our true love to Thee make unlovely things shine in the light of Thy great love, through Jesus Christ our Lord.

*George Dawson*

374 O Lord, I have a busy world around me; eye, ear, and thought will be needed for all my work to be done in that busy world. Now, before I enter upon it, I would commit eye, ear, and thought, to thee! Do thou bless them and keep their work thine, such as, through thy natural laws, my heart beats and my blood flows without any thought of mine for them, so may my spiritual life hold on its course at those times when my mind cannot consciously turn to thee to commit each particular thought to thy service. Hear my prayer for my dear Redeemer's sake. Amen

*Thomas Arnold*

375 God, make each moment of our lives a miracle; God, make us laugh at the utterly impossible; God, give us hope when all things seem hopeless, peace where no peace could be, love for the unlovable. Make us to gamble all on Your Almightiness, and to dare everything in Your great service.

*M. E. Procter*

376 Blessed are You, Lord, God of our fathers. You turn the shadow of death into morning, bringing light to my eyes. O

Lord may Your sun dispel the night-mist of my sins. Grant that I may become a child of the light and of the day. Keep me this day from sin. Uphold me when I stumble and pick me up if I should fall. Let this day add some knowledge or good deed to yesterday. Oh, let me hear Your loving-kindness in the morning for in You is my trust.

*Lancelot Andrewes*

377 Let our prayer, O Lord, come before Thee in the morning. Thou didst take upon Thee our feeble and suffering nature; grant us to pass this day in gladness and peace, without stumbling and without stain; that reaching the eventide free from evil, we may praise Thee, the eternal King: through Thy mercy, O our God, Who art blessed, and dost live, and govern all things, world without end.

*St Anselm*

378 Thou, who very early in the morning while the sun was yet arising, didst rise from the dead;
Raise us up daily unto newness of life,
and save us, O our Lord and Saviour Jesus Christ.

*Lancelot Andrewes*

379 Thou who at the third hour of the morning didst send down thy Holy Spirit on the Apostles;
Take not away the same Spirit from us,
but renew him daily within us,
and save us, O our Lord and Saviour Jesus Christ.

*Lancelot Andrewes*

380 O God, our Father, help us all through this day so to live that we may bring help to others, credit to ourselves and to the name we bear, and joy to those that love us, and to you.
Cheerful when things go wrong;
Persevering when things are difficult;
Serene when things are irritating.
Enable us to be;
Helpful to those in difficulties;
Kind to those in need;
Sympathetic to those whose hearts are sore and sad.
Grant that;
Nothing may make us lose our tempers;
Nothing may take away our joy;
Nothing may ruffle our peace;

Nothing may make us bitter towards anyone.
So grant that through all this day all with whom we work, and all those whom we meet, may see in us the reflection of the master, whose we are, and whom we seek to serve. This we ask for your love's sake.

*William Barclay*

381 Lord God, make us watchful to benefit, and not to injure the minds and souls of those with whom we have to do this day; and give us grace, by word and influence and good example to promote their happiness and their good; through Jesus Christ our Lord.

*Charles J. Vaughan*

382 O Lord, the day is thine, and the night is thine;
thou hast prepared the light and the sun;
they continue this day according to thine ordinance,
for all things serve thee.
Blessed art thou, O Lord,
who turnest the shadow of death into the morning,
and dost renew the face of the earth.

*Lancelot Andrewes*

383 Warm our cold hearts, Lord, we beseech Thee. Take away all that hinders us from giving ourselves to Thee.
Mould us according to Thine own image. Give us grace to obey Thee in all things, and ever to follow Thy gracious leading.
Make us this day to be kind to our fellows, to be gentle and unselfish, careful to hurt no one by word or deed, but anxious to do good to all, and to make others happy.
Give us a meek and a loving spirit, which in Thy sight is of great price. We would not live just for ourselves, but for Thee.

*Ashton Oxenden*

384 O eternal Son of God, who came from the Father, the fountain of light, to enlighten the darkness of the world. Shine upon us today that in whatever we do we shall reflect your light, for your Name's sake.

*Jeremy Taylor\**

385 O Thou, Whose name is Love, Who never turnest away from the cry of Thy needy children, give ear to my prayer this morning. Make this a day of blessing to me, and make me a

blessing to others. Keep all evil away from me. Preserve me from outward transgression and from secret sin. Help me to control my temper. May I check the first risings of anger or sullenness. If I meet with unkindness or ill-treatment, give me that charity which suffereth long and beareth all things. Make me kind and gentle towards all, loving even those who love me not. Let me live this day as if it were to be my last. O my God, show me the path that Thou wouldest have me to follow. May I take no step that is not ordered by Thee, and go nowhere except Thou, Lord, go with me. Amen

*Ashton Oxenden*

**386** We commend to you, Lord,
our souls and our bodies,
our minds and our thoughts,
our prayers and our hopes,
our health and our work,
our life and our death;
our parents and brothers and sisters,
our benefactors and friends,
our neighbours, our countrymen,
and all Christian folk
this day and always.

*Lancelot Andrewes*

**387** O Jesus, watch over me always, especially today, or I shall betray you like Judas.

*Philip Neri*

**388** I want to begin this day with thankfulness, and continue it
with eagerness.
I shall be busy; let me set about things in the spirit of service
to you and to my fellows, that Jesus knew in the
carpenter's shop in Nazareth.
I am glad that he drew no line between work sacred and
secular.

Take the skill that resides in my hands, and use it today;
Take the experience that life has given me, and use it;
Keep my eyes open, and my imagination alert, that I may see
how things look to others, especially the unwell, the
worried, the overworked. For your love's sake. Amen

*Rita Snowden*

**389** Make us of quick understanding and tender conscience, O Lord; that understanding, we may obey every word of thine this day, and discerning, may follow every suggestion of thine indwelling Spirit. Speak, Lord, for thy servant heareth, through Jesus Christ our Lord. Amen

*Christina Rossetti*

**390** O my God, make me happy this day in Thy service. Let me do nothing, say nothing, desire nothing, which is contrary to Thy will. Give me a thankful spirit, and a heart full of praise for all that Thou hast given me, and for all Thou hast withheld from me. Amen

*Ashton Oxenden*

**391** Grant us, O Lord, to pass this day in gladness and peace, without stumbling and without stain; that, reaching the eventide victorious over all temptations, we may praise you, the eternal God, who are blessed, and governs all things, world without end. Amen

*Mozarabic Sacramentary*

**392** Father, may nothing this day come between me and Thee. May I will, do, and say, just what Thou, my loving and tender Father, willest me to will, do, and say. Work Thy holy will in me and through me this day. Protect me, guide me, bless me, within and without, that I may do something this day for love of Thee; something which shall please Thee; and that I may, this evening, be nearer to Thee, though I see it not, nor know it. Lead me, O Lord, in a straight way unto Thyself, and keep me in Thy grace unto the end. Amen

*E. B. Pusey*

**393** As I begin this day
become flesh again
in me, Father.
Let your timeless and everlasting love
live out this sunrise to sunset
within the possibilities,
and the impossibilities
of my own, very human life.

Help me to become
Christ to my neighbour,
food to the hungry,
health to the sick,

friend to the lonely,
freedom to the enslaved,
in all my daily living.

*J. Barrie Shepherd**

**394** Lord Jesus Christ, I thank thee; thou hast watched over and protected me, thy unworthy servant, with thy presence all the night past, bringing me whole, safe and unharmed to this hour. I thank thee for all the blessings given, of thy great goodness, to me.

*St Edmund of Abingdon*

**395** Help us this day, O God, to serve thee devoutly, and the world busily. May we do our work wisely, give succour secretly, go to our meat appetitely, sit thereat discreetly, arise temperately, please our friends duly, go to our bed merrily, and sleep surely; for the joy of our Lord, Jesus Christ.

*Medieval Prayer*

**396** Helper of men who turn to you,
Light of men in the dark,
Creator of all that grows from seed,
Promotor of all spiritual growth,
have mercy, Lord, on me
and make me a temple fit for yourself.
Do not scan my transgressions too closely,
for if you are quick to notice my offences,
I shall not dare to appear before you.
In your great mercy,
in your boundless compassion,
wash away my sins, through Jesus Christ,
your only Child, the truly holy,
the chief of our souls' healers.
Through him may all glory be given you,
all power and honour and praise,
throughout the unending succession
of ages. Amen

*From a second-century papyrus*

**397** Living each day to the full
Lord, let me live this day
as if it were my first day,
or my last.
Let me bring to it

all the wonder and amazement of a new-born child;
the trust
that welcomes all I meet,
expects of them only the best,
and grants them the benefit
of every possible doubt;
But let me also bring
the wisdom and experience of the aged to this day;
the tenderness
that grows from years of care and gentle giving;
the hope
that has been forged through all the fires of doubt.

*J. Barrie Shepherd**

**398** O Lord, Who, in infinite wisdom and love, orderest all things for Thy children, order everything this day for me in Thy tender pity. Thou knowest my weakness, Who madest me; Thou knowest how my soul shrinks from all pain. Lord, I know Thou wilt lay no greater burden on me than Thou canst help me to bear. Teach me to receive all things this day from Thee. Enable me to commend myself in all things to Thee; grant me in all things to please Thee; bring me through all things nearer unto Thee; bring me, day by day, nearer to Thyself, to life everlasting. Amen

*E. B. Pusey*

**399** Be with me, Lord, at my rising in the morning. Have kindly regard to me, my Lord, and guide my actions, my words and my thoughts. Keep me in the right path that I spend the day according to thy will. Give me reverence of thee and a repentant heart. Guide my hearing that I pay no attention to backbiting, nor to untrue and foolish talk, but let my ears be alert for the voice of God. Watch my steps that I go not about from place to place with idle mind, but united with the thought of God in my mind. Restrain my hands, that they be not ever seeking undeserved rewards, but let them be, as it were in service, offered to the Lord of this world, that the prophet's prayer may be mine. The lifting up of my hands shall be my evening sacrifice.

*Book of Cerne*
*(of the tenth century)*

**400** For joys of service, thee we praise,
whose favour crowneth all our days;
For humble tasks that bring delight,

when done, O Lord, as in thy sight.
Accept our offerings, Lord most high,
our work, our purpose sanctify,
and with our gifts may we have place,
now in the Kingdom of thy grace.

*Venantius Fortunatus*

**401** We beseech thee, O Lord, to purify our consciences by thy
daily visitation; that when thy Son our Lord cometh, he may
find in us a mansion prepared for himself; through the same
Jesus Christ our Lord.

*Gelasian Sacramentary*

**402** Into your hands, O Lord, we commend ourselves this day. Let
your presence be with us to its close. Strengthen us to remember that in whatsoever good work we do we are serving you.
Give us a diligent and watchful spirit, that we may seek in all
things to know your will, and knowing it, gladly to perform it,
to the honour and glory of your name; through Jesus Christ
our Lord.

*Gelasian Sacramentary*

**403** Glory to Thee, who safe hast kept,
And hast refresh'd me whilst I slept.
Heaven is, dear Lord, where'er Thou art;
O never, then, from me depart.

Lord, I my vows to Thee renew,
Scatter my sins as morning dew;
Guard my first springs of thought and will,
And with Thyself my spirit fill.

Direct, control, suggest, this day,
All I design, or do, or say;
That all my powers, with all their might,
In Thy sole glory may unite.

Praise God, from whom all blessings flow,
Praise Him, all creatures here below;
Praise Him above, ye heavenly host,
Praise Father, Son, and Holy Ghost.

*Thomas Ken*

**404** Lord Jesus Christ, to whom belongs all that is in heaven and
earth, I desire to consecrate myself wholly to you and to be

yours for evermore. This day I offer myself to you in single-
ness of heart, to serve and obey you always, and I offer you
without ceasing, a sacrifice of praise and thanksgiving. Receive me, O my Saviour, in union with the holy oblation of
your precious blood which I offer to you this day, in the
presence of angels, that this sacrifice may avail unto my
salvation and that of the whole world.

*Thomas à Kempis*

405 Be thou a bright flame before me,
Be thou a guiding star above me,
Be thou a smooth path below me,
Be thou a kindly shepherd behind me,
Today – tonight – and forever.

*St Columba of Iona*

406 Who can tell what a day may bring forth? Cause me therefore,
gracious God, to live every day as if it were to be my last, for I
know not but that it may be such. Cause me to live now as I
shall wish I had done when I come to die. O grant that I may
not die with any guilt on my conscience, or any known sin
unrepented of, but that I may be found in Christ, who is my
only Saviour and Redeemer.

*Thomas à Kempis*

407 Eternal God, who knows neither morning nor evening, yet
wraps us in love both night and day, lift the curtain of night
from the world and the veil from our hearts. Rise with thy
morning sun upon our souls and enliven our work and prayer.
May we walk this day in the steps of Him who worked in
harmony with your will. Amen

*James Martineau*

408 Eternal God, who committest to us the swift and solemn trust
of life; since we know not what a day may bring forth, but only
that the hour for serving Thee is always present, may we wake
to the instant claims of Thy holy will; not waiting for tomorrow, but yielding today.

Lay to rest, by the persuasion of Thy spirit, the resistance of
our passion, indolence or fear. Consecrate with Thy presence
the way our feet may go; and the humblest work will shine,
and the roughest places be made plain.

Lift us above unrighteous anger and mistrust into faith and
hope and charity by a simple and steadfast reliance on Thy

sure will. In all things draw us to the mind of Christ, that Thy lost image may be traced again, and Thou mayest own us as at one with Him and Thee.

*James Martineau*

**409** The privilege of yielding unto Thee,
The day with all it holds in store for me,
In every act to do it as for Thee.
A housewife's humble prayer.

To start the day with all its duties small
And claim Thy strength and promised help in all.
To know that Thou wilt answer ere I call.
A housewife's answered prayer.

To offer unto Thee when night draws nigh
A humble worship – penitential sigh.
To have Thy Blessings as Thou passest by.
A housewife's grateful prayer.

*Margaret H. Hancock*

**410** Teach us, O gracious Lord, to begin our daily tasks with fear, to go on with obedience, and to finish them in love, and then to wait patiently in hope, and with cheerful confidence to look up to thee, whose promises are faithful and rewards infinite; through Jesus Christ our Lord.

*George Hickes*

**411** O merciful Lord God and heavenly Father, I offer you praise and thanks for preserving me this night and continually throughout my life. I offer myself and my day to you, but not only today, every day while I live. May your Holy Spirit direct and guide me this day, driving all darkness away from my heart that I may walk in the light of the truth, through Jesus Christ our Lord and Saviour. Amen

*Henry VIII's Primer*

**412** Keep us from sin in all we do today, Lord. Fill us with a holy simplicity, content to seek and do your will. Help us to be wholehearted in the work you have given us to do, not giving short measure in return for what we have been given in energy, strength and talent. Preserve us in the true peace that comes from unity with your will and purpose. Amen

*James Martineau*

**413** O Lord, when I awake and day begins,
waken me to Thy Presence;
waken me to Thine indwelling;
waken me to inward sight of Thee,
and speech with Thee,
and strength from Thee;
that all my earthly walk may waken into song
and my spirit leap up to Thee all day, all ways.

O my God
all times are Thy times,
and every day Thy day,
made lovely only with Thy light.
Bring us, O Lord, to that blessed eternal day
which Thy Son our Saviour hath won for us,
and to the perfect light.

*Eric Milner-White*

**414** Father in heaven, you have given us a mind to know you, a will to serve you, and a heart to love you. Be with us today in all that we do, so that your light may shine out in our lives.

We pray that we may be today what you created us to be, and may praise your name in all that we do.

We pray for your Church: may it be a true light to all nations; May the Spirit of your Son Jesus guide the words and actions of all Christians today.

We pray for all who are searching for truth: bring them your light and your love.

Give us, Lord, a humble, quiet, peaceable, patient, tender and charitable mind, and in all our thoughts, words and deeds a taste of the Holy Spirit. Give us, Lord, a lively faith, a firm hope, a fervent charity, a love of you. Take from us all luke-warmness in meditation, dullness in prayer. Give us fervour and delight in thinking of you and your grace, your tender compassion towards me. The things that we pray for, good Lord, give us grace to labour for: through Jesus Christ our Lord.

*Thomas More*

# EVENING PRAYERS

**415** Holy Spirit, I thank you for the quiet moments of this busy day when you spoke to me of your abiding love. Teach me now as I lie down to rest how to listen to you when you speak in the silence of the night, in the silence of my heart. Teach me waking or sleeping how to watch and how to listen for your still, small voice which gives meaning and direction to every moment of my life.

*Michael Buckley*

**416** My thanks, O holy Lord, Father Almighty, Eternal God, for thy divine mercy has kept me safe throughout this day; grant that I pass this night tranquilly and in cleanness of mind and body, that rising chaste in the morning hours, I may again do thee grateful service.

*Alcuin*

**417** Holy Spirit, I thank you for being with me this day, for all the happiness your will has brought, and for all the toil and hardships I have had to accept. Forgive me for the times when I have forgotten you amid the cares of life. Forgive me also if I have not accepted any suffering in the same spirit as Christ my Lord. Help me to rest in peace this night, that I may wake truly refreshed and willing to spend a new day in your service. Guard me this night, as the good shepherd guards his flock. Grant that, in your mercy and love, when I close my eyes on this world for the last time, I may wake in the joy of your presence to a new everlasting day.

*Harold Winstone*

**418** Almighty and Everlasting God, Who commandest Thy mercy in the day time, and in the night declarest the same: We humbly beseech Thee, Who hast preserved us this day in safety, that tonight Thou wilt guard our rest; through Jesus Christ our Lord.

*Mozarabic Sacramentary*

**419** Be present, O merciful God, and protect us through the silent hours of this night, so that we who are wearied by the changes and chances of this fleeting world may repose upon thy eternal changelessness; through Jesus Christ our Lord.

*Leonine Sacramentary*

**420** Before we go to rest, we would commit ourselves to God's care through Christ, beseeching him to forgive us for all our sins of this day past, and to keep alive his grace in our hearts, and to cleanse us from all sin, pride, harshness, and selfishness, and to give us the spirit of meekness, humility, firmness, and love. O Lord, keep thyself present to us ever, and perfect thy strength in our weakness. Take us and ours under thy blessed care, this night and evermore; through Jesus Christ our Lord.

*Thomas Arnold*

**421** Into Thy hands, O Lord, we commend our souls and bodies, beseeching thee to keep us this night under thy protection, and to strengthen us for thy service on the morrow, for Christ's sake.

*William Laud\**

**422** Save us, O Lord, while waking, and guard us while sleeping, that when we wake, we may watch with Christ, and when we sleep we may rest in peace.

*Roman Breviary*

**423** O Merciful God, Eternal Light, shining in darkness, thou who dispellest the night of sin and all blindness of heart, since thou hast appointed the night for rest and the day for labour, we beseech thee grant that our bodies may rest in peace and quietness, that afterward they may be able to endure the labour they must bear. Temper our sleep that it be not disorderly, that we may remain spotless both in body and soul, yea that our sleep itself may be to thy glory. Enlighten the eyes of our understanding that we may not sleep in death, but always look for deliverance from this misery. Defend us against all assaults of the devil and take us into thy holy protection. And although we have not passed this day without greatly sinning against thee, we beseech thee to hide our sins with thy mercy, as thou hidest all things on earth with the darkness of the night, that we may not be cast out from thy presence. Relieve and comfort all those who are afflicted in mind, body, or estate. Through Jesus Christ our Lord. Amen

*John Calvin*

**424** Let our night's peaceful rest, we beseech thee, O Lord our God, renew our strength after the burdens of the day, for it is thy divine appointment that, as night and day succeed each other, our weak human nature may be restored.

*Leonine Sacramentary*

425  God that madest earth and heaven,
Darkness and light,
Who the day for toil hast given,
For rest the night;
Guard us waking, guard us sleeping,
And when we die:
May we in thy mighty keeping
All peaceful lie.

*Reginald Heber*

426  Glory to Thee, my God, this night
For all the blessings of the light;
Keep me, O keep me, King of kings,
Beneath Thine own almighty wings.

Forgive me, Lord, for Thy dear Son,
The ill that I this day have done,
That with the world, myself, and Thee,
I, ere I sleep, at peace may be.

Teach me to live, that I may dread
The grave as little as my bed;
Teach me to die, that so I may
Rise glorious at the awful day.

Praise God, from whom all blessings flow,
Praise him, all creatures here below,
Praise him above, ye heavenly host,
Praise Father, Son, and Holy Ghost.

*Thomas Ken*

427  Into thy hands, O Lord and Father, we commend our souls and our bodies, our parents and our homes, friends and servants, neighbours and kindred, our benefactors and brethren departed, all thy people faithfully believing, and all who need thy pity and protection. Enlighten us with thy holy grace, and suffer us never more to be separated from thee, who art one God in Trinity, God everlasting.

*St Edmund of Abingdon*

428  Abide with us, Lord, for it is toward evening and the day is far spent; abide with us and with your whole Church. Abide with

us in the evening of the day, in the evening of life, in the evening of the world. Abide with us and with all your faithful ones, O Lord, in time and eternity.

*Lutheran Manual of Prayer*

**429** O Lord our God, what sins I have this day committed in word, deed, or thought, forgive me, for thou art gracious, and thou lovest all men. Grant me peaceful and undisturbed sleep, send me thy guardian angel to protect and guard me from every evil, for thou art the guardian of our souls and bodies, and to thee we ascribe glory, to the Father and the Son and the Holy Ghost, now and for ever and unto the ages of ages.

*Russian Orthodox Prayer*

**430** Show your loving kindness tonight, O Lord, to all who stand in need of your help. Be with the weak to make them strong, and with the strong to make them gentle. Cheer the lonely with your company and the worried with your peace. Prosper your Church in the fulfilment of her mighty task, and grant your blessing to all who have toiled today in Christ's name.

*John Baillie*

**431** O Lord my God, I thank thee that thou has brought this day to a close; I thank thee for giving me rest in body and soul. Thy hand has been over me and has guarded and preserved me. Forgive my lack of faith and any wrong that I have done today, and help me to forgive all who have wronged us. Let me sleep in peace under thy protection, and keep me from all the temptations of darkness. Into thy hands I commend my loved ones and all who dwell in this house; I commend to thee my body and soul. O God, thy holy name be praised.

*Dietrich Bonhoeffer*

**432** Eternal and ever-blessed God, we give thee thanks, as the day comes to an end, for those who mean so much to us, and without whom life could never be the same.

We thank thee for those to whom we can go at any time and never feel a nuisance.

We thank thee for those to whom we can go when we are tired, knowing that they have, for the weary feet, the gift of rest.

We thank thee for those with whom we can talk, and keep nothing back, knowing that they will not laugh at our dreams or mock our failures.

We thank thee for those in whose presence it is easier to be good.

We thank thee for those in whose company joys are doubly dear, and sorrow's bitterness is soothed.

We thank thee for those who by their warning counsel and their rebuke have kept us from mistakes we might have made, and sins we might have committed.

And above all we thank thee for Jesus, the pattern of our lives, the Lord of our hearts, and the Saviour of our souls.

Accept this our thanksgiving, and grant us tonight a good night's rest; through Jesus Christ our Lord.

*William Barclay*

**433** Father in Heaven! humbly before thee
Kneeling in prayer thy children appear;
We in our weakness, we in our blindness,
Thou in thy wisdom, hear us, oh hear!

God watching o'er us sleeps not nor slumbers,
Faithful night watches his angels keep.
Through all the darkness, unto the dawning,
To his beloved he giveth sleep.

*Edward Rowland Sill*

**434** O Thou, whose captain I account myself,
To Thee I do commend my watchful soul,
Ere I let fall the windows of mine eyes:
Sleeping and waking, O! defend me still.

*William Shakespeare*

**435** O Lord Jesus Christ, our Watchman and Keeper, take us to Thy care: grant that, our bodies sleeping, our minds may watch in Thee, and be made merry by some sight of that celestial and heavenly life wherein Thou art the King and Prince, together with the Father and the Holy Spirit, where Thy angels and holy souls be most happy citizens. Oh purify our souls, keep clean our bodies, that in both we may please Thee, sleeping and waking, for ever.

*Book of Christian Prayers, 1578*

**436** Into thy hands, most blessed Jesus, I commend my soul and body, for thou hast redeemed both by thy most precious blood. So bless and sanctify my sleep to me, that it may be temperate, holy, and safe, a refreshment to my weary body, to enable it so to serve my soul, that both may serve thee with never-failing duty. Visit, I beseech thee, O Lord, this habitation with thy mercy, and me with thy grace and favour. Teach me to number my days, that I may apply my heart unto wisdom, and ever be mindful of my last end. Amen

*Jeremy Taylor*

**437** We come before Thee, O Lord, at the end of Thy day with thanksgiving. The service of the day is over, and the hour come to rest. We resign into Thy hands our sleeping bodies, our cold hearths and open doors. Give us to awaken with smiles, give us to labour smiling. As the sun returns in the east, so let our patience be renewed with dawn; as the sun lightens the world, so let our loving kindness make bright this house of our habitation.

*Robert Louis Stevenson*

**438** The busy day now takes its rest,
as mother evening enfolds us in embrace.
The distant stars and galaxies signal
messages about a Creator so vast
that our minds stagger
and our hearts are filled
with loving awe.

O Lord, our Lord,
glorious in your name in all the universe.
What are earth's children
that you notice us?
And what is the mystery of divine grace
that you love us?
You give us faith to trust you,
even though we cannot see you.
You touch our minds with fingers of light,
and our hearts with forgiveness and peace.

As the evening moves on,
we go to rest
able to sleep the sleep of children
who know that, in life or death,
we are surrounded by love eternal.

O Lord, our Lord, glorious is your name
on earth and in the heavens!

*Bruce Prewer*

# CHILDREN'S NIGHT PRAYERS

**439**  Ere on my bed my limbs I lay,
God grant me grace my prayers to say:
O God! preserve my mother dear
In strength and health for many a year;
And, O! preserve my father too,
And may I pay him reverence due;
And may I my best thoughts employ
To be my parents' hope and joy;
And O! preserve my brothers both
From evil doings and from sloth,
And may we always love each other
Our friends, our father, and our mother:
And still, O Lord, to me impart
An innocent and grateful heart,
That after my great sleep I may
Awake to thy eternal day! Amen

*Samuel Taylor Coleridge*

**440**  Hear my prayer, O! Heavenly Father,
Ere I lay me down to sleep;
Bid thy Angels, pure and holy,
Round my bed their vigil keep.

Keep me through this night of peril
Underneath its boundless shade;
Take me to thy rest, I pray thee,
When my pilgrimage is made.

*Charles Dickens*

**441**  My Prayer is such a little thing, it might get lost and go
     astray.
Are you, dear God, now listening to what I say?
I wish to thank You for the sun that kissed, this morn, my
     sleeping eyes;
for all the happy things I've done since I did rise.

For gift of sound and gift of sight; for feet that skip so
     merrily;
for food and warmth, and each delight You gave to me.
I thank You for my mother dear; I thank You for my father
     kind;
and for the star that watches near – behind the blind.

So many Grown-ups show me love, though I'm a child and
    still quite small.
Look down upon them from above – and please God, bless
    them all.
And, now, dear God, I'll say, 'Goodnight', and may Your
    angels guard my bed
until You send Your morning light to wake this Sleepy
    Head.

*Wilhelmina Stitch*

**442** Jesus, tender Shepherd, hear me,
Bless thy little lamb tonight;
Through the darkness be thou near me,
Watch my sleep till morning light.

All this day thy hand has led me,
And I thank thee for thy care;
Thou hast clothed me, warmed and fed me,
Listen to my evening prayer.

Let my sins be all forgiven;
Bless the friends I love so well;
Take me, when I die, to heaven,
Happy there with thee to dwell.

*Mary L. Duncan*

**443** From Witches, Warlocks and Wurricoes,
From Ghoulies, Ghosties and Long-leggit Beasties,
From all Things that go bump in the night –
Good Lord, deliver us!

*Traditional Cornish Prayer*

# GRACES

**444** Come Lord Jesus be our guest,
And may our meal by you be blest. Amen

*Attributed to Martin Luther*

**445** Heavenly Father, make us thankful to thee and mindful of
others as we receive these blessings, in Jesus' name.

*Book of Common Worship*

**446** To God who gives our daily bread
A thankful song we raise,
And pray that he who sends us food
May fill our hearts with praise.

*Thomas Tallis*

**447** Praise God from whom all blessings flow,
Praise him, all creatures here below,
Praise him above, angelic host,
Praise Father, Son and Holy Ghost.

*Thomas Ken*

**448** Gracious God, may the food which we are about to receive strengthen our bodies, and may thy Holy Spirit strengthen and refresh our souls; through Jesus Christ.

*The Tent and the Altar*

**449** Be present at our table, Lord,
Be here and everywhere ador'd;
These creatures bless and grant that we
May feast in paradise with thee.

*John Cennick*

**450** Here, a little child, I stand,
Heaving up my either hand:
Cold as paddocks* though they be,
Here I lift them up to Thee,
For a benison to fall
On our meat and on our all.

*Robert Herrick*

*Frogs or toads

**451** We thank you, Father, for the holy resurrection, which you made known to us through Jesus, your Child. As the ingredients of the bread on this table, though once separate, were gathered together and made one, so may your Church be built up from the ends of the earth and gathered into your kingdom; for power and glory are yours through all the endless succession of ages. Amen

*Pseudo-Athanasius*

**452** O Lord our God, you are the Bread that is eaten in heaven, the Bread that gives life, the Food that really nourishes the whole world. You came down from heaven and gave the world life; you guide us through this present existence, and you have promised that there will be another for us to enjoy after this. Bless, then, our food and drink and enable us to take them without sinning. May we receive them thankfully and give you glory for them, for you it is who confer all good gifts upon us.

Blessed and glorious is your name, ever worthy of honour.

*Third-century Prayer*

# III PRAYERS OF DEPENDENCE

## ADORATION

**453** O God, Who has chosen the weak things of the world to confound the mighty, do Thou shed forth continual day upon us who watch for Thee; that our lips may praise Thee, our life may bless Thee, and our meditations glorify Thee.

*Sarum Breviary*

**454** O most high, almighty, good Lord God, to thee belong praise, glory, honour and all blessing!

Praised be my Lord God with all his creatures, and especially our brother the sun, who brings us the day and who brings us the light; fair is he and shines with a very great splendour;

O Lord, he signifies to us thee.

Praised be my Lord for our sister the moon, and for the stars, the which he has set clear and lovely in heaven.

Praised be my Lord for our brother the wind, and for air and cloud, calms and all weather, by the which thou upholdest life in all creatures.

Praised be my Lord for our sister water, who is very serviceable unto us and humble and precious and clean.

Praised be my Lord for our brother fire, through whom thou givest us light in the darkness; and he is bright and pleasant and very mighty and strong.

Praised be my Lord for our mother the earth, the which doth sustain us and keep us, and bringeth forth divers fruits, and flowers of many colours, and grass.

Praised be my Lord for all those who pardon one another for his love's sake, and who endure weakness and tribulation; blessed are they who peaceably shall endure, for thou, O Most Highest, shall give them a crown.

Praised be my Lord for our sister the death of the body,

from which no man escapeth. Woe to him who dieth in mortal sin!

Blessed are they who are found walking by thy most holy will, for the second death shall have no power to harm them.

Praise ye and bless ye the Lord, and give thanks unto him, and serve him with great humility. Amen

*St Francis of Assisi*

455 O God our Father, we would thank thee for all the bright things of life. Help us to see them, and to count them, and to remember them, that our lives may flow in ceaseless praise; for the sake of Jesus Christ our Lord.

*J. H. Jowett*

456 Holy, holy, holy, Lord God almighty!
Early in the morning our song shall rise to thee;
Holy, holy, holy, merciful and mighty,
God in three persons, blessed Trinity!
Holy, holy, holy, though the darkness hide thee,
Though the eye of sinful man thy glory may not see,
Only thou art holy; there is none beside thee,
Perfect in power, in love and purity.

*Reginald Heber*

457 Glory be to God for dappled things –
For skies of couple-colour as a brinded cow;
For rose-moles all in stipple upon the trout that swim;
Fresh-firecoal chestnut-falls; finches' wings;
Landscape plotted and pieced – fold, fallow and plough;
And all trades, their gear and tackle and trim.
All things counter, original, spare, strange;
Whatever is fickle, freckled (who knows how?)
With swift, slow; sweet, sour; adazzle, dim;
He fathers-forth whose beauty is past change:
Praise him.

*Gerard Manley Hopkins*

458 God of bright colours: rainbows, peacocks,
And the shot-silk gleam of springing
Wind-shaken wheat
On rolling red-ribbed Earth:
Thou Who dost bring to birth
From out the womb
Of darkness golden flowers,

Filling the hollows
With daffodils in March,
Cowslips in April,
Dog-roses in May;
Who in the smouldering forest
Makes the huge
Red flare of Autumn:
God of all the colours
On Earth, and hues (too bright for mortal eyes)
In Paradise –
Unblind me to Thy glory,
That I may see!

*F. W. Harvey*

**459** May none of God's wonderful works
keep silence, night or morning.
Bright stars, high mountains, the depths of the seas,
sources of rushing rivers:
may all these break into song as we sing
to Father, Son and Holy Spirit.
May all the angels in the heavens reply:
Amen! Amen! Amen!
Power, praise, honour, eternal glory
to God, the only Giver of grace.
Amen! Amen! Amen!

*Third-century Prayer*

**460** Almighty God, whose glory the heavens proclaim, the earth
thy power, the sea thy might, and whose greatness all feeling
and thinking creatures trumpet forth. To thee belongeth all
glory, honour, power, greatness and magnificence, now and
for evermore. Amen

*Liturgy of St James*

**461** I offer thee
Every flower that ever grew,
Every bird that ever flew,
Every wind that ever blew.

Good God!

Every thunder rolling,
Every church bell tolling,
Every leaf and sod.

Laudamus Te!

I offer thee
Every wave that ever moved,
Every heart that ever loved,
Thee, thy Father's well-beloved.

                                                Dear Lord!

Every river dashing,
Every lightning flashing,
Like an angel's sword.

                                                Benedicimus Te!

I offer thee
Every cloud that ever swept
O'er the skies, and broke and wept
In rain, and with the flowerets slept.

                                                My King!

Every communicant praying,
Every angel staying,
Before thy throne to sing.

                                                Adoramus Te!

I offer thee
Every flake of virgin snow,
Every spring of earth below,
Every human joy and woe,

                                                My love!

O Lord! And all thy glorious
Self o'er death victorious,
Throned in heaven above.

                                                Glorificamus Te!
                                                *Ancient Irish Prayer*

462  O Thou in whom all things live, who commandest us to seek
     thee, and art ever ready to be found: To know thee is life, to
     serve thee is freedom, to praise thee is our souls' joy. We bless
     thee and adore thee, we worship thee and magnify thee, we
     give thanks to thee for thy great glory; through Jesus Christ
     our Lord.
                                         *St Augustine of Hippo*

463  You are holy, Lord, the only God,
     And your deeds are wonderful.
     You are strong,
     You are great.
     You are the Most High,
     You are almighty.
     You, holy Father, are

King of heaven and earth.
You are Three and One,
Lord God, all good.
You are good, all good, supreme good,
Lord God, living and true.
You are love,
You are wisdom.
You are humility,
You are endurance.
You are rest,
You are peace.
You are joy and gladness,
You are justice and moderation.
You are all our riches,
And you suffice for us.
You are beauty,
You are gentleness.
You are our protector,
You are our guardian and defender.
You are courage,
You are our haven and our hope.
You are our faith,
Our great consolation.
You are our eternal life,
Great and wonderful Lord,
God almighty,
Merciful Saviour.

*St Francis of Assisi*


**464** Blessing and honour, and thanksgiving and praise, more than
we can utter, more than we can conceive, be yours, holy and
glorious Trinity, Father, Son and Holy Spirit, by all angels, all
men, all creatures, for ever and ever.

*Lancelot Andrewes\**


**465** Tune me, O Lord, into one harmony
With Thee, one full responsive vibrant chord;
Unto Thy praise, all love and melody,
Tune me, O Lord.

*Christina Rossetti*


**466** We praise thee, O God; we acknowledge thee to be the
Lord.
All the earth doth worship thee, the Father everlasting.

To thee all angels cry aloud,
the heavens and all the powers therein.
To thee cherubim and seraphim continually do cry:
Holy, holy, holy, Lord God of Sabaoth;
Heaven and earth are full of the majesty of thy glory.
The glorious company of the apostles praise thee.
The goodly fellowship of the prophets praise thee.
The noble army of martyrs praise thee.
The holy Church throughout all the world doth acknowledge
    thee,
the Father, of an infinite majesty,
thine adorable, true and only Son,
also the Holy Ghost the Comforter.

Thou art the King of glory, O Christ.
Thou art the everlasting Son of the Father.
When thou tookest upon thee to deliver man,
thou didst humble thyself to be born of a virgin.
When thou hadst overcome the sharpness of death,
thou didst open the kingdom of heaven to all believers.
Thou sittest at the right hand of God, in the glory of the
    Father.
We believe that thou shalt come to be our judge.

We therefore pray thee, help thy servants,
whom thou hast redeemed with thy precious blood.
Make them to be numbered with thy saints,
in glory everlasting.

*Te Deum*
*(Fourth-century hymn)*

**467** A hymn of glory let us sing,
New songs throughout the world shall ring;
By a new way none ever trod
Christ mounteth to the throne of God.

Be thou our present joy, O Lord!
Who wilt be ever our reward;
And, as the countless ages flee,
May all our glory be in Thee!

*The Venerable Bede*

**468** O Light Invisible, we praise Thee!
Too bright for mortal vision.
O Greater Light, we praise Thee for the less;

The eastern light our spires touch at morning,
The light that slants upon our western doors at evening,
The twilight over stagnant pools at batflight,
Moon light and star light, owl and moth light,
Glow-worm glowlight on a grassblade.
O Light Invisible, we worship Thee!

We thank Thee for the lights that we have kindled,
The light of altar and of sanctuary;
Small lights of those who meditate at midnight
And lights directed through the coloured panes of windows
And light reflected from the polished stone,
The gilded carven wood, the coloured fresco.
Our gaze is submarine, our eyes look upward
And see the light that fractures through unquiet water.
We see the light but see not whence it comes.
O Light Invisible, we glorify Thee!

*T. S. Eliot*

**469** Grant, I pray, O Lord, that with that lowliness of mind
which befits my humble condition, and that elevation of
soul which your majesty demands, I may ever adore you.
May I continually live in that fear which your justice inspires,
and ever adore you.
May I continually live in that hope which your clemency
permits, and ever adore you.
May I submit myself to you as all-powerful, abandoning
myself into your hands, and ever adore you.
May your burning fire purify me, your clear light illuminate
me, and may I ever adore you.
May your pure love so advance me that I may never be held
back from finally coming to you, and then ever adore you.

*Vittoria Colonna\**

**470** Glory be to Thee, O Heavenly Father, for our being and
preservation, health and strength, understanding and memory, friends and benefactors, and for all our abilities of mind
and body. Glory be to Thee for our competent livelihood, for
the advantages of our education, for all known and un-
observed deliverances, and for the guard which Thy holy
Angels keep over us. Glory be to Thee, O Lord, O Blessed
Saviour, for those ordinary gifts by which sincere Christians
have in all ages been enabled to work for their salvation,
for all the spiritual strength and support, comfort and

illumination which we receive from Thee, and for all Thy preserving, restraining and sanctifying grace.

*Thomas Ken*

471 O Lord, how wonderful you are!
Your greatness and love overwhelms me.
You catch and hold me in your shining darkness.
You take me out of myself into the light of your being
which blinds me with its brightness.
You fill me with yourself, and my being is suffused
with the beauty of your glory.
I am speechless, silent, held by your overwhelming love.
Lord, never let me go, keep me hidden in yourself, always.

*Etta Gullick*

472 O God, whose name is holy of itself, we pray that it may be hallowed also by us. To this end help us, O blessed Father in heaven, that thy word may be taught in truth and purity, and that we, as thy children, may lead holy lives in accordance with it; through Jesus Christ, thy Son, our Lord. Amen

*Martin Luther*

473 Justify my soul, O God, but also from your fountains fill my will with fire . . . Let my eyes see nothing in the world but your glory, and let my hands touch nothing that is not for your service . . . let me use all things for one sole reason; to find my joy in giving You great glory.

*Thomas Merton*

474 O Lord, Whom all Thy good creatures bless and praise according to Thy gift unto each of them, grant, we pray Thee, that we on whom Thou hast bestowed reason and speech may ever bless Thee with heart and lips, and may of Thine infinite mercy inherit a blessing, even the eternal blessedness of heaven. Amen

*Christina Rossetti*

475 I worship you, Lord, I bless you, God the good; I beseech you, Most Holy; I fall down before you, Lover of men.
I give you glory, O Christ, because you, the Only Begotten, the Lord of all things, who alone are without sin, gave yourself to die for me, a sinner, unworthy of such a blessing: you died the death of the cross to free my sinful soul from the bonds of sin.

What shall I give you, Lord, in return for all this kindness?
Glory to you for your love.
Glory to you for your mercy.
Glory to you for your patience.
Glory to you for forgiving us all our sins.
Glory to you for coming to save our souls.
Glory to you for your incarnation in the virgin's womb.
Glory to you for your bonds.
Glory to you for receiving the cut of the lash.
Glory to you for accepting mockery.
Glory to you for your crucifixion.
Glory to you for your burial.
Glory to you for your resurrection.
Glory to you that were preached to men.
Glory to you in whom they believed.
Glory to you that were taken up into heaven.
Glory to you who sit in great glory at the Father's right
hand and will come again with the glory of the Father and the
holy angels to judge the souls of those who have despised your
holy sufferings. When that time of awe and terror comes, the
powers in the heavens will quake with dread; angels,
archangels, cherubim and seraphim will come together in fear
and trembling before your glory; the foundations of the earth
will shake, and everything that breathes will shudder before
the incomparable greatness of your glory.

When that time comes, fold your hand about me and hide
me, that my soul may escape the terrible fire, the gnashing of
teeth, the darkness without and the endless weeping. So may I
bless you and say:

Glory to you whose will it is that the sinner should be saved
through your great mercy and compassion.

*Ephrem Syrus*

**476** We praise Thee, O unseen Father, giver of immortality. Thou
art the fount of life, the fount of light, the fount of all grace
and all truth, O lover of men, O lover of the poor, who dost
reconcile Thyself to all, and draw all to Thyself through the
coming of Thy beloved Son. We beseech Thee, make us living
men. Give us a spirit of light that we may know Thee, the
True, and Him whom Thou didst send, Jesus Christ. Give us
this Holy Spirit, that we may be able to tell forth and declare
Thine ineffable mysteries. May the Lord Jesus speak in us,
and the Holy Spirit hymn Thee through us.

*Serapion of Thmuis*

**477** Lord, be it thine,
Unfaltering praise of mine!
To thee my whole heart's love be given,
Of earth and heaven thou king divine.

Lord, be it thine,
Unfaltering praise of mine!
And, O pure prince, make clear my way
To serve and pray at thy sole shrine!

Lord, be it thine,
Unfaltering praise of mine!
O father of all souls that long,
Take my song and make it thine.

*Celtic Prayer*

**478** Thine are goodness, grace, love, kindness, O Thou Lover of
men! Gentleness, tenderness, forbearance, longsuffering,
manifold mercies, great mercies, abundant tender compassions. Glory be to Thee, O Lord.

*Lancelot Andrewes*

**479** O God, to whom glory is sung in the highest, while on earth
peace is proclaimed to men of good will: Grant that good will
to us thy servants, cleanse us from all our sins, and give
perpetual peace to us and to all people; through thy mercy, O
God, who are blessed, and dost govern all things, world
without end.

*Mozarabic Sacramentary*

**480** We praise you, God our Father, for the richness of your
creation,
for the uniqueness of each person,
for the creativity which sustains and renews our cultures,
for your faithfulness towards your people.
We praise you, Jesus our Lord, for your constant meddling
in our affairs,
for your identification with the poor,
for your sacrifice for all men on the cross,
for revealing the true man to all people.
We praise you, God the Spirit, for your inspiration of life,
for your insistence to draw us always to Christ,
for the infusion of unrest among men,
for your patient preparation of the fulfilment of history.

We praise you, blessed Trinity, for not doing for us
    according to our sins,
for continuing your love to all that lives,
for continuing your disturbing call to repentance,
for continuing life on earth.

*WCC Bangkok Conference, 1973*

**481** Glory be to the Father
and to the Son
and to the Holy Spirit.
As it was in the beginning
is now and ever shall be
world without end. Amen

*Traditional Prayer*

# THANKSGIVING

**482** Lord Jesus, I thank you
not just with my lips and heart
but with my spirit, with which I recognise
and love you.
You are my all, and everything is in you.
In you I live, move and have being.

You are my brother, my all.
You are the true God, the true Son of God
to whom all honour, glory and thanks
are due.

*Gallican Formularies*

**483** Almighty Giver of all good, may our hearts sing with gratitude
for the overwhelming number of blessings you have showered
upon us. Make us to sing your song of love and thanks in the
light and in the night feel the touch of your hand, and be at
peace. May you be our trusted Lord and King for evermore.
Amen

*Henry W. Foote*

**484** Giver of all good things, we thank thee: for health and vigour;
for the air that gives the breath of life, the sun that warms us,
and the good food that makes us strong; for happy homes and
for the friends we love; for all that makes it good to live. Make

us thankful and eager to repay, by cheerfulness and kindliness, and by a readiness to help others. Freely we have received; let us freely give, in the name of him who gave his life for us, Jesus Christ our Lord.

*Thomas Ken*

**485** Almighty God, Father of all mercies, we thine unworthy servants do give thee most humble and hearty thanks for all thy goodness and loving-kindness to us, and to all men.

We bless thee for our creation, preservation, and all the blessings of this life; but above all for thine inestimable love in the redemption of the world by our Lord Jesus Christ; for the means of grace, and for the hope of glory.

And, we beseech thee, give us that due sense of all thy mercies, that our hearts may be unfeignedly thankful, and that we shew forth thy praise, not only with our lips but in our lives, by giving up ourselves to thy service, and by walking before thee in holiness and righteousness all our days.

*Book of Common Prayer, 1559*

**486** O Infinite God, the brightness of whose face is often hidden from my mortal gaze, I thank you that you sent your Son, Jesus Christ, to be a light in a dark world.

I thank you Christ, light of light, that in your most holy life you pierced the eternal mystery as with a great shaft of light, so that on seeing you we see him whom no one has ever seen.

*John Baillie\**

**487** We give thee humble and hearty thanks, O most merciful Father, for all thy goodness and loving-kindness to us and to all men, for the blessings of this life and for the promise of everlasting happiness. And as we are bound, we specially thank thee for the mercies which we have received; for health and strength, for outward prosperity and well-being, for the many enjoyments of our daily life, and the hope of the future; for the opportunities of learning, for the knowledge of thy will, for the means of serving thee in thy holy church, for the love thou hast revealed to us in thy Son, our Saviour; for every blessing of soul and body, we thank thee, O God. Add this, O Lord, to thy other mercies, that we may praise thee not with our lips only, but with our lives, always looking to thee as the author and giver of all good things; for Jesus Christ's sake.

*Brooke Foss Westcott*

**488** My God, from my heart I thank you for the many blessings you have given me. I thank you for having created and baptised me, for having placed me in your holy Church, and for having given me so many graces and mercies through the merits of Jesus Christ. I thank your Son Jesus, for having died upon the cross that I might receive pardon for my sins and obtain my eternal salvation. I thank you for all your other mercies you have given me through Jesus Christ, Our Lord.

*Michael Buckley*

**489** We thank Thee, O Lord, for all those good things which are in our world and in our lives through Thy love. Save us from being ungrateful. Save us from magnifying our sorrows and forgetting our blessings. Give strength of spirit to rise into joyfulness of heart. By Thy help may we learn to live as those should who have trusted the promises of good which are incarnate in Jesus, and who know that in the end love must conquer all.

*A. Herbert Gray*

**490** Thou hast given so much to me
Give one thing more – a grateful heart:
Not thankful when it pleaseth me,
As if thy blessings had spare days,
But such a heart whose pulse may be
Thy Praise.

*George Herbert*

**491** Infinite and Holy One, Whom we know as our Father and the Father of our Lord Jesus Christ, we devoutly thank Thee for the mercy that created us from the dust, and for the greater mercy that has created us anew by a heavenly adoption as Thy children. For the undying yearnings, which Thou hast implanted in us, after things unseen, for their satisfaction in Thyself, we thank Thee; and we rejoice that Thou hast been willing to encourage our frail and mortal spirits, by revealing to us something of the perfections of Thy nature, and calling us to follow after Thee. Grant, we pray, that Thy loving-kindness may be followed by our obedience. And do Thou so confirm our best purposes by renewing our sense of Thy presence, that we may both imitate Thy nature, and accept Thy dealings with us in the spirit of childlike trust, and by the help of Thy dear Son, Jesus Christ our Lord. Amen

*Henry W. Foote*

**492** To the Spirit great and good,
Felt, although not understood,
By whose breath, and in whose eyes,
The green earth rolls in the blue skies,
Who we know, from things that bless,
Must delight in loveliness;
And who, therefore, we believe,
Means us well in things that grieve,
Gratitude! Gratitude!
Heav'n be praised as heavenly should
Not with slavery, or with fears,
But with a face as towards a friend,
And with thin sparkling tears.

*Leigh Hunt*

**493** O God, who hast given us life and all good things in this world: thou hast created us for thy service, and when we have forsaken thee in our wanderings thou hast sought us out; thou hast vouchsafed to us the precious treasure of thy gospel; thou hast ordained that we should be born in the bosom of thy Church; thou hast revealed to us thy exceeding great riches in Jesus Christ our Lord. For all these gifts of thy grace, and for thy benefits which we remember not, we thine unworthy servants do give thee thanks, and bless thy holy name for ever and ever.

*Eugène Bersier*

**494** O Lord, fill us, we beseech Thee, with adoring gratitude to Thee for all Thou art for us, to us, and in us; fill us with love, joy, peace, and all the fruits of the Spirit. Amen

*Christina Rossetti*

**495** O Lord, my God, I cried to you in my trouble and you heard me; I put my trust in you and have not been confounded. You have turned my heaviness into joy, and guided me with gladness. Therefore I praise you with all my heart, and give thanks to your holy name for ever. Hear me and accept me, for the sake of Jesus Christ our Lord.

*Laurence R. Tuttiett*

**496** O most merciful God, Whose mercies are as high as the heavens, great and many as the moments of eternity; fill my soul, I beseech Thee, with great thoughts of Thy unspeakable blessings, that my thankfulness may be as great as my needs of mercy are. Let Thy loving-kindness endure for ever and ever upon me; and, because I cannot praise Thee according to Thy excellence, take my soul, in due time, into the land of everlasting praises, that I may spend a whole eternity in ascribing to Thy Name praise, and honour, and dominion. Grant this for Jesus Christ's sake. Amen

*Jeremy Taylor*

497  I thank Thee, God, that I have lived
In this great world and known its many joys;
The song of birds, the strong, sweet scent of hay
And cooling breezes in the secret dusk,
The flaming sunsets at the close of day,
Hills, and the lonely, heather-covered moors,
Music at night, and moonlight on the sea,
The beat of waves upon the rocky shore
And wild, white spray, flung high in ecstasy:
The faithful eyes of dogs, and treasured books.
The love of kin and fellowship of friends,
And all that makes life dear and beautiful.
I thank Thee, too, that there has come to me
A little sorrow and, sometimes, defeat,
A little heartache and the loneliness
That comes with parting, and the word, 'Goodbye',
Dawn breaking after dreary hours of pain,
When I discovered that night's gloom must yield
And morning light break through to me again.
Because of these and other blessings poured
Unasked upon my wondering head,
Because I know that there is yet to come
An even richer and more glorious life,
And most of all, because Thine only Son
Once sacrificed life's loveliness for me –
I thank Thee, God, that I have lived.

*Elizabeth, Countess of Craven*

498  For eyes whereby I clearly see
The many lovely things there be;
For lungs to breathe the morning air,
For nose to smell its fragrance rare;
For tongue to taste the fruits that grow,
For birds that sing and flowers that blow;
For limbs to climb, and swing, and run,
For skin to feel the cheerful sun;

For sun and moon and stars in heaven,
Whose gracious light is freely given;
The river where the green weed floats,
And where I sail my little boats;
The sea, where I can bathe and play,
The sands where I can race all day,
The pigeons wheeling in the sun,
Who fly more quickly than I run;
The winds that sing as they rush by,
The clouds that race across the sky;
The shelter of the shady woods,
Where I may spend my lonely moods;
The gabled house that is my home,
The garden where I love to roam,
And bless my parents, every day,
Though they be very far away,
Take thou my thanks, O God above,
For all these tokens of thy love.
And when I am a man do thou
Make me as grateful then as now.

*Richard Molesworth Dennis*


**499** Thanks be to thee,
my joy and my glory
and my hope and my God.
Thanks be to thee for thy gifts;
but do thou preserve them in me,
thus thou wilt preserve me,
and the things thou hast given me
will increase and be made perfect,
and I shall be with thee:
because even that I exist is thy gift.

*St Augustine of Hippo*


**500** Thank you, God, for filling things:
filling the world with people,
filling words with meaning,
filling life with happenings,
filling our plates with food
and our wallets with money.
May we ask one more thing?
Please fill our hearts with thankfulness,
and, as our gratitude overflows
in gifts to you and your Church,

bless what we give
and make it useful
in the doing of what you want done,
through Jesus Christ our Lord.

*Jamie Wallace*

# FAITH

**501** Give me, Lord, eyes to behold the truth;
A seeing sense that knows the eternal right;
A heart with pity filled, and gentlest ruth;
A manly faith that makes all darkness light.

*Theodore Parker*

**502** Behold, Lord, an empty vessel that needs to be filled. My
Lord, fill it. I am weak in the faith; strengthen me. I am cold in
love; warm me and make me fervent, that my love may go out
to my neighbour. I do not have a strong and firm faith; at times
I doubt and am unable to trust you altogether. O Lord, help
me. Strengthen my faith and trust in you.

*Martin Luther*

**503** O God, by whose command the order of time runs its course:
Forgive, we pray thee, the impatience of our hearts; make
perfect that which is lacking in our faith; and, while we tarry
the fulfilment of thy promises, grant us to have a good hope
because of thy word; through Jesus Christ our Lord.

*St Gregory of Nazianzus*

**504** Teach me, O God, not to torture myself, not to make a martyr
out of myself through stifling reflection, but rather teach me to
breathe deeply in faith.

*Søren Kierkegaard*

**505** God in heaven, I thank thee that thou hast not required of
man that he should comprehend Christianity; for if that were
required, I should be of all men most miserable. The more I
seek to comprehend it, the more incomprehensible it appears
to me, and the more I discover merely the possibility of
offense. Therefore I thank thee that thou dost only require
faith, and I pray thee to increase it more and more. Amen

*Søren Kierkegaard*

**506** Father, as we remember the victorious faith of your servants of old, we acknowledge that we are not people of faith.

Sometimes your promises seem so unlikely as to be laughable. They are almost more than we can believe.

Father, forgive us. Increase our faith, and save us from concentrating on our doubts.

Open our eyes to see what you can do with us when we put ourselves at your disposal.

Help us to hold firm to your promises, to laugh at impossibilities, and to believe that all things are possible, through Jesus Christ our Lord.

*Frank Colquhoun*

**507** We read in one of the Psalms, O God, the assertion of Thy saint of old who said, 'I have trusted in the Lord without wavering.' We thank Thee for his certain faith and for his strength of conviction whereby nothing could move him from his implicit trust. And we pray for that kind of faith to be in us. Our lives are beset by many challenges. When sorrow comes, or disappointment, or failure, or discouragement, we tend to lose faith. It is as if a little voice within us says, 'Where is your God now?' But we know that in all these experiences, Thou art faithful. Make us as unwavering in our trust as Thou art unwavering in Thy care over us. We pray in Jesus' name. Amen

*William H. Kadel*

**508** Most merciful and gracious Father, I bless and magnify Thy name that Thou hast adopted me into the inheritance of sons, and hast given me a portion of my elder Brother. Thou Who art the God of patience and consolation, strengthen me that I may bear the yoke and burden of the Lord, without any uneasy and useless murmurs, and ineffective unwillingness. Let me pass through the valley of tears, and the valley of the shadow of death with safety and peace, with a meek spirit, and a sense of the divine mercies, through Jesus Christ. Amen

*Jeremy Taylor*

**509** Lord, perfect for me what is lacking of thy gifts; of faith, help Thou mine unbelief; of hope, establish my trembling hope; of love, kindle its smoking flax.

*Lancelot Andrewes*

# HOPE

**510** My Lord God, give me once more the courage to hope; merciful God, let me hope once again, fructify my barren and infertile mind.

*Søren Kierkegaard*

**511** My God, who has graciously promised every blessing, even heaven itself, through Jesus Christ, to those who keep your commandments. Relying on your infinite power, goodness, and mercy, and confiding in your sacred promises, to which you are always faithful, I confidently hope to obtain pardon of all my sins, grace to serve you faithfully in this life, by doing the good works you have commanded, which, with your assistance, I will perform; and eternal happiness in the next, through my Lord and Saviour Jesus Christ. Amen

*Michael Buckley*

**512** Lord God,
the scripture says you make all things new.
Make all things new this day.
Give us such hope in you
that we become optimistic about everyone and everything
   else,
Lord of all hopefulness, Lord of the future,
lead us forward with a light step and a courageous heart;
to your honour and glory,
and for the sake of Jesus Christ,
your Son, our Saviour.

*Jamie Wallace*

**513** You are the Lord of fire
Present in the fiery furnace,
Present in the heat of life,
Present in situations of horror and despair,
Present in the prisons that incarcerate men for their beliefs.
Shadrach, Meshach and Abednego were lucky ones, Lord.
They came out unscathed.
Not all are so lucky,
Not all understand the tyrannies of life and remain
   unharmed.
You are with men in their suffering, in their aloneness and
   ignominy and death.

Be with them.
Be with them through us who are your limbs.
Give us a glimmering of hope in hopeless situations;
For where there is no hope there is nothing.

*Rex Chapman*

**514** Thou, who art the eternal protection and salvation of our
souls, arm us, we entreat Thee, with the helmet of hope, and
the shield of Thy invincible defence; that so, helped by Thee
in the straits of our necessities, we may be filled with joy and
gladness with those who love Thee, through Jesus Christ our
Lord.

*Sarum Breviary*

# FOR LIGHT AND LOVE

**515** Oh blessed Lord! How much I need
Thy Light to guide me on my way!
So many hands, that, without heed,
Still touch Thy wounds and make them bleed,
So many feet that day by day
Still wander from Thy fold astray!
Feeble at best is my endeavour!
I see but cannot reach the height
That lies for ever in the Light;
And yet for ever and for ever,
When seeming just within my grasp,
I feel my feeble hands unclasp,
And sink discouraged into night; –
For Thine own purpose Thou has sent
The strife and the discouragement.

*Henry Longfellow*

**516** Glory be to thee, O Lord, for that thou didst create not only
the visible light, but the light invisible, that which may be
known of God, the law written in the heart.
    Give us a mind to perceive this light in the oracles of
prophets, the melody of psalms, the prudence of proverbs, the
experience of histories, and the life and love of our Lord Jesus
Christ, for his sake.

*Lancelot Andrewes*

**517** Give me grace, O Lord, to be in all things strong, prudent and just with a wise restraint at need. Grant me an exact faith, unshakeable trust in thee, and perfect charity. Fill me with the spirit of intelligence and wisdom. Let me be always thoughtful for others and courageous, with loyalty and reverence. O Light, perfect and eternal, enlighten me.

*Alcuin*

**518** We beseech you, O Lord, to graciously enlighten our hearts by your pure radiance; that we may serve you without fear in holiness all our lives. May we escape the darkness that can enfold us in this world and one day, by your guidance, arrive at the land of eternal brightness. Amen

*Sarum Breviary*

**519** How easy it is for me to live with you, Lord!
How easy it is for me to believe in you!
When my mind is distraught and my reason fails,
When the cleverest people do not see further than this
evening what must be done tomorrow
You grant me the clear confidence
that you exist, and that you will take care
that not all the ways of goodness are stopped.
At the height of earthly fame I gaze with wonder
at that path through hopelessness –
to this point from which even I have been able
to convey to men some reflection of the Light
which comes from you.
And you will enable me to go on doing
as much as needs to be done.
And in so far as I do not manage it –
that means that you have allotted the task to others.

*Alexander Solzhenitsyn*

**520** Grant unto us, O Lord, the royalty of inward happiness and the serenity which comes from living close to thee. Daily renew in us the sense of joy, and let thy eternal spirit dwell in our souls and bodies, filling every corner of our hearts with light and gladness: so that, bearing about with us the infection of a good courage, we may be diffusers of life, and meet all that comes, of good or ill, even death itself, with gallant and high-hearted happiness: giving Thee thanks always for all things.

*The Splendour of God*

**521** In me there is darkness,
   But with thee there is light,
   I am lonely, but thou leavest me not.
   I am feeble in heart, but thou leavest me not.
   I am restless, but with thee there is peace.
   In me there is bitterness, but with thee there is patience;
   Thy ways are past understanding, but
   Thou knowest the way for me.

   *Dietrich Bonhoeffer*

**522** Lord, make me like crystal that your light may shine through me.

   *Katherine Mansfield*

**523** O Thou who sendest forth the light, createst the morning, and makest the sun to rise on the good and the evil; enlighten the blindness of our minds with the knowledge of the truth; lift up the light of thy countenance upon us, that in thy light we may see light, and, at the last, in the light of grace the light of glory; through Jesus Christ our Lord.

   *Lancelot Andrewes*

**524** O everlasting Light, surpassing all created luminaries, flash forth Thy lightning from above, piercing all the most inward parts of my heart. Make clean, make glad, make bright and make alive my spirit, with all the powers thereof, that I may cleave unto thee in ecstasies of joy.

   *Thomas à Kempis*

**525** Lord, enfold me in the depths of your heart; and there hold me, refine, purge and set me on fire; raise me aloft until my own self knows utter annihilation.

   *Teilhard de Chardin*

**526** O Almighty Father, giver of every good and perfect gift, who hast made the light of thy truth to shine in our hearts. Make us to walk as children of the light in all goodness and righteousness, that we may have no fellowship with the unfruitful works of darkness, through Jesus Christ our Lord.

   *W. Walsham How*

**527** Fill us, we pray, Lord, with your light and life that we may show forth your wondrous glory. Grant that your love may

so fill our lives that we may count nothing too small to do
for you, nothing too much to give and nothing too hard to
bear.

*Ignatius of Loyola*

**528** Eternal Light, before Whom all darkness is light, and, in
comparison with Whom, every other light is but darkness!
May it please Thee to send forth Thy light and Thy truth, that
they may lead us. Purify, we pray Thee, our souls from all
impure imaginations, that Thy most beautiful and holy image
may be again renewed within us, and, by contemplating Thy
glorious perfections, we may feel daily improved within us
that Divine similitude, the perfection whereof we hope will at
last make us forever happy in that full and beatific vision we
aspire after. Till this most blessed day break, and the shadows
fly away, let Thy Spirit be continually with us, and may we feel
the powerful effects of Thy Divine grace constantly directing
and supporting our steps; that all our endeavours, throughout
the whole remaining part of our lives, may serve to promote
the honour of Thy blessed Name, through Jesus Christ our
Lord. Amen

*Robert Leighton*

**529** Lord, am I losing my mind?
Or is this what you want?
It would not matter, except that I am alone, I am alone.
You have taken me far, Lord; trusting I followed you,
And you walked by my side.
And now, at night, in the middle of the desert,
Suddenly you have disappeared.
I call, and you do not answer.
I search, and I do not find you.
I left everything, and now am left alone,
Your absence is my suffering.
Lord it is dark.

Lord, are you here in my darkness?
Where are you, Lord?
Do you love me still?
Or have I wearied you?
Lord, answer,
Answer.
It is dark.

*Michel Quoist*

**530** Lord Jesus Christ, very Sun of the world, ever arising and never going down; who by thine appearing givest health and gladness, creating, preserving, and nourishing all things in heaven and in earth; I pray thee graciously to enlighten my spirit that the night of sin and the mists of error may be driven away by thine inward shining; so that I may go all my life long without stumbling, and walk as in the daytime, pure and undefiled by the works of darkness; who with the Father and the Holy Spirit livest and reignest for ever. Amen

*Erasmus*

**531** Father, in Thy mysterious Presence kneeling,
Fain would our souls feel all Thy kindling love;
For we are weak, and need some deep revealing
Of trust and strength and calmness from above.

*Rev. Samuel Johnson*

**532** Lord Jesus Christ, that our prayer may be rightly directed, we pray first for one all important need. Help us to love you, increase our love, inflame it. This prayer you will surely hear, for you are not love of a crude selfish sort, merely an uncaring object of regard. If you were you would not be the love that casts out all fear. No, you are compassionate love; more than that you are love of such a sort that draws out the love that loves you, nurturing and encouraging us to increase daily in your love. Love divine, increase our love.

*Søren Kierkegaard*

**533** O God, men think the heroes of tragedy great, and they admire them. But Abraham's contemporaries could not understand him. What then did he achieve? That he was true to his love. And he who loves God has no need of admiration, no need that others weep for him. He forgets his suffering in love, forgets it so thoroughly that no one even suspects his pain except thee, O God, who seest in secret, and knowest the need, and countest the tears and forgettest nothing.

*Søren Kierkegaard*

**534** O Love Divine and Great,
Why dost Thou still besiege my heart?
Of me infatuate Thou art,
From me Thou canst not rest!

If I come forth by way of Light,
Love, Love is all around;
In radiance painted on the skies,
In colour on the ground:
They plead with me, in beauty drowned,
To take Thee to my breast.

If I come forth by Heaven's gate,
O what is this I hear?
What is this woven mist of sound
That breaks upon mine ear?
Here's no escape! Thy voice is clear, –
'Tis Love, in music drest.

O Love, why do I flee from Thee?
Why should I fear to yield?
Because Thou wouldst re-make my heart,
In fires of love annealed?
No more myself, in Thee concealed,
And by Thy love possessed.

Lead me to Christ, who died for me,
Draw me from sea to shore:
And make me mourn in penitence
The wounds and griefs He bore:
Why did He suffer pains so sore?
That I might be at rest.

*Jacopone da Todi*

## LOVE OF GOD

535 O God, reign over us in spite of our infidelities; may the fire of
your love quench every other fire. What can we see that is
lovable outside of you, and which we do not find perfectly in
you, who are the source of all good? Grant us the grace of
loving you; we shall then love you only, and we shall love you
eternally.

*François Fénelon*

536 O my God, let me walk in the way of love which knoweth not
how to seek self in anything whatsoever. Let me love thee for
thyself, and nothing else but in and for thee. Let me love

nothing instead of thee, for to give all for love is a most sweet bargain. Let thy love work in me and by me, and let me love thee as thou wouldst be loved by me.

*Gertrude More*

537 Thyself, O my God, thyself for thine own sake, above all things I love. Thyself as my last end I long for. Make me therefore in this present life always to love thee before all things, to seek thee in all things, and at the last in the life to come to find and to keep thee for ever.

*Thomas Bradwardine*

538 Lord, give us hearts never to forget Thy love; but to dwell therein whatever we do, whether we sleep or wake, live or die, or rise again to the life that is to come. For Thy love is eternal life and everlasting rest; for this is life eternal to know Thee and Thy infinite goodness. O let its flame never be quenched in our hearts; let it grow and brighten, till our whole souls are glowing and shining with its light and warmth. Be Thou our Joy and Hope, our Strength and Life, our Shield and Shepherd, our Portion for ever. For happy are we if we continue in the love wherewith Thou hast loved us; holy are we when we love Thee steadfastly. Therefore, O Thou, Whose name and essence is Love, enkindle our hearts, enlighten our understandings, sanctify our wills, and fill all the thoughts of our hearts, for Jesus Christ's sake. Amen

*Johann Arndt*

539 O God, my God and my all,
    without thee I am nothing, less than nothing,
    a rebel to thy love,
    a despiser of thy grace.
    O God have pity on me a sinner;
    grant me a new vision of thy love
    and of thy will for me;
    give me a stillness in my soul
    that I may know thee and love thee,
    and grant me strength to do thy will, O my God,
    my all.

*Gilbert Shaw*

540 Open Thou my heart for Thy love, keep Thy love in me, prepare me by Thy love for greater fullness of Thy love, until I

have reached the fullest measure of love, which Thou, in
Thine eternal love, hast willed for me.

Make me, in thought, word, and deed, to love Thee, and
thank Thee, and praise Thee, and praising Thee to love Thee
more, and know Thee more, how worthy Thou art of all love
and praise, until I be fitted with all Thy saints and angels to
love Thee and praise Thee everlastingly, and breathe out my
soul to Thee in loving Thee and praising Thee for all Thy
boundless, undeserved love to me, Thy poor sinner, yet,
though a sinner, Thine, O God my God. Amen

*E. B. Pusey*

**541** Lord,
How do I love thee? Let me count the ways.
I love thee to the depth and breadth and height
my soul can reach, when feeling out of sight
for the ends of being and of ideal grace.
I love thee to the level of every day's
most quiet need, by sun and candlelight.
I love thee purely, as they turn from praise.
I love thee with a passion put to use
in my old griefs, and with my childhood faith.
I love thee with a love I seemed to lose
with my lost saints – I love thee with the breath,
smiles, tears, of all my life!
And, God, if thou dost choose
I shall love thee better after death.

*Elizabeth Browning**

**542** Let my heart be free from every unworthy thing that I may be
free to love thee, my Lord God, with all my heart and soul and
with all my strength. Free me from such narrow-mindedness
as would make me set my affections upon anything apart from
thee, O thou, who art the only true Lover and true Lord of all.
When I love anything for the reason that it is from thee, then
do I truly love thee, in that I love it for thy sake, for thou alone
hast every claim over it for our good. Our service of thee, what
else is it but a working out of thy loving salvation? Thou didst
first show us love to win our love, not needing it, but solely
because we cannot become what thou wouldst have us be
unless we love thee.

*William of Saint Thierry*

543 Lord, it is my chief complaint,
   That my love is weak and faint;
   Yet I love Thee and adore,
   Oh for grace to love Thee more.

*William Cowper*

544 You who are love itself give me the grace of love, give me
   yourself, so that all my days may finally empty into the one day
   of your eternal life.

*Karl Rahner*

545 Teach us, O Lord, to fear without being afraid; to fear thee in
   love that we may love thee without fear; through Jesus Christ
   our Lord.

*Christina Rossetti*

546 O beloved Saviour, show yourself to us who knock, that
   knowing you, we may love you alone, desire only you, think
   always of you alone, meditating day and night on your words.
   Awaken in us such a love as may be rightly and fittingly
   rendered to you.
      O God, may your love take possession of our whole being
   and make it totally yours.

*St Columbanus*

547 O Lord, who hast taught us that all our doings without charity
   are nothing worth; send thy Holy Ghost, and pour into our
   hearts that most excellent gift of charity, the very bond of
   peace and of all virtues, without which whosoever liveth is
   counted dead before thee: Grant this for thine only Son Jesus
   Christ's sake.

*Thomas Cranmer*

548 O Father, help us to know that the hiding of Thy face is wise
   love. Thy love is not fond, doting and reasonless. Thy bairns
   must often have the frosty cold side of the hill, and set down
   both their bare feet amongst the thorns: Thy love hath eyes,
   and in the meantime is looking on. Our pride must have
   winter weather.

*George Macdonald*

549 You know better than I how much I love you, Lord. You
   know it and I know it not, for nothing is more hidden from me
   than the depths of my own heart. I desire to love you; I fear

that I do not love you enough. I beseech you to grant me the fullness of pure love. Behold my desire; you have given it to me. Behold in your creature what you have placed there. O God, who love me enough to inspire me to love you for ever, behold not my sins. Behold your mercy and my love.

*François Fénelon*

550 Dear Lord,
   Love is kind and suffers long,
   Love is meek and thinks no wrong,
   Love than Death itself more strong,
   Therefore give us Love!

*Christopher Wordsworth*

551 O God, Who through the grace of Thy Holy Spirit, dost pour the gift of love into the hearts of Thy faithful people, grant unto us health, both of mind and body, that we may love Thee with our whole strength, and with entire satisfaction may perform those things which are pleasing unto Thee, through Christ our Lord. Amen

*Sarum Breviary*

552 O God, the God of all goodness and all grace, Who art worthy of a greater love than we can either give or understand; fill my heart, I beseech Thee, with such love towards Thee as may cast out all sloth and fear, that nothing may seem too hard for me to do or to suffer in obedience to Thee; and grant that, by thus loving, I may become daily more like unto Thee, and finally obtain the crown of life, which Thou hast promised to those that love Thee; through Jesus Christ our Lord. Amen

*Pocket Manual of Prayers*

553 O God, we have known and believed the love that thou hast for us. May we, by dwelling in love, dwell in thee, and thou in us. Teach us, O heavenly Father, the love wherewith thou hast loved us; fashion us, O blessed Lord, after thine own example of love; shed abroad, O thou Holy Spirit of love, the love of God and man in our hearts. For thy name's sake.

*Henry Alford*

554 Lord, you are the living flame, burning ceaselessly with love for man. Enter into me and inflame me with your fire so that I might be like you.

*John Henry Newman*

**555** Give us, O Lord God, a deep sense of Thy wonderful love towards us; how Thou wouldst not let us alone in our ruin, but didst come after us, in the Person of Thy Son Jesus Christ to bring us back to our true home with Thee.

Quicken in us, O Lord, the Spirit of gratitude, of loyalty and of sacrifice, that we may seek in all things to please Him who humbled Himself for us, even to the death of the Cross, by dying unto sin and living unto righteousness; through the same Jesus Christ our Lord.

*Charles J. Vaughan*

**556** My God, I love you with my whole heart and soul, and above all things, because you are infinitely good and perfect, and most worthy of all my love; and for your sake I love my neighbour as myself. Mercifully grant, O my God, that having loved you on earth, I may love and enjoy you for ever in heaven. Amen

*Traditional Prayer*

**557** Late have I loved you, O beauty so ancient and so new;
late have I loved you.
For behold you were within me, and I outside;
and I sought you outside and in my ugliness fell
upon those lovely things that you have made.
You were with me and I was not with you.
I was kept from you by those things,
yet had they not been in you, they would not have
been at all.
You called and cried to me and broke upon my deafness;
and you sent forth your light and shone upon me,
and chased away my blindness;
You breathed fragrance upon me,
and I drew in my breath and do now pant for you:
I tasted you and I now hunger and thirst for you;
you touched me, and I have burned for your peace.

*St Augustine of Hippo*

**558** O God, who by love alone are great and glorious, who are present and live with us by love alone: grant us likewise by love to attain another self, by love to live in others, and by love to come to our glory to see and accompany your love throughout all eternity.

*Thomas Traherne*

**559** O that my Lord Jesus would grant me but a tiny spark of that charity which is his gift! So might all that is close to his heart be my care also, yet always with the surety that I give myself, before all else, to what I know he asks of me, or whatever my clear duty lays upon me.

*St Bernard of Clairvaux*

**560** O Jesus, Master and Lord, pour into our hearts thine own heroic love; that being filled with love we may know the love which passeth knowledge, and live in the unknown power of love to win men to trust in love, to the glory of God who is love.

*William Temple*

**561** O my sweet Saviour Christ, which in thine undeserved love towards mankind so kindly wouldst suffer the painful death of the cross, suffer me not to be cold nor lukewarm in love again towards thee.

*Thomas More*

**562** Lord Jesus, may the sweet burning ardour of your love absorb my soul entirely and make it a stranger to all that is not you or for you.

*St Francis of Assisi*

**563** O my blessed Saviour Lord Jesus, thou askest my love, thou desirest to have my heart, and for my love thou wilt give me thy love in return. O my sweet Lord, what is this for thee to desire, who art so excellent? If my poor heart were of so much value as all the hearts of men and women that ever were if they were put together into one, and if it were as precious and noble as there is price and nobleness in all the orders of angels, if furthermore it did contain in it all the bodily and spiritual treasure that is within the compass of heaven and without, yet it were but a little gift to give unto so great a Lord to have his most precious and delicate love in return . . . Nevertheless, such as it is, since it is thy pleasure to have it, and thy goodness doth ask it of me saying: Give me thy heart, I freely give it unto thee, and I most humbly beseech thy goodness and mercy to accept it, and so to order me by thy grace that I may receive into it the love of nothing contrary to thy pleasure.

*John Fisher*

**564** O my Jesus! I am not worthy to love thee! Yet because thou biddest me love thee, and has told me that my soul was created on purpose to love thee, I cheerfully resign my love and affection to thee! I desire to love thee! I wish for nothing more than that I may passionately love thee. Whom have I in heaven to love but thee? And there is none on earth that I desire to love more than thyself. For thou art altogether lovely, and thy love surpasses all the love of friends, and the dearest relations I have.

O my blessed Redeemer! I desire to love thee with all my heart, and with all my strength. Thou gavest me this heart and this strength: And on whom can I bestow it better, than on thee, the Author of it?

*Anthony Horneck*

**565** We are the mediocre,
   we are the half givers,
   we are the half lovers,
   we are the savourless salt.
Lord Jesus Christ,
   restore us now,
to the primal splendour
   of first love.
To the austere light
   of the breaking day.
Let us hunger and thirst,
   let us burn in the flame.
Break the hard crust
   of complacency.
Quicken in us
   the sharp grace of desire.

*Caryll Houselander*

**566** O God, I love Thee, I love Thee –
   Not out of hope of heaven for me
   Nor fearing not to love and be
   In the everlasting burning.
   Thou, Thou, my Jesus, after me
   Didst reach Thine arms out dying,
   For my sake sufferedst nails and lance,
   Mocked and marred countenance,
   Sorrows passing number,
   Sweat and care and cumber,
   Yea and death, and this for me,

And Thou couldst see me sinning:
Then I, why should not I love Thee,
Jesu, so much in love with me?
Not for heaven's sake; not to be
Out of hell by loving Thee;
Not for any gains I see;
But just the way that Thou didst me
I do love and I will love Thee:
What must I love Thee, Lord, for then?
For being my king and God. Amen

*Gerard Manley Hopkins*

**567** Set our hearts on fire with love of thee, O Christ Our God, that in that flame we may love thee with all our hearts, with all our mind, with all our soul, and with all our strength, and our neighbours as ourselves; so that, keeping thy commandments, we may glorify thee, the giver of all good gifts.

*Eastern Orthodox Prayer*

## LOVE OF OTHERS

**568** O God, who out of your great love for our world did reconcile earth to heaven through your only-begotten Son; grant that we, who by the darkness of our sins are turned aside from brotherly love, may, by your light, shed forth in our souls your own sweetness and embrace our friends in you, forgiving our enemies, even as you forgive us for your Son's sake.

*Mozarabic Sacramentary\**

**569** O merciful Father, who has made of one blood all nations of men; grant us a universal love towards all men. Give to us such a tenderness of heart that we may feel deeply the miseries and calamities of our brethren, and diligently remember them in love. Grant that we may not only seek our own things, but also the things of others. Let this mind be also in us which was in Christ Jesus, that we may love as brethren, that we may be sympathetic and courteous, and may endeavour heartily and vigorously to keep the unity of the spirit in the bond of peace; and may the God of grace, mercy and peace be with us all.

*Thomas à Kempis*

**570** O You who are love, and dwell in love, teach us to be children of love in our actions, thoughts and words. May we never turn our love away from those who are ignorant of your love. May we be instruments of your mercy reaching out to those in distress and need, giving such an example of your loving concern that all may find unity in the discovery that they are your children. Amen

*James Martineau\**

**571** Soften our hearts, O Lord, that we may be moved no less at the necessities and griefs of our neighbours, than if they concerned ourselves, or the cases that touched us nearest, and let us think them to befall even to our dearest friends. Let us pity them as ourselves, and, in their adversity, let us have compassion upon them, that, as we would have pitied ourselves for the like cause, so we may be moved with pity towards those whom we see oppressed with the same adversities. Amen

*Johannes Ludovicus Vives*

**572** O God, perfect us in love, that we may conquer all selfishness and hatred of others; fill our hearts with Thy joy, and shed in them Thy peace which passeth understanding; that so those murmurings to which we are too prone may be overcome. Make us long-suffering and gentle, and thus subdue our hastiness and angry tempers, and grant that we may bring forth the blessed fruits of the Spirit, to Thy praise and glory, through Jesus Christ our Lord. Amen

*Henry Alford*

**573** O Lord, the author and persuader of peace, love and good-will, soften our hard and steely hearts, warm our icy and frozen hearts that we may wish well to one another, and may be the true disciples of Jesus Christ. And give us grace even now to begin to show forth that heavenly life, wherein there is no disagreement nor hatred, but peace and love on all hands, one towards another.

*Johannes Ludovicus Vives*

**574** O Lord, give us more charity, more self-denial, more likeness to Thee.

Teach us to sacrifice our comforts to others, and our likings for the sake of doing good.

Make us kindly in thought, gentle in word, generous in deed.

Teach us that it is better to give than to receive; better to forget ourselves than to put ourselves forward; better to minister than to be ministered unto.

And unto Thee, the God of Love, be glory and praise for ever.

*Henry Alford*

575 Almighty and eternal God, who hast revealed thy nature in Christ Jesus thy son as love, we humbly pray thee give us thy Holy Spirit to glorify thee also in our hearts as pure love, and thus constrain us by thy divine power to love thee with our whole souls, and our brethren as ourselves; that so by thy grace we may be fulfilled with love, and evermore abide in thee, and thou in us, with all joyfulness, and free from fear or distrust; through Jesus Christ our Lord.

*Christian K. J. Bunsen*

576 O God, who hast bound us together in this bundle of life, give us grace to understand how our lives depend on the courage, the industry, the honesty, and integrity of our fellow men; that we may be mindful of their needs, grateful for their faithfulness, and faithful in our responsibilities to them; through Jesus Christ our Lord.

*Reinhold Niebuhr*

577 Lord God, heavenly Father, who hast bound us together in one body through thy Holy Spirit; help us, we pray thee, to serve one another willingly and forgive one another from our hearts, through Jesus Christ our Lord. Amen

*Thomas Bradwardine*

578 Lord, save us from being self-centred in our prayers and teach us to remember to pray for others. May we be so bound up in love with those for whom we pray, that we may feel their needs as acutely as our own, and intercede for them with sensitivity, with understanding and with imagination. We ask this in Christ's name.

*John Calvin* *

579 Help me, Lord, to be more like you:
to draw a circle that includes rather than excludes.
Give me a genuine love for others,

both those I like and those I don't like.
Help me to overcome my fears and prejudices
and to see your image in all men.

*Richard Harries*

580 Almighty and most merciful Father, who has given us a new
commandment that we should love one another, give us also
grace that we may fulfil it. Make us gentle, courteous, and
forbearing. Direct our lives so that we may look each to the
good of others in word and deed. And hallow all our
friendships by the blessing of thy spirit, for his sake, who
loveth us and gave himself for us, Jesus Christ our Lord.
Amen

*Brooke Foss Westcott*

581 Bless me, O God, with the love of Thee, and of my neighbour.
Give me peace of conscience, the command of my affections;
and for the rest, Thy will be done! O King of peace, keep us in
love and charity. Amen

*Thomas Wilson*

582 Heavenly Father, we thank you for our neighbours and for
    the people around us with whom we share our daily lives.
We pray for those who are old and lonely;
those isolated because of ill-health;
and those who find it difficult to make friends.
Show us what we can do to help, and teach us to be good
    neighbours; for Jesus' sake.

*Llewellyn Cumings*

583 O God, fountain of love, pour thy love into our souls, that we
may love those whom thou lovest with the love thou givest us,
and think and speak of them tenderly, meekly, lovingly; and
so loving our brothers and sisters for thy sake, may grow in thy
love, and dwelling in love may dwell in thee; for Jesus Christ's
sake.

*E. B. Pusey*

584 Grant me, I beseech thee, my God, in the name of Jesus
Christ thy Son, the charity which never fails, that my light may
shine, warming my own heart and enlightening others.

*St Columbanus*

**585** Almighty God, who thyself art love, fill us with the spirit of thy holy love; that our hearts being enkindled by thee, we may for ever love thee, and each other in thee, and all men for thee; through Jesus Christ our Lord, who liveth and reigneth with thee and the Holy Ghost, one God, world without end.

*Eric Milner-White*

**586** Give us patience and fortitude to put self aside for you in the most unlikely people: to know that every man's and any man's suffering is our own first business, for which we must be willing to go out of our way and to leave our own interests.

*Caryll Houselander*

**587** O God of love, who has given us a new commandment through your only begotten Son, that we should love one another even as You loved us, the unworthy and the wandering: We pray that you will give us, your servants, all our life on this earth, a mind forgetful of past injuries, a pure conscience and a heart of love for our brothers and sisters; for the sake of Jesus Christ our Lord.

*Coptic Liturgy of St Cyril*

**588** Pray God make all bad people good, and all good people nice.

*Little Child's Prayer*

# IV   FOR THE COMING OF THE KINGDOM

## FOR THE COMING OF THE KINGDOM

**589** O Lord, who hast set before us the great hope that thy kingdom shall come on earth, and hast taught us to pray for its coming: Give us grace to discern the signs of its dawning, and to work for the perfect day when thy will shall be done on earth as it is in heaven; through Jesus Christ our Lord.

*Percy Dearmer*

**590** O most merciful Father, we confess that we have done little to forward thy kingdom in the world and to advance thy glory. Pardon, we pray thee, our shortcomings; give us greater zeal for thy glory; and make us more ready and diligent by our prayers, our gifts and our example to spread abroad the knowledge of thy truth and to enlarge the boundaries of thy kingdom; through Jesus Christ our Lord.

*W. Walsham How*

**591** O Lord, you have warned us that you will require much of those to whom much is given. Grant that we, who have received so much, may strive together, by our prayers, hard work and gifts to extend to those who know you not, what we so richly enjoy. So may your will be fulfilled with the salvation of all mankind.

*Fifth-century Prayer*

**592** O God, who makest men to be of one mind and hast called us into the fellowship of thy dear Son: Draw into closer unity, we beseech thee, the people of all races in this and every land; that in fellowship with thee they may understand and help one another, and that, serving thee, they may find their perfect freedom; through the same thy Son Jesus Christ our Lord.

*Joost de Blank*

**593** Make us receptive and open
and may we accept your kingdom
like children taking bread
from the hands of their father.
Let us live in your peace,
at home with you
all the days of our lives.

*Huub Oosterhuis*

**594** O God, the Father, good beyond all that is good, fair beyond
all that is fair, in whom is calmness, peace, and concord: do
thou make up the dissensions that divide us from each other,
and bring us into a unity of love, which may bear some
likeness to thy sublime nature; through Jesus Christ our Lord.

*Liturgy of St Dionysius*

**595** Almighty and everlasting God, whose beloved Son became
man for us men and for our salvation, and gave commandment to his disciples that they should go and teach all nations,
and baptise them in the name of the Father and of the Son and
of the Holy Ghost: Give us grace to be obedient to his
command, and grant that all men may have new birth in him,
and, being delivered out of the power of darkness, may be
received into the kingdom of thy love: through the same Jesus
Christ our Lord.

*George Appleton*

**596** O God, who hast made of one blood all nations of men for to
dwell on the face of the earth, and didst send thy blessed Son
Jesus Christ to preach peace to them that are afar off, and to
them that are nigh: Grant that all the peoples of the world may
feel after thee and find thee; and hasten, O God, the fulfilment of thy promise, to pour out thy Spirit upon all flesh;
through Jesus Christ our Lord.

*George E. Cotton*

**597** O God of all the nations of the earth, remember those who,
though created in your image, are ignorant of your love; and,
in fulfilment of the sacrifice of your Son Jesus Christ, let the
prayers and labours of your Church deliver them from false
faith and unbelief, and bring them to worship you; through
him who is the resurrection and the life of all who put their
trust in you, Jesus Christ our Lord.

*Francis Xavier*

**598** Almighty and everlasting God, who hast willed to restore all things in thy well-beloved Son, the King and Lord of all: Mercifully grant that all peoples and nations, divided and wounded by sin, may be brought under the gentle yoke of his most loving rule; who with thee and the Holy Spirit liveth and reigneth, ever one God, world without end.

*Sarum Breviary*

**599** O Jesus, Son of God, carpenter of Nazareth, grant sight to those blinded by luxury, and deliverance to those bound by want, that the rich may joyfully follow the simplicity of thy most holy life, and the poor may obtain their inheritance, and that the hearts of all may be set with one accord to discover the way of salvation; through thy mercy, who for our sake didst become poor, that we through thy poverty might become rich. And this we ask for thy Name's sake.

*Twentieth-century Prayer*
*(unknown source)*

**600** O God, our Leader and our Master and our Friend, forgive our imperfections and our little motives, take us and make us one with Thy great purpose, use us and do not reject us, make us all servants of Thy kingdom, weave our lives into Thy struggle to conquer and to bring peace and union to the world.

We are small and feeble creatures, we are feeble in speech, feebler still in action, nevertheless let but Thy light shine upon us, and there is not one of us who cannot be lit by Thy fire and who cannot lose himself in Thy salvation. Take us into Thy purposes, O God. Let Thy kingdom come into our hearts and into this world.

*H. G. Wells*

**601** Lord, hear: Lord, forgive: Lord, do: hear what I speak not, forgive what I speak amiss, do what I leave undone: that, not according to my word or my deed, but according to Thy mercy and truth, all may issue to Thy glory and the good of Thy Kingdom.

*Maria Hare*

**602** Almighty God, our heavenly Father, whose Son Jesus Christ came to cast fire upon the earth: Grant that by the prayers of thy faithful people a fire of burning zeal may be kindled, and pass from heart to heart, till all our hardness is melted in the warmth of thy love; through him who loved us and gave himself for us, Jesus Christ our Lord.

*G. C. Binyon*

**603** Enlarge our souls with a divine charity, that we may hope all things, endure all things; and become messengers of Thy healing mercy to the grievances and infirmities of men. In all things attune our hearts to the holiness and harmony of Thy kingdom. And hasten the time when Thy kingdom shall come, and Thy will be done on earth as it is in heaven. Amen

*James Martineau*

**604** Almighty God, the giver of all good things, without whose help all work is ineffectual, and without whose grace all wisdom is folly; Grant, we beseech thee, that in our undertakings thy Holy Spirit may not be withheld from us, but that we may promote thy glory, and the coming of thy kingdom; through Jesus Christ our Lord.

*Rev. Samuel Johnson*

**605** Almighty Father, whose blessed Son at his coming among us brought redemption to his people, and peace to men of goodwill; Grant that, when he shall come again in glory to judge the world and to make all things new, we may be found ready to receive him, and enter into his joy; through the same Christ our Lord.

*Frederick B. Macnutt*

# FOR THE CHURCH

**606** O God, Redeemer and Governor of mankind: We beseech thee to grant that thy Church may continually be enlarged by the gathering in of new children to thee, and perfected by the increasing devotion of those who have been regenerated; through Jesus Christ our Lord.

*Gelasian Sacramentary*

**607** Almighty and everlasting God, who hast revealed thy glory in Christ to all nations: Protect, we beseech thee, what thy compassion has created, that thy Church which is spread abroad throughout the world may persevere with steadfast

faith in the confession of thy name; through the same Jesus
Christ our Lord.

*Gelasian Sacramentary*

**608** Almighty God, whose mercy reaches unto the heavens and
thy faithfulness unto the clouds: We bless thee for thy gracious
providence towards our nation in the creation, preservation
and reformation of thy Church within its borders; and we
beseech thee to stretch forth thy mighty hand in this our day to
purge us from sin, to establish us in truth, to unite us in love,
and to inspire us with zeal for the extension of thy kingdom;
through Jesus Christ our Lord.

*John R. W. Stott*

**609** Thou, O God, didst name thy Church thy spouse. As it
becomes graceful in thy sight by its devout and trusting faith,
so may it ever have a lover's loyalty. Grant that all peoples
honouring thy name may be worthy of the title they bear. May
all in thy Church, closely united to thee, reverence thee, love
thee, follow thee, that walking always in thy footsteps, they
may deserve under thy guidance to attain the heavenly kingdom of thy promise.

*Abbot Grimald*

**610** O God, let thy mercy descend upon thy whole Church;
preserve her in truth and peace, in unity and safety, in all
storms and against all enemies; that she, offering to thy glory
the never-ceasing sacrifice of prayer and thanksgiving, may
advance the honour of her Lord and be filled with his Spirit,
and partake of his glory, through the same Jesus Christ our
Lord.

*Jeremy Taylor*

**611** Be merciful, O Father of all mercies, to thy Church universal
dispersed throughout the whole world, that all thy faithful people may have grace to confess thy holy name; and
especially be merciful to such as are under persecution for
their testimony, and their profession of the gospel; that as
they stand fast for thy holy Word, so they may be upheld by it;
through thy Son our Saviour Jesus Christ.

*After Prayers of 1585*

**612** O Heavenly Father, who saveth not by might, nor by power,
but by thy Spirit: We humbly beseech thee to pour out thy

Holy Spirit from on high and to revive thy work in the midst of the years. Grant to thy Church Universal, a new vision of thy glory, a new experience of thy power, a new fidelity to thy Word, a new consecration to thy service; that through the witness of a renewed and dedicated people thy holy name may be glorified and thy blessed kingdom advanced in all the world; through Jesus Christ our Lord.

*Frank Colquhoun*

**613** O Lord, we beseech thee to maintain thy Church in truth and patience; that her pastors may be faithful, her watchmen vigilant, her flock loyal, her camp united, her war spiritual, her weapons heavenly, her lamp burning and shining; and as thy Son Jesus Christ hath given so great a price for us, let us not count it a hard thing to give up all for him, and to spend and be spent for the souls he hath redeemed; who liveth and reigneth with thee and the Holy Ghost, now and for evermore.

*Percy Dearmer*

**614** O God, our Shepherd, give to the Church a new vision and a new charity, new wisdom and fresh understanding, the revival of her brightness and the renewal of her unity; that the eternal message of Thy Son, undefiled by the traditions of men, may be hailed as the good news of the new age; through him who maketh all things new, Jesus Christ our Lord. Amen

*Percy Dearmer*

**615** We pray you, Lord, to direct and guide your Church with your unfailing care, that it may be vigilant in times of quiet, and daring in times of trouble; through Jesus Christ our Lord.

*Franciscan Breviary*

**616** O most gracious Father, we most humbly beseech thee for thy holy Catholic church. Fill it with all truth; in all truth with all peace. Where it is corrupt, purge it; where it is in error, direct it; where anything is amiss, reform it; where it is right, strengthen and confirm it; where it is in want, furnish it; where it is divided, heal it and unite it in thy love; through Jesus Christ our Lord.

*William Laud*

**617** Eternal Father, who wouldst make the Church of thy dear Son a city great and fair, the joy of the whole earth: we beseech thee, by the sending of thy Holy Spirit, direct its counsels in all manner of wisdom, love, and might; remove perplexity, establish concord, kindle flame, and gather a people single and strong of faith; to the praise of him, who with thee and the same Spirit liveth and reigneth, one God, world without end.

*Lambeth Conference, 1930*

**618** O heavenly Father, the same yesterday, today and forever, pour your blessing upon the ministers and laymen of your church, in this country and in all lands. May we grasp your majesty and might; may we be filled with your Holy Spirit, that the church today, like the early church, may preach and live the gospel of Christ in eagerness, power and love. Grant this, O Lord, that your name may be honoured before the world. Amen

*Unknown Source*

# THE COMMUNION OF SAINTS

**619** O Lord our God, from whom neither life nor death can separate those who trust in thy love, and whose love holds in its embrace thy children in this world and in the next: So unite us to thyself that in fellowship with thee we may always be united to our loved ones whether here or there: give us courage, constancy and hope; through him who died and was buried and rose again for us, Jesus Christ our Lord.

*William Temple*

**620** O King, eternal, immortal, invisible, before whom stand the spirits of the living and the dead, who in the righteousness of thy saints hast given us an example of godly life, and in their blessedness a glorious pledge of the hope of our calling, we beseech thee that, being compassed about with so great a cloud of witnesses, we may run with patience the race that is set before us, and with them receive the crown of glory that fadeth not away; through Jesus Christ our Lord.

*Acts of Devotion*

**621** Lord, help us to perceive that we are all linked together through you, and that because of our union with you, we share each others' burdens and joys. Lord, make us realise that we are never alone in suffering for you and all our brothers are with us in it. By our prayers for each other made through you and by the prayers of the saints on earth and in heaven, make us conscious of the great support we have as members of your Body. Lord, I thank you for the most wonderful gift of the communion of Saints.

*Michael Hollings and Etta Gullick*

**622** Lord of all worlds,
We thank Thee for all those who are now perfected in Thee.
We thank Thee that now they are released from their
    apprenticeship,
and behold Thee face to face at last,
Dwelling for ever in light and joy with Thyself.

We thank Thee for their steadfast faithfulness,
For their loyalty and trusty friendship,
For their ready answer to Thy call.

We thank Thee for the high inspiration of their example,
For the hope which is given us, as we think of them,
That we also – though our probation here be longer –
May like them be faithful and self-denying, pure, humble,
    and loving,
That so we may all in heaven and earth be bound together
    into one new creation in Thyself.

*John S. Hoyland*

**623** Almighty God, we praise your holy name for all the saints throughout the ages who have kept the lamp of faith burning brightly. Grant that we who are following in their steps may keep that light shining, that the darkness of this world may be lit by him who is the light of the world, even your Son our Saviour, Jesus Christ. Amen

*William Hampson*

**624** We thank you, God, for the saints of all ages, for those who in times of darkness kept the lamp of faith burning, for the great souls who saw visions of larger truths and dared to declare them, for the multitude of quiet, gracious souls whose presence purified and sanctified the world; and for those known and loved by us, who have passed from this earthly fellowship into the fuller life with you. Accept this, our thanksgiving, through Jesus Christ, to whom be praise and dominion for ever. Amen

*Fellowship Litanies*

**625** Truly fearless, truly fortunate martyrs, called and chosen to glorify our Lord Jesus Christ! If any man magnifies the Lord, honours and adores him, these are the models for him. If he reads about them, he will find that though they are modern, they are not inferior to the ancient ones: they will edify the Church just as much. These new examples of virtue will prove that it is one and the same Holy Spirit who was active then and is active now, one and the same omnipotent God the Father and his Son, Jesus Christ, our Lord, whose glory and power are boundless and always will be, age after age. Amen

*Tertullian*

**626** O Christ our God incarnate, whose Virgin Mother was blessed in bearing thee, but still more blessed in keeping thy word: Grant us, who honour the exaltation of her lowliness, to follow the example of her devotion to thy will; who livest and reignest with the Father and the Holy Ghost, ever one God, world without end.

*William Bright*

(See also 745–748 *All Saints*)

# GUARDIAN ANGELS

**627** Guardian angel, to whose care this poor soul and body of mine have been given, do not abandon me because I am a sinner, nor hold aloof from me because I am not clean. Take my limp hand and bring me to the path that leads to salvation.

Yes, holy angel, God has given you charge of my miserable little soul and body. Protect me during the coming night and keep me safe from the machinations and contrivances of the Enemy, that I may not sin and arouse God's anger.

Intercede for me with the Lord; ask him to make me fear him more and more, and to enable me to give him the service his goodness deserves. Amen

*Macarius of Egypt*

**628** O everlasting God, who hast ordained and constituted the services of Angels and men in a wonderful order; mercifully grant, that as Thy holy Angels always do Thee service in heaven, so by Thy appointment they may succour and defend us on earth; through Jesus Christ our Lord.

*Book of Common Prayer, 1928*

**629** Holy Michael, the archangel defend us in the day of battle; be our safeguard against the wickedness and snares of the devil: May God rebuke him we humbly pray; and may the prince of the heavenly host, by the power of God thrust down to hell Satan and all wicked spirits, who wander through the world for the ruin of souls. Amen

*Traditional Prayer*

**630** O sweet angel, to me so dear,
That night and day standeth me near,
Full lovingly with mildest mood:
Offer for me, to Jesu our king,
Thanking, loving, love, praising,
For his gifts all great and good;
As thou goest 'twixt him and me,
And know'st my life in each degree,
Saying it in his presence.
Ask me grace to love him truly,
To serve my Lord with full heart duly,
With my daily diligence.
Keep me from vice and every peril,
While thou with me dost daily travel;
In this world of wickedness
Set me my petitions granted,
By thy prayers daily haunted, –
If it please thy holiness.

*Richard Rolle*

# MINISTER'S PRAYERS

**631** Listen to me, O merciful God, on behalf of these children for whom my bounden duty, no less than my affection, urges me to pray. Thou, my sweet Lord, knowest how much I love them, how they are all my life, how my heart yearns after them. Thou knowest, too, Lord, how little I wish to rule them harshly, or dominate over them; how I would rather benefit them by affection than by command, be quite spent for their good; how I deem myself their servant, desiring always to be in full sympathy with them. Therefore, hear me, Lord, hear me, and let thy eyes be upon them day and night. Overshadow them with thy wings to shield them. Stretch forth thy holy right hand upon them to keep them ever united and at peace.

*St Aelred of Rievaulx*

632 O Lord, grant all who contend for the faith, never to injure it by clamor and impatience; but, speaking Thy precious truth in love, so to present it that it may be loved, and that men may see in it Thy goodness and beauty.

*William Bright*

633 We pray thee, almighty God, open the hearts of thy people to thy law and give them humble minds to receive thy heavenly commandments. Whatever our mortal tongue shall utter for the salvation of their souls, do thou in thy heavenly pity make acceptable to them. Speak thou from heaven through us and give them life; and may they and we who watch over them be counted worthy to attain to Christ unharmed.

*Mozarabic Sacramentary*

634 The chief service I owe you in my life, as I well know, O God, all-powerful Father, is that every word and thought of mine should speak of you. The power of speech that you have bestowed on me can give me no greater pleasure than to serve you by preaching and to show an ignorant world what you are: the Father, the Father whose only Son is God.

But in saying this, I am merely saying what I want to do. If I am actually to do it, I must ask you for your help and mercy, ask you to fill with wind the sails I have hoisted for you and to carry me forward on my course – to breathe, that is, your Spirit into my faith and my confession of it, and to enable me to continue the preaching I have begun.

*St Hilary of Poitiers\**

635 O Lord, I humbly beseech and implore thee, grant me always the humble knowledge that edifies. Give unto me that gentle and wise eloquence which is innocent of all arrogance and exaltation of one's own gifts above the brethren. Put into my mouth, I pray thee, the word of consolation and edification and exhortation through thy Holy Spirit, that I may exhort those that are good to be better and, by word and example, recall those who are going contrary to thy straight path. May the words which thou shalt grant to thy servant be

as sharp javelins and burning arrows which will pierce the hearts of the hearers and kindle them to fear and love thee. Amen

*St Ambrose of Milan*

**636** O God our Father, let us find grace in thy sight so as to have grace to serve thee acceptably with reverence and godly fear; and further grace not to receive thy grace in vain, nor to neglect it and fall from it, but to stir it up and grow in it, and to persevere in it unto the end of our lives; through Jesus Christ our Lord.

*Lancelot Andrewes*

**637** Help me to spread your fragrance everywhere I go – let me preach you without preaching, not by words but by my example – by the catching force, the sympathetic influence of what I do, the evident fullness of the love my heart bears to you.

*John Henry Newman*

**638** O Lord, let me stand before thee. Thou art the beginning, the middle, and the end. Holy art thou, and holy is thy day, holy art all the hours of service to thee.

Lead me by thy Spirit. Help me; be thou my strength. Renew and quicken me. Give me the Bread of Life. Gather my thought, O Lord, and keep me from wandering and weariness. Preserve me from the curse of much speaking, from the death of vain busyness. Let all that I do and say be done in spirit and in truth. Keep my love ready and willing to serve thee among men. In the midst of all our labour thou art a refuge of peace. Thou dost strengthen us ever anew from the living fountain. There is no end to thy mercy.

Praise, honour, and glory be to thee, the Father, and the Son, and the Holy Spirit. By thy mercy, accept my ministry to the praise of thy glory. Amen

*Karl B. Ritter*

**639** Trouble me with the smallness of my work.
Trouble me with the greatness of thy command.
Trouble me with my unholiness and my slowness to obey.
Trouble me with time running out and every lost hour.
Trouble me with my sins and the sins of all men.
Trouble me with the troubles of thy church which are the work of men.

Trouble me, and make me to watch continually for thy
   judgment.
Let me go forth desiring the coming of thy glory.
Let me go forward; for thy glory shall be revealed.
I thank thee that my work ends and thy work begins.
Lord, I believe, help thou my unbelief.

*Karl B. Ritter*

**640** O God, the fountain of all wisdom, in a deep sense of my own
ignorance, and of that great charge which lies upon me, I am
constrained to come often before thee, from whom I have
learned whatever I know, to ask that help without which I
shall disquiet myself in vain; most humbly beseeching thee to
guide me with thine eye; to enlighten my mind, that I may see
myself, and teach others the wonders of thy law; that I may
learn from thee what I ought to think and speak concerning
thee. Direct and bless all the labours of my mind, give me a
discerning spirit, a sound judgment, and an honest and religious heart. And grant that, in all my studies, my first aim
may be to set forth thy glory, and to set forward the salvation
of mankind; that I may give a comfortable account of my time
at the great day, when all our labours shall be tried.

And if thou art pleased that by my ministry sinners shall be
converted, and thy kingdom enlarged, give me the grace of
humility, that I may never ascribe the success to myself, but to
thy Holy Spirit, which enables me to will and to do according
to thy good pleasure. Grant this, O Father of all light and
truth, for the sake of Jesus Christ. Amen

*Thomas Wilson*

**641** Lord, make us bold to run the way of thy commandments and
help us to stand still before thy presence, that, leading lives of
quiet confidence, we may bear witness to thy grace and carry
thy power into the world. Let thy light shine through us, that
men may see good works in us and give glory to the Father in
heaven. So direct our lives, that in the end none to whom we
have failed to show mercy and love may accuse us, and we may
be received into the eternal habitations; through Jesus Christ,
our Lord. Amen

*Hermann Bezzel*

**642** Holiness of life we crave after. Grant that our speech, our
thoughts, our actions, may all be holiness, and 'holiness unto
the Lord'. We know that there be some that seek after moral

virtue apart from God; let us not be of their kind, but may our desire be that everything may be done as unto the Lord, for thou hast said, 'Walk before me and be thou perfect.' Help us to do so; to have no master but our God; no law but his will; no delight but himself. O, take these hearts, most glorious Lord, and keep them, for 'out of them are the issues of life', and let us be the instruments in thy hand, by daily vigilance, of keeping our hearts, lest in heart we go astray from the Lord our God. Until life's latest hour may we keep the sacred pledges of our early youth.

*Charles H. Spurgeon*

**643** Praise be to thee, O Christ, and all glory, for in thy going about among men, thou didst with wondrous gentleness console them and mercifully ease their sufferings and sadness. Give me also that gift of kindliness of heart and easy affection and understanding, that I may sympathize with every affliction, feel for every misfortune, as if it were my own; that I may be calm and tolerant with the shortcomings of others and gladly help them at need.

*Nakatenus*

**644** Hail, sweet Jesus, praise, honour and glory be to thee who didst give thy Holy Spirit to thy chosen disciples who were with one mind persevering in prayer, and sent them hence to teach all nations. Cleanse my heart, I beseech thee; give me a sincere mind, a stable mind that the Paraclete himself, finding a worthy dwelling-place in my heart, may enrich me with yet fuller graces, comfort and strengthen me, rule and possess me.

*Nakatenus*

**645** Lord Jesus, merciful and patient, grant us grace, we beseech Thee, ever to teach in a teachable spirit; learning along with those we teach, and learning from them whenever Thou so pleasest; that we and they may all be taught of God.

*Christina Rossetti*

**646** Lord Jesus, teach me, that I may teach them; sanctify and enable all my powers, that in their full strength I may deliver thy message reverently, readily, faithfully, and fruitfully. Make thy word a swift word, passing from the ear to the heart, from the heart to life and conversation; that as the rain returns not empty, so neither may thy word, but accomplish that for which it is given. O Lord, hear; O Lord, forgive; O Lord, hearken; and do so for thy blessed Son's sake.

*George Herbert*

**647** O Son of David, I approach you with a humbled spirit. In the hope and strength that you have given me, I dare to speak to you. With the key of your cross open up the secrets of my heart; send one of the seraphim with a burning coal from your altar to cleanse my soiled lips. Grant that my tongue, in loving service of my neighbour, may never speak in error but bravely and without ceasing proclaim your truth.

*St Julian of Toledo*

**648** O Jesus, Son of the living God, who became man and made the supreme sacrifice of yourself in order to reveal the mystery of the Father's love and his plan of mercy and salvation for all peoples, we adore you and praise you, because you have enlightened and redeemed us.

O Jesus, you who sent out your apostles to gather in the harvest from all the fields of the world and did promise to draw all men to yourself on the Cross, we thank you for having sent to us those who have taught us the truth and made us sharers in your grace.

We implore your grace for our bishops and priests so that they may be sanctified, and that their ministry may be faithful; in accordance with your divine will may they be as the salt, and the light, of our lands and our peoples.

*Pope John XXIII*

# V  THE CHURCH'S YEAR

## ADVENT

**649** O Lord our God, make us watchful and keep us faithful, as we await the coming of your Son our Lord; that when he shall appear, he may not find us sleeping in sin, but active in his service and joyful in his praise, for the glory of your holy name.

*Gelasian Sacramentary*

**650** Visit, O Lord, we pray thee, and cleanse our consciences, that thy Son our Lord Jesus Christ, when he comes, may find in us a dwelling prepared for himself; who liveth and reigneth with thee in the unity of the Spirit, one God, world without end.

*Roman Missal*

**651** Merciful God, who sent your messengers the prophets to preach repentance and prepare the way of our salvation: give us grace to heed their warnings and forsake our sins, that we may greet with joy the coming of Jesus Christ our Redeemer; who lives and reigns with you and the Holy Spirit, now and for ever.

*Episcopal Church, USA*

**652** Let me love Thee, O Christ,
in Thy first coming,
when Thou wast made man, for love of men,
and for love of me.

Let me love Thee, O Christ,
in Thy second coming,
when with an inconceivable love
Thou standest and knockest at the door,
and wouldest enter into the souls of men,
and into mine.

Plant in my soul, O Christ, Thy likeness of love;
that when by death Thou callest,
it may be ready,
and burning
to come unto Thee.

*Eric Milner-White*

**653** Almighty God, we give thee thanks for the mighty yearning of the human heart for the coming of the Saviour, and the constant promise of thy word that he was to come. In our own souls we repeat the humble sighs and panting aspirations of ancient men and ages, and own that our souls are in darkness and infirmity without faith in him who comes to bring God to man and man to God. We bless thee for the tribute we can pay to him from our very sense of need and dependence, and that our own hearts can so answer from their wilderness, the cry, 'Prepare ye the way of the Lord'. In us the rough places are to be made smooth, the crooked straight, the mountains of pride brought low and the valleys of despondency lifted up. O God, prepare thou the way in us now, and may we welcome anew thy Holy Child. Hosanna! Blessed be he who cometh in the name of the Lord. Amen

*Samuel Osgood*

# CHRISTMAS

**654** Glory be to God in the highest, and on earth peace, goodwill towards men; for unto us is born this day a Saviour who is Christ the Lord. We praise thee, we bless thee, we glorify thee, we give thanks to thee, for this greatest of thy mercies, O Lord God, heavenly King, God the Father Almighty.

*Thomas Ken*

**655** God, who makest us glad with the yearly remembrance of the birth of Thy only Son Jesus Christ; Grant that as we joyfully receive Him as our Redeemer, so we may with sure confidence behold Him, when He shall come to be our Judge, who liveth and reigneth with Thee and the Holy Ghost, now and forever.

*Book of Common Prayer, 1928*

**656** The shepherds sing; and shall I silent be?
My God, no hymn for thee?
My soul's a shepherd too; a flock it feeds
Of thoughts and words and deeds:
The pasture is thy word; the streams thy grace,
Enriching all the place.
Shepherd and flock shall sing, and all my powers
Out-sing the daylight hours.

*George Herbert*

**657** Merciful and most loving God, by whose will and bountiful
gift Jesus Christ our Lord humbled himself that he might exalt
mankind; and became flesh that he might restore in us the
most celestial image; and was born of the Virgin that he might
uplift the lowly: Grant unto us the inheritance of the meek,
perfect us in thy likeness, and bring us at last to rejoice in
beholding thy beauty, and with all thy saints to glorify thy
grace; through the same Jesus Christ our Lord.

*Gallican Sacramentary*

**658** Loving Father, as we think of the little Child of Bethlehem,
make us glad that Thou the Almighty, the Creator, the
Infinite, Whose Being is utterly beyond even the power of our
loftiest thought and most daring imagination, canst speak to
us in a little human Child. Save us from being impressed too
much by the impressive. Help us to see Thee in simple things:
a child's love, birdsong, the quiet loveliness of dawn, human
friendship and the peace of our homes. We bow in worship
before the majesty of heaven revealed in a human life. Accept
our worship and make our lives more like His. We ask it for
His sake. Amen

*Leslie D. Weatherhead*

**659** O Thou, whose glorious yet contracted light,
Wrapt in Night's mantle, stole into a manger,
Since my dark soul and brutish, is Thy right,
To man, of all beasts, be not Thou a stranger:
Furnish and deck my soul, that Thou mayest have
A better lodging than a rack or grave.

*George Herbert*

**660** O God, who hast made this most sacred night to shine with the
illumination of the true light: grant, we beseech thee, that, as
we have known the mystery of that light upon earth, we may

also perfectly enjoy it in heaven; through the same Jesus
Christ our Lord.

*Gelasian Sacramentary*

**661** Sweet Child of Bethlehem, grant that we may share with all
our hearts in this profound mystery of Christmas. Pour into
the hearts of men the peace which they sometimes seek so
desperately, and which you alone can give them. Help them to
know one another better and to live as brothers, children of
the same Father. Awaken in their hearts love and gratitude
for your infinite goodness; join them together in your love;
and give us all your heavenly peace.

*Pope John XXIII*

**662** My heart for very joy doth leap,
My lips no more their silence keep;
I too must sing with joyful tongue
That sweetest ancient cradle-song:

Glory to God in highest heaven,
Who unto man his Son hath given;
While angels sing with pious mirth
A glad new year to all the earth.

*Martin Luther*

**663** We beseech thee, O gracious Lord, let our hearts be enlightened by the holy radiance of Thy Son's Incarnation; that so we
may escape the darkness of this world, and by His guidance
attain to the country of everlasting clearness.

*Sarum Missal*

**664** O God, our loving Father, help us rightly to remember the
birth of Jesus, that we may share in the songs of the angels, the
gladness of the shepherds, and the worship of the wise men.
May the Christmas morning make us happy to be your
children, and the Christmas evening bring us to our beds with
grateful thoughts, forgiving and forgiven, for Jesus' sake.
Amen

*Robert Louis Stevenson*

**665** O Christ, whose wondrous birth meanest nothing unless we be
born again, whose death and sacrifice nothing if thou be risen
alone: raise up and exalt us, O Saviour, both now to the estate
of grace and hereafter to the seat of glory; where with the

Father and the Holy Spirit thou livest and reignest, God for ever and ever.

*Eric Milner-White*

# EPIPHANY

**666** Almighty and everlasting God, who hast made known the incarnation of thy Son by the bright shining of a star, which when the wise men beheld they adored thy majesty and presented costly gifts: Grant that the star of thy righteousness may always shine in our hearts, and that for our treasure we may give to thy service ourselves and all that we have; through the same Jesus Christ our Lord.

*Gelasian Sacramentary\**

**667** Almighty and everlasting God, the brightness of faithful souls, who didst bring the Gentiles to thy light, and made known unto them him who is the true light, and the bright and morning star: fill, we beseech thee, the world with thy glory, and show thyself by the radiance of thy light unto all nations; through Jesus Christ our Lord.

*Gregorian Sacramentary*

**668** May Jesus Christ, the king of glory, help us to make the right use of all the myrrh that God sends, and to offer to him the true incense of our hearts; for his name's sake. Amen

*Johann Tauler*

**669** O God, who didst manifest thine only begotten Son to the Gentiles, and hast commanded thy Church to preach the gospel to every creature: bless all thy servants who are labouring for thee in distant lands. Have compassion upon those who know thee not. Lead them by the Holy Spirit to him who is the light of the world, that, walking in the light, they may at length attain to the light of everlasting life; through Jesus Christ our Lord.

*Robert Nelson*

**670** Lord Jesus Christ, who in the offerings of the wise men didst receive an earnest of the worship of the nations: Grant that thy Church may never cease to proclaim the good news of thy love, that all men may come to worship thee as their Saviour and King, who livest and reignest world without end.

*George Appleton*

# LENT

**671** O God, who by thy Son dost marvellously work out the salvation of mankind: Grant, we beseech thee, that, following the example of our blessed Lord, and observing such a fast as thou dost choose, we may both be subjected to thee with all our hearts, and united to each other in holy charity; through the same Jesus Christ our Lord.

*Gelasian Sacramentary*

**672** Heavenly Father,
we have decided for your kingdom
and dared to take your cup.

But we confess that we do not understand
the fearsome consequences of obedience.

When we are brought to the test,
steady our nerve and hold us in our faith,

That we may sail through heavy seas,
and ride the frightening storm.

Through Jesus Christ, our Lord. Amen

*Caryl Micklem*

**673** Almighty God, Father of our Lord Jesus Christ, Maker of all things, Judge of all men: we acknowledge and bewail our manifold sins and wickedness, which we, from time to time, most grievously have committed, by thought, word, and deed, against thy Divine Majesty, provoking most justly thy wrath and indignation against us. We do earnestly repent, and are heartily sorry for these our misdoings; the remembrance of them is grievous unto us; the burden of them is intolerable. Have mercy upon us, have mercy upon us, most merciful Father; for thy Son our Lord Jesus Christ's sake, forgive us all that is past; and grant that we may ever hereafter serve and please thee in newness of life, to the honour and glory of thy Name; through Jesus Christ our Lord.

*Book of Common Prayer, 1548*

**674** O Lord, grant that we may not be conformed to the world, but may love it and serve it. Grant that we may never shrink from being instruments of your peace because of the judgment of the world. Grant that we may love you without fear of the world, grant that we may never believe that the inexpressible majesty of yourself may be found in any power of this earth. May we firstly love you and our neighbours as ourselves. May we remember the poor and the prisoner, and the sick and the lonely, and the young searchers, and the tramps and vagabonds, and the lost and lonely, as we remember Christ, who is in them all.

*Alan Paton*

**675** Lord and Master of my life, take from me the spirit of sloth, faintheartedness, lust of power and idle talk. Give me rather the spirit of chastity, humility, patience and love. Grant me, my Lord and King, to see my own errors and not to judge my brother, for you are blessed for ever and ever.

*Ephrem Syrus*

**676** Give me that tranquil courage which is content to await your gift. I live by what comes to me from you. Your word proceeding forth from your mouth, at your own time, in your way: not by my deliberate self-occupied use of the power you give. Sometimes my need and exhaustion seem very great, and you seem very silent: surrounding conditions seem very stony, and hard. Those are the moments when my faith is purified, when I am given my chance of patience and fortitude and tranquillity: abiding among the stones in the wilderness and learning the perfection of dependence on you.

*Evelyn Underhill*

**677** Bestow on me, O Lord, a genial spirit and unwearied forbearance; a mild, loving, patient heart; kindly looks, pleasant, cordial speech and manners in the intercourse of daily life; that I may give offence to none, but as much as in me lies live in charity with all men.

*Johann Arndt*

**678** I pray thee, Lord, the Father, and the Guide of our reason, that we may remember the nobleness with which Thou hast adorned us; and that Thou would'st be always on our right hand and on our left, in the motion of our own wills; that so we may be purged from the contagion of the body and the

affections of the brute, and overcome them and rule, and use,
as it becomes men to use them, for instruments. And then that
Thou would'st be in fellowship with us for the careful correction of our reason, and for the conjunction by the light of truth
with the things that truly are.

*George Chapman*

679 Keep me, O Lord, while I tarry on this earth, in a daily serious
seeking after thee and in a believing affectionate walking with
thee; that when thou comest, I may be found not hiding my
talent, nor yet asleep with my lamp unfurnished; but waiting
and longing for my Lord, my glorious God, for ever and ever.

*Richard Baxter*

680 Have mercy upon our efforts, that we
Before thee, in love and in faith,
Righteousness and humility,
May follow thee, with self-denial,
Steadfastness and courage,
And meet thee in the silence.
Give us a pure heart that we may see thee,
A humble heart that we may hear thee,
A heart of love that we may serve thee,
A heart of faith that we may love thee.

*Dag Hammarskjöld*

681 Christ,
In this dark hour,
Be near,
Be swift to save:
We thank thee for the price which must be paid,
We thank thee for each stab which marks the cost,
We thank thee for all weariness, all pain
Which lays upon us, all too late, our share,
Our share so little of thy cross;
Oh, make us zealous, Lord, to bear, to pay
In secret ways,
That burden and that price:
Oh, give us grace,
That valiantly and uncomplainingly
We may bear on, pay on,
Unto the end,
With thee.

*John S. Hoyland*

**682** O Lord Christ, Lamb of God, Lord of Lords,
call us, who are called to be saints,
along the way of thy cross:
draw us, who would draw nearer our king,
to the foot of thy cross:
cleanse us, who are not worthy to approach,
with the pardon of thy cross:
instruct us, the ignorant and blind,
in the school of thy cross:
arm us, for the battles of holiness,
by the might of thy cross:
bring us in the fellowship of thy sufferings
to the victory of thy cross:
and seal us in the kingdom of thy glory
among the servants of thy cross,
O crucified Lord;
who with the Father and the Holy Ghost
livest and reigneth one God
almighty, eternal,
world without end.

*Eric Milner-White*

**683** Thank you, Lord Jesus Christ,
for all the benefits which you have given me,
for all the pains and insults you have borne for me.
O most merciful redeemer, friend and brother,
may I know you more clearly,
love you more dearly,
and follow you more nearly,
day by day.

*St Richard of Chichester*

**684** O Lord Jesu Christ, take us to thyself, draw us with cords to
the foot of the cross; for we have no strength to come, and we
know not the way. Thou art mighty to save, and none can
separate us from thy love. Bring us home to thyself, for we are
gone astray. We have wandered; do thou seek us. Under the
shadow of thy cross let us live all the rest of our lives, and there
we shall be safe.

*Frederick Temple*

**685** Blessed Lord, who for our sakes wast content to bear sorrow
and want and death: Grant to us such a measure of thy Spirit
that we may follow thee in all self-denial and tenderness of

soul. Help us by thy great love to succour the afflicted, to relieve the needy, to share the burdens of the heavy laden, and ever to see thee in all that are poor and destitute; for thy great mercy's sake.

*Brooke Foss Westcott*

**686** O Christ, my Master, let me keep very close to thee. When I am tempted to be undisciplined or self-indulgent, let me remember thy forty days of prayer and fasting. When the fires of my spirit burn low, let me remember thee continuing all night in prayer. When I flinch from hardship, let me go with thee to thy Gethsemane. When I am lonely, let me turn to thee, my risen Lord. Whatever the outer facts may be, grant me thy gift of inner joy; in thy name and through thy grace. Amen

*Walter Russell Bowie*

**687** Son of Man, our Saviour, we remember that your sternest judgments were reserved for the religious people of your day, because they failed to live up to their profession.

Forbid it, Lord, that we, who so often and so readily take your name upon our lips, should come under the same condemnation.

Help us in this season of Lent to search our hearts and examine our lives and to have done with all hypocrisy and pretence; that we may be what we seem to be, put our creed into practice, and bear a witness that will honour you before men.

*Frank Colquhoun*

## HOLY WEEK

**688** And so we come: O draw us to thy feet,
Most patient Saviour, who canst love us still;
And by this food, so awful and so sweet,
Deliver us from every touch of ill;
In thine own service make us glad and free,
And grant us never more to part with thee.

*William Bright*

**689** Lord Jesus Christ, who when thou wast about to institute thy holy Sacrament at the Last Supper didst wash the feet of the

apostles, and teach us by thy example the grace of humility:
Cleanse us, we beseech thee, from all stain of sin, that we may
be worthy partakers of the holy mysteries; who livest and
reignest with the Father and the Holy Ghost, one God, world
without end.

*The Royal Maundy*

**690** Lord, thou goest forth alone to thy sacrifice: thou dost offer
thyself to death, whom thou art come to destroy. What can we
miserable sinners plead, who know that for the deeds that we
have done thou dost atone? Ours is the guilt, Lord: why then
must thou suffer torture for our sins? Make our hearts so to
share in thy passion, that our fellow-suffering may invite thy
mercy. This is that night of tears, and the three days' eventide
of sadness, until the day break with the risen Christ, and
with the joy of those that mourn. May we so suffer with thee,
Lord, that we may be partakers of thy glory, and our three
days' mourning shall pass away and become thine Easter
joy.

*Peter Abelard*

**691** My God, I love thee: not because
I hope for heaven thereby,
nor yet because who love thee not
are lost eternally.

Thou, O my Jesus, thou didst me
upon the cross embrace;
for me didst bear the nails and spear
and manifold disgrace.

And griefs and torments numberless
and sweat of agony;
even death itself – and all for one
who was thine enemy.

Then why, O blessed Jesu Christ,
should I not love thee well;
not for the sake of winning heaven
or of escaping hell;
not with the hope of gaining aught,
nor seeking a reward:
but as thyself has loved me,
O ever-loving Lord!

Even so I love thee, and will love
and in thy praise will sing,
solely because thou art my God
and my eternal king.

*Francis Xavier*

**692** Almighty God, who hast shown us in the life and teaching of thy Son the true way of blessedness, thou hast also shown us in his suffering and death that the path of love may lead to the Cross, and the reward of faithfulness may be a crown of thorns. Give us grace to learn these hard lessons. May we take up our cross and follow Christ in the strength of patience and the constancy of faith; and may we have such fellowship with him in his sorrow that we may know the secret of his strength and peace, and see even in our darkest hour of trial and anguish the shining of the eternal light.

*John Hunter*

**693** O Christ, give us patience and faith and hope as we kneel at the foot of thy Cross, and hold fast to it. Teach us by thy Cross that however ill the world may go, the Father so loved us that he spared not thee.

*Charles Kingsley*

**694** O Holy and adorable Redeemer, by whose condemnation we are acquitted, by whose stripes we are healed, by whose death we have life, by whose cross we gain our crown: Keep us, we beseech thee, ever mindful of thy boundless love; and when thou dost call on us to bear for a while thy cross, like Simon of old, make us to rejoice that we are counted worthy to suffer for thy sake, and accept our feeble sacrifice, through the merits of thine eternal redemption.

*W. E. Scudamore**

**695** Almighty and most merciful Father, we are about to commemorate the death of thy Son, Jesus Christ our Saviour and Redeemer. Grant, O Lord, that our whole hope and confidence may be in his merits and thy mercy. Enforce and accept our imperfect repentance, make this commemoration available to the confirmation of our faith, the establishment of our hope, and the enlargement of our love, and make the death of thy dear Son Jesus Christ effectual to our redemption. Have mercy upon us, and pardon the multitude of our offences. Bless our friends. Have mercy upon all men.

Support us by the Holy Spirit throughout life, and receive
us at last into everlasting happiness.

*Dr Johnson*

**696** O Jesus, poor and abject, unknown and despised, have
mercy upon me, and let me not be ashamed to follow thee.
O Jesus, hated, calumniated, and persecuted, have mercy
upon me, and make me content to be as my master.
O Jesus, blasphemed, accused, and wrongfully condemned,
have mercy upon me, and teach me to endure the
contradiction of sinners.
O Jesus, clothed with a habit of reproach and shame, have
mercy upon me, and let me not seek my own glory.
O Jesus, insulted, mocked, and spit upon, have mercy upon
me, and let me not faint in the fiery trial.
O Jesus, crowned with thorns and hailed in derision;
O Jesus, burdened with our sins and the curses of the people;
O Jesus, affronted, outraged, buffeted, overwhelmed with
injuries, griefs and humiliations;
O Jesus, hanging on the accursed tree, bowing the head,
giving up the ghost, have mercy upon me, and conform my
whole soul to thy holy, humble, suffering Spirit.

*John Wesley*

**697** O loving Saviour, we would linger by Thy Cross, that the light
of Thy perfect love may shine into the secret places of our
souls, showing what is vile there, so that it may shrink away;
and nurturing whatever there is pure or lovely or of good re-
port, so that beholding Thee, we may become more like Thee,
Thou Revealer of God to men, Thou Guide of men to God.

*William Temple*

**698** Lord Jesus Christ, who for us endured the horror of deep
darkness; teach us by the depth of your agony the vileness of
our sin, and so bind us to yourself in bonds of gratitude and
love, that we may be united with you in your perfect sacrifice,
our Saviour, our Lord and our God.

*William Temple\**

**699** Good, kind and gentle Jesus
I kneel before you.
I see and consider your five wounds.
My eyes behold what David prophesied:
'They have pierced my hands and my feet;
they have counted all my bones'.

Engrave upon me this image of yourself.
Fulfil the yearnings of my heart;
give me faith, hope, and love,
repentance for all my sins
and a true turning to you for life.

*Traditional Prayer*

**700** I kiss the wounds in your sacred head,
   with sorrow deep and true,
   may every thought of mine this day
   be an act of love for you.

   I kiss the wounds in your sacred hands,
   with sorrow deep and true,
   may every touch of my hands this day
   be an act of love for you.

   I kiss the wounds in your sacred feet,
   with sorrow deep and true,
   may every step I take this day
   be an act of love for you.

   I kiss the wound in your sacred side,
   with sorrow deep and true,
   may every beat of my heart this day
   be an act of love for you.

*George Spencer*

**701** Soul of Christ, sanctify me.
   Body of Christ, save me.
   Blood of Christ, fill me.
   Water from the side of Christ, wash me.
   Passion of Christ, strengthen me.
   O good Jesus, hear me.
   Within your wounds hide me.
   Suffer me not to be separated from you.
   From the malicious enemy defend me.
   In the hour of my death call me.
   And bid me come unto you.
   That with your saints I may praise you.
   For ever and ever.

*Fourteenth-century prayer*

**702** O Christ, my Lord, who for my sins did hang upon a tree,
   grant that your grace in me, poor wretch,
      may still ingrafted be.

Grant that your naked hanging there may kill in me all pride,
and care of wealth since you did then in such poor state
abide.
Grant that your crown of pricking thorns, which you for me
did wear,
may make me willing for your sake all shame and pain to
bear.
Grant that your pierced hand, which did of nothing all things
frame,
may move me to lift up my hands and ever praise your name.
Grant that your wounded feet, whose steps were perfect
evermore,
may learn my feet to tread those paths which you have gone
before.
Grant that your blessed grave, wherein your body lay awhile,
may bury all such vain delights as may my mind defile.
Grant, Lord, that your ascending then may lift my mind to
thee,
that there my heart and joy may rest, though here in flesh I
be.

*Philip Howard*

# EASTER

**703** Almighty God, who by the death of thy Son hast destroyed sin
and death, and by his resurrection hast restored innocence
and everlasting life, in order that, delivered from the power of
the devil, we may live in thy kingdom; grant unto us that we
may believe this with our whole heart, and, steadfast in this
faith, may praise and thank thee evermore; through the same
Jesus Christ, thy Son, our Lord.

*Martin Luther*

**704** It is the Pasch; the Pasch of the Lord . . .
O you, who are truly all in all! . . .
The joy, the honour, the food and the delight of every
creature;
through you the shadows of death have fled away,
and life is given to all,
the gates of heaven are flung open.
God becomes man
and man is raised up to the likeness of God.

O divine Pasch! . . .
O Pasch, light of new splendour . . .
The lamps of our souls will no more burn out.
The flame of grace,
divine and spiritual,
burns in the body and soul,
nourished by the resurrection of Christ.

We beg you, O Christ, Lord God,
eternal king of the spiritual world,
stretch out your protecting hands
over your holy Church
and over your holy people;
defend them, keep them, preserve them . . .

Raise up your standard over us
and grant that we may sing with Moses
the song of victory,
for yours is the glory and the power for all eternity! Amen

*St Hippolytus of Rome**

**705** Glory be to Thee, O Lord, glory to Thee, Creator of the light
and enlightener of the world . . . O by Thy Resurrection raise
us up into newness of life. The God of peace, who did bring
again from the dead the great Shepherd of the sheep, through
the blood of the everlasting covenant, our Lord Jesus Christ,
perfect us in every good work to do His will, working in us
what is acceptable before Him, through Jesus Christ, to whom
be glory for ever.

*Lancelot Andrewes*

**706** O Lord, who by triumphing over the power of darkness
prepared our place in the New Jerusalem; grant us, who have
this day given thanks for your resurrection, to praise you in
that city of which you are the light; where with the Father and
the Holy Spirit you live and reign, now and for ever.

*William Bright**

**707** Most glorious Lord of life! that on this day,
Didst make thy triumph over death and sin;
And, having harrowed hell, didst bring away
Captivity thence captive, us to win:
This joyous day, dear Lord, with joy begin;
And grant that we, for whom Thou didst die,
Being, with thy dear blood, clean washed from sin,

May live for ever in felicity!
And that Thy love we weighing worthily,
May likewise love Thee for the same again,
And for Thy sake that all like dear didst buy,
With love may one another entertain.
So let us love, dear Love, like as we ought;
Love is the lesson which the Lord us taught.

*Edmund Spenser*

**708** God, through the mighty resurrection of your Son Jesus Christ you have liberated us from the power of darkness and brought us into the kingdom of your love; grant that as he was raised from the dead by the glory of the Father, so we may walk in newness of life, and look for those things which are in heaven, where with you, Father, and the Holy Spirit, he is alive and reigns for ever and ever.

*Gelasian Sacramentary*

**709** O heavenly Father, whose blessed Son has 'risen from the dead, and become the first fruits of them that slept', grant that we may so live and die in him that when he shall appear again in his glory we may rise to everlasting life. We pray also for all our brethren in Christ, especially our relations and friends, and neighbours, that we may all share in a joyful resurrection, and be partakers of thy heavenly kingdom, through Christ our Lord.

*W. Walsham How*

**710** Merciful and gracious God, who deigned to make Mary Magdalene the first witness and herald of the glorious resurrection of your Son. Grant to those who have fallen into the torment and captivity of sin to hear that wondrous voice of Jesus, which is able to subdue and cast out all evil passions, that there may be none without hope of mercy, or beyond help of grace, through the same Jesus Christ our Saviour.

*William E. Orchard*

**711** O God of unchangeable power and eternal light, look favourably on your whole Church, that wonderful and sacred mystery, and carry out the work of man's salvation; and let the whole world feel and see that things which were cast down are being raised up, and things which had grown old are being made new, and all things are returning to perfection, through Jesus Christ our Lord. Amen

*Gelasian Sacramentary*

**712** O God, who by the glorious death and resurrection of thy Son Jesus Christ hast brought life and immortality to light; grant us so to die daily unto sin that we may evermore live with thee in the joy of his resurrection; through the same Jesus Christ our Lord, to whom be glory and dominion for ever and ever.

*Gregorian Sacramentary*

**713** Lord Jesus, risen from the dead and alive for evermore: Stand in our midst today as in the upper room; show us thy hands and thy side; speak thy peace to our hearts and minds; and send us forth into the world as thy witnesses; for the glory of thy name.

*John R. W. Stott*

**714** God of the inner light,
come to us
on the golden rays of the morning,
warming moods that are frosty,
enlightening minds that are gloomy;
and, as the sun swings higher,
so may our lives rise to you
in the active praise of this day's duties:
through Jesus, our risen Light.

*Bruce Prewer*

**715** Lord of creation and God of grace, we thank you for the yearly miracle of the spring, as the earth awakes from its winter sleep and is arrayed again in the glory of resurrection life.

May a similar miracle of grace take place in our lives this Easter. Send into our hearts the Spirit of the living Christ, to raise us to newness of life and to clothe us with the beauty of his holiness, for your honour and glory.

*Frank Colquhoun*

**716** Pour upon us, O Lord, thy heavenly blessing, that we may be armed with the faith of the resurrection so as not to fear any army of men sent against us.

*Mathew Parker*

**717** O Lord Jesus Christ, who art the very bright Sun of the world, ever rising, never going down: Shine, we beseech Thee, upon our spirit, that the night of sin and error being driven away by

Thy inward light, we may walk without stumbling, as in the day. Grant this, O Lord, who livest and reignest with the Father and the Holy Ghost for evermore.

*Primer of 1559*

**718** Lord Jesus, our risen Saviour, we rejoice in your mighty victory over sin and death. You are the Prince of life: you are alive for evermore. Help us to know your presence, not only as we worship you here, but at home, and at work, and wherever we go; for your great name's sake. Amen

*Michael Botting*

**719** O risen and victorious Christ, whose power and love destroyed the darkness and death of sin; ascend, we pray thee, the throne of our hearts, and so rule our wills by the might of that immortality wherewith thou hast set us free, that we may evermore be alive unto God, through the power of thy glorious resurrection, world without end.

*John W. Suter*

**720** I adore and praise and bless thee, O Lord, Jesus Christ, giving thanks for the love and confidence with which having overcome death, rising from the tomb thou hast glorified our human flesh; and, ascending into heaven, hast placed it at the right hand of God; beseeching thee on behalf of the souls for which I pray, that thou wilt deign to make them partakers of thy glory and thy victory.

*St Gertrude and Mechthild of Magdeburg*

**721** Lord, come alive within my experience,
within my sorrows and disappointments and doubts,
within the ordinary movements of my life.
Come alive as the peace and joy and assurance that is
stronger than the locked doors within, with which we
try to shut out life.
Come alive as the peace and joy and assurance that
nothing in life or death can kill.

*Rex Chapman*

**722** O Risen Saviour, bid me rise with Thee
and seek those things which are above;
not only seek, but set my whole heart upon them.

Thou art in heaven, ever raising lives to Thyself;
O, by Thy grace, may mine be making that ascent
not in dreams, but in truth,
now, tomorrow, always.

Daily in spirit, in Thy Holy Spirit,
Let me behold Thee on the throne of God,
Thou King reigning in holiness,
Thou Conqueror of all evil,
Thou Majesty of love,
very God and very Man,
of glory unimaginable and eternal,
in whom all hope is sure.

*Eric Milner-White*

# ASCENSION

**723** Glory to our ascended Lord that He is with us always.
Glory to the Word of God, going forth with His armies
conquering and to conquer.
Glory to Him Who has led captivity captive and given gifts
for the perfecting of His saints.
Glory to Him Who has gone before to prepare a place in His
Father's home for us.
Glory to the Author and Finisher of our Faith; that God in
all things may be glorified through Jesus Christ,
To Whom be all worship and praise, dominion and glory;
now and for ever and ever. Amen

*Sursum Corda*

**724** O Glorious Christ, who in thy ascension didst enter into thy
kingdom: Remember, we pray thee, the countless millions
who have not heard of the redemption which thou hast won
for them.
Grant that they may learn, through thy Church, of the new
and living way which thou hast opened for them. Let them
draw near in fullness of faith, to enter with thee into the holy
place of the Father's presence, and receive forgiveness and
peace. So may they worship, with the innumerable company
of angels and with the spirits of just men made perfect, Father,
Son and Holy Spirit, one God, blessed for evermore.

*George Appleton*

**725** O God, who hast exalted the Crucified, the Son, by a triumphant resurrection and ascension into heaven: May His triumphs and glories so shine in the eyes of our hearts and minds, that we may more clearly comprehend His sufferings, and more courageously pass through our own; for His sake who with Thee and the Holy Ghost liveth and reigneth, one God, for ever and ever.

*Eric Milner-White*

**726** Almighty and merciful God, into whose gracious presence we ascend, not by the frailty of the flesh, but by the activity of the soul: make us ever by thine inspiration to seek after the courts of the heavenly city, whither our Saviour Christ hath ascended, and by thy mercy confidently to enter them both now and hereafter; through the same Jesus Christ our Lord.

*Phillips Brooks*

**727** O Lord Jesus Christ, who after thy resurrection from the dead didst gloriously ascend into heaven, grant us the aid of thy loving-kindness, that, according to thy promise, thou mayst ever dwell with us on earth, and we with thee in heaven, where with the Father and the Holy Spirit, thou livest and reignest one God for ever and ever.

*Gelasian Sacramentary*

**728** Who shall speak of Thy power, O Lord, and who shall be able to tell the tale of all Thy praises? Thou didst descend to human things, not leaving behind heavenly things. Thou art returned to things above, not abandoning things below. Everywhere Thou art Thy whole self, everywhere wonderful. In the flesh, Thou hast yet thy being in the Father; in thine Ascension Thou art not torn away from Thy being in man. Look upon the prayer of Thy people, holy Lord, merciful God; that in this day of Thy holy Ascension, even as glory is given to Thee on high, so grace may be vouchsafed to us below.

*Mozarabic Sacramentary*

**729** You are not only risen and alive, you are Lord.
This your ascension, your ascendency over the whole
    universe.
You stand over and above all that is best in life as its source.
You stand above all that is worst as ultimate victor.
You stand above all powers and authorities as judge.

You stand above all failure and weakness and sin as
    forgiveness and love.
You alone are worthy of total allegiance, total commitment.
You are Lord,
'My Lord and my God'.

*Rex Chapman*

**730** Come forth out of Thy royal chambers, O Prince of all the
kings of the earth; put on the visible robes of Thy imperial
majesty, take up that unlimited sceptre which Thy Almighty
Father hath bequeathed Thee, for now the voice of Thy bride
calls Thee, and all creatures sigh to be renewed.

*John Milton*


# PENTECOST


**731** O God, who at this time didst send down thy Holy Spirit from
above upon thine apostles, and dost evermore send him to
renew thine image in our souls: mercifully grant that by the
effectual working of his grace we may be preserved from all
sin, and may glorify thee both in our bodies and in our spirits,
which are thine; through the merits and mediation of thy Son
our Saviour Jesus Christ, who liveth and reigneth with thee in
the unity of the same Spirit, one God, world without end.

*W. E. Scudamore*

**732** God, who in generous mercy sent upon your disciples the
Holy Spirit in the burning fire of your love; grant that your
people may be fervent in the fellowship of faith; so that,
always abiding in you, they may be found steadfast in faith and
active in service; through Jesus Christ our Lord.

*Gelasian Sacramentary*

**733** O God, may the fire of the Holy Spirit burn up the dross in our
hearts, warm them with love and set them on fire with zeal for
your service.

*Ancient Collect*

**734** O Lord Jesus Christ, who on the first day of the week didst rise
again: Raise up our souls to serve the living God; and as thou
didst also on this day send down on thy apostles thy most Holy

Spirit, so take not the same Spirit from us, but grant that we may be daily renewed and plentifully enriched by his power; for thine own mercy's sake, who livest and reignest with the Father and the Holy Spirit, ever one God, world without end.

*Lancelot Andrewes*

**735** Lord Jesus, we thank you that you have fulfilled your promise and given us your Spirit to abide with us for ever: grant us to know his presence in all its divine fullness.

May the fruit of the Spirit be growing continually in our lives;

may the gifts of the Spirit be distributed among us as he wills to equip us for your service;

and may the power of the Spirit be so working in us that the world around may increasingly come to believe in you.

We ask it, Lord, in your victorious name.

*Michael Botting*

**736** Holy Spirit of God,
great gift of our exalted Lord,
on the day of Pentecost you came to the Church
as he promised, to abide with us for ever.
Come to us in your grace and power today,
to make Jesus real to us,
to teach us more about him,
and to deepen our trust in him;
that we may be changed into his likeness
and be his witnesses in the world,
to the glory of God the Father.

*Unknown Source*

**737** Praise to the Holy Spirit who alone enables us to call God
our Father and Jesus our Lord.
May we live and walk by the same Spirit,
that we may grow in the likeness of Jesus Christ
and pray with the freedom of the sons of God.

Praise to the Holy Spirit for his fruit of love and joy and
peace.
May he put to death in us the works of the flesh,
that his fruit may grow and prosper
and our lives be lived to the glory of God.

Praise to the Holy Spirit for his gifts of power and
inspiration.
May he lead the Church to desire the best gifts
and to distinguish the true from the false,
for the sake of the health of the Body.

Praise to the Holy Spirit who is the promise of the Father
and the gift of the Son, in whose name we pray, Jesus
Christ our Lord.

*Christopher Idle*

# HARVEST THANKSGIVING

**738** Almighty and everlasting God, who hast given to us the fruits
of the earth in their season, and hast crowned the year with thy
goodness: Give us grateful hearts, that we may unfeignedly
thank thee for all thy loving-kindness, and worthily magnify
thy holy name; through Jesus Christ our Lord.

*John Dowden*

**739** O God, from whose unfailing bounty we draw our life and all
that we possess, forgive our pride and self-sufficiency. Teach
us to reverence the earth, which thou hast made fruitful. Help
us to remember our unity with those by whose work we are fed
and clothed. Touch us with compassion for all who have not
enough to eat. As thou hast given us the knowledge which can
produce plenty, so give us also the wisdom to bring it within
the reach of all: through Jesus Christ our Lord.

*John H. Oldham*

**740** Creator of heaven and earth, you have studded the sky with
stars and made it bright with lights, enriched the earth with
fruits to satisfy men's needs, given to the race that took shape
under your hands the clear light and the shining stars to enjoy,
the earth's produce to feed on. We pray you, send us rain,
abundant, plentiful, fertilising; and make the earth yield fruit
and to spare; for we know how you love men, we know what
your kindness is.

Hear our petitions and prayers and bless the whole earth,
through your only Son, Jesus Christ. Through him may glory
and power be yours, in the Holy Spirit, now and age after age.
Amen

*Serapion of Thmuis*

**741** Lord God, out of your kindness to men, bless the fruits you have given us and bless your servants who have gathered in the harvest. Grant salvation, too, to those who possess these fruits, that having the abundance that comes from you, they may show to the poor the kindness that is also yours. To that end, accept the worship of us all, for all glory is yours, Father, Son and Spirit for ever and ever. Amen

*Euchologium Sinaiticium*

**742** The eyes of all things do look up and trust in thee, O Lord, thou givest them their meat in due season, thou dost open thy hand and fillest with thy blessing everything living. Good Lord, bless us and all thy gifts, which we receive of thy bountiful liberality; through Jesus Christ our Lord.

*Queen Elizabeth's Primer, 1558*

**743** Creator God, we thank you for your promise that while the earth endures seed time and harvest, summer and winter, day and night, shall not fail. We thank you for the reliability of this good earth, for the variety of the seasons and for all the unity and contrasts of creation. We thank you for this world's agenda for the labours of men and for permitting us to be partners to the earth's activity. We thank you that we can nourish the miracle of life upon the miracle of harvest and we praise you for the dignity of sharing in the work of your almighty hands, O God our Father, blessed for ever. Amen

*Dick Williams*

**744** Almighty God, Lord of heaven and earth, in whom we live and move and have our being; who doest good unto all men, making thy sun to rise on the evil and on the good, and sending rain on the just and on the unjust: favourably behold us thy servants, who call upon thy Name, and send us thy blessing from heaven, in giving us fruitful seasons, and satisfying us with food and gladness; that both our hearts and mouths shall be continually filled with thy praise, giving thanks to thee in thy holy Church; through Jesus Christ our Lord.

*John Cosin*

# ALL SAINTS

**745** Almighty and everlasting God, who dost enkindle the flame of thy love in the hearts of the saints: grant to our minds the same faith and power of love; that as we rejoice in their triumphs, we may profit by their examples; through Jesus Christ our Lord.

*Gothic Missal*

**746** Eternal God, help us always to remember the great unseen cloud of witnesses round about us. When in danger, give us their courage and when in difficulty, their perseverance; so that we too may be faithful until we rejoice with all the saints in your eternal kingdom, through Jesus Christ our Lord. Amen

*William Hampson*

**747** God, whom all the saints adore, assembled in thy glorious presence from all times and places of thy dominion; who gathered us far dwellers of the islands of the sea into the kingdom of thy Son; and has adorned our land with many splendid lamps of holiness; grant us worthily to celebrate the saints of our country by following their footsteps throughout the world and here, wherever thou shalt send us, each lowly serving, till all nations confess thy Name and all humankind know and fulfil its destiny in Christ; to whom with thee and the Holy Spirit be all honour and glory, world without end.

*Alexander Nairne*

**748** O God, before whose face the generations rise and pass away, the strength of those who labour and suffer, and the repose of the holy and blessed dead: we rejoice in the communion of saints, we bless thy holy Name for all thy servants who have fought a good fight, and have finished their course in faith – for patriots and statesmen, for prophets and martyrs, for artists and poets and musicians, for all noble men and women in every walk of life – and we beseech thee to grant us grace to follow their good examples and to carry on the work which they began, for their country and for humanity. May we and all the people hear the call to nobler living which sounds in our ears from the graves of those who have given of their best to make life stronger and more beautiful; through Jesus Christ our Lord.

*John Hunter*

(See also 619–626 The Communion of Saints)

# VI  THE HUMAN CONDITION

## THE FAMILY

**749** O God, our heavenly Father, from whom every family in heaven and on earth is named: We entrust to thy loving care the members of our families, both near and far. Supply their needs; guide their footsteps; keep them in safety of body and soul; and may thy peace rest upon our homes and upon our dear ones everywhere; for Jesus Christ our Saviour's sake.

*Frank Colquhoun*

**750** We thank you, Father, for the gift of Jesus your Son who came to our earth and lived in a simple home. We have a greater appreciation of the value and dignity of the human family because he loved and was loved within its shelter. Bless us this day; may we grow in love for each other in our family and so give thanks to you who are the maker of all human families and our abiding peace.

*Michael Buckley*

**751** Father in heaven, pattern of all parenthood and lover of children, we pray for homes and families across the world (or in this community).

Sustain and comfort them in need and sorrow.

In times of bitterness, tension and division, draw near to heal.

May parents and children together be learners in the school of Christ, daily increasing in mutual respect and understanding, in tolerance and patience, and in all-prevailing love; through Jesus Christ our Lord.

*Timothy Dudley-Smith*

**752** Lord God, from you every family in heaven and on earth takes its name.

Father, you are Love and Life.

Through your Son, Jesus Christ, born of woman,
and through the Holy Spirit, fountain of divine charity,
grant that every family on earth
may become for each successive generation
a true shrine of life and love.
Grant that your grace may guide
the thoughts and actions of husbands and wives
for the good of their families
and of all the families in the world.
Grant that the young may find in the family
solid support for their human dignity
and for their growth in truth and love.
Grant that love,
strengthened by the grace of the sacrament of marriage,
may prove mightier than all the weaknesses and trials
through which our families sometimes pass.
Through the intercession of the Holy Family of Nazareth,
grant that the Church may fruitfully carry out her worldwide
mission in the family and through the family.
We ask this of you, who are Life, Truth, and Love,
with the Son and the Holy Spirit. Amen

*Pope John Paul II*

**753** Lord God, to come to you is to come home, for you are
eternally the Father of all men. From you every family takes
its name, and your household of faith gives the pattern for
every human household.

We thank you for showing us, in Jesus, that we belong to
you and that you care for us. Help us to believe it, and to
believe that we ought not to live so selfishly. Show us the
deeper joy of service, and give us pardon and peace through
the Holy Spirit. For Jesus Christ's sake.

*Caryl Micklem and Roger Tomes*

**754** O living bread, that came down from heaven to give life to the
world! O loving shepherd of our souls, from your throne of
glory whence, a 'hidden God', you pour out your grace on
families and peoples, we commend to you particularly the
sick, the unhappy, the poor and all who beg for food and
employment, imploring for all and every one the assistance of
your providence; we commend to you the families, so that
they may be fruitful centres of Christian life. May the
abundance of your grace be poured out over all.

*Pope John XXIII*

**755** Almighty God, by whose goodness we were created, and whose mercies never fail, we commend to thee all who have a place in our hearts and sympathies; all who are joined to us by the sacred ties of kindred, friendship, and love; keep them both outwardly in their bodies and inwardly in their souls; through Jesus Christ our Lord.

*John Hunter*

**756** O Lord, we pray for those who, full of confidence and love, once chose a partner for life, and are now alone after final separation. May they receive the gift of time, so that hurt and bitterness may be redeemed by healing and love, personal weakness by your strength, inner despair by the joy of knowing you and serving others; through Jesus Christ our Lord.

*Susan Williams*

**757** Lord, behold our family here assembled.
We thank you for this place in which we dwell,
for the love that unites us,
for the peace accorded us this day,
for the hope with which we expect the morrow;
for the health, the work, the food and the bright skies
that make our lives delightful;
for our friends in all parts of the earth.
Give us courage and gaiety and the quiet mind.
Spare us to our friends, soften us to our enemies.
Bless us, if it may be, in all our innocent endeavours;
if it may not, give us the strength
to endure that which is to come
that we may be brave in peril,
constant in tribulation, temperate in wrath
and in all changes of fortune
and down to the gates of death,
loyal and loving to one another.
We beseech of you this help and mercy
for Christ's sake.

*Robert Louis Stevenson*

**758** Dear Lord, who hast blessed us with the gift of family life, that we may learn to love and care for others: We praise thee for the example of thy Son Jesus Christ, who even when deserted and betrayed by closest friends took thought for his mother and his disciple. Open our eyes to recognize in all men the claims of kinship, and stir our hearts to serve them as brethren called with us into the sonship of thy love.

*Basil Naylor**

## For children

**759** Almighty God and heavenly Father, we thank thee for the children whom thou hast given to us; give us also grace to train them in thy faith, fear and love; that as they advance in years thy may grow in grace, and be found hereafter in the number of thine elect children; through Jesus Christ our Lord.

*John Cosin*

**760** O Lord Jesus, be near to all young children, that in the peril and confusion of this age their growing spirits may take no hurt at our hands, and grant to parents such sure knowledge of thy love that they may guide their children with courage and faith.

*New Every Morning*

**761** Bless my children with healthful bodies, with good understandings, with the grace and gifts of Thy Spirit, with sweet dispositions and holy habits, and sanctify them throughout in their bodies, souls and spirits, and keep them unblameable to the coming of the Lord Jesus.

*Jeremy Taylor*

**762** God our Father, we pray for our young people growing up in an unstable and confusing world.

Show them that your ways give more meaning to life than the ways of the world, and that following you is better than chasing after selfish goals.

Help them to take failure not as a measure of their worth but as a chance for a new start.

Give them strength to hold their faith in you, and to keep alive their joy in your creation; through Jesus Christ our Lord.

*Episcopal Church, USA*

**763** O God, who hast commanded us to remember thee in the days of our youth, and dost promise that those who seek thee early shall find thee; make our vision bright, our allegiance unfaltering, our service loyal; through him who as a boy was

always about his Father's business, Jesus Christ thy Son our
Lord.

*John R. W. Stott*

## *For parents*

**764** O Lord God, whose will it is that, next to yourself, we should
hold our parents in highest honour; it is not the least of our
duties to beseech your goodness toward them. Preserve, we
pray, our parents and home, in the love of your religion and in
health of body, and mind. Grant that through us no sorrow
may befall them; and finally as they are kind to us, so may you
be to them, O supreme Father of all.

*Erasmus*

**765** Give, I pray Thee, to all children grace reverently to love their
parents, and lovingly to obey them. Teach us all that filial duty
never ends or lessens; and bless all parents in their children,
and all children in their parents.

*Christina Rossetti*

**766** Heavenly Father, creator and giver of life, there is such joy
in our hearts at the news of a baby's birth,
a most special and complete gift of your love,
a new being and a wonder of creation.
Be with the mother and father of this little baby in their
happiness, and accept their praise and ours as we give
thanks to you, through Jesus Christ our Lord.

*Mothers' Union*

# THE ELDERLY

**767** O Lord, evening is at hand, furnish it with brightness. As day
has its evening so also has life; the even of life is age, age has
overtaken me, furnish it with brightness. Cast me not away in
the time of age; forsake me not when my strength faileth me.
Do Thou make, do Thou bear, do Thou carry and deliver me.
Abide with me, Lord, for it is toward evening, and the day is
far spent of this fretful life. Let Thy strength be made perfect
in my weakness.

*Lancelot Andrewes*

**768** Lord, Jesus Christ, King of kings; you have power over life
and death, you know even what is uncertain and obscure, our
secret thoughts and feelings are not hidden from you. Cleanse
me from my faults, for I have done evil in your sight.

Day by day my life draws nearer to its end and my sins seem
to increase as time passes. O Lord, God of soul and body, you
know how frail I am. Give me strength, Lord, in my weakness
and uphold me in my sufferings. Give me a prudent judgment,
good Lord, and let me always remember your blessings. Do
not think of my many sins; put my faults out of your mind.

Lord, do not disdain my prayer, a sinner though I am; but
leave with me that grace of yours that has been my protection
until now. Your grace it was that taught me wisdom. Blessed
are they that keep to its paths, a glorious crown awaits them.

I am unworthy and sinful, Lord, but I still want to bless and
praise you, for you have poured your mercies lavishly over
me, you have been my Helper and Protector; your great name
deserves eternal glory.

Glory to you, O Lord, our God.

*Ephrem Syrus*

**769** When the signs of age begin to mark my body and still more
when they touch my mind; when the illness that is to diminish
me or carry me off strikes from without or is born within me;
when the painful moment comes in which I suddenly awaken
to the fact that I am ill or growing old; in all those dark
moments, O God, grant that I may understand that it is you,
provided only my faith is strong enough, who are painfully
parting the fibres of my being in order to penetrate to the
very marrow of my substance and bear me away within
yourself.

*Teilhard de Chardin*

**770** It's not very nice to be an old fogey, Lord.
I don't feel an old fogey,
even if I might look one.
Inside one doesn't feel old,
it's the outside that decays so quickly.
Lined face,
sagging muscles,
greying hair
And young folk class you as an old fogey,
thinking that you have forgotten what it is to be young.

You were never old, Master.
You died in young manhood,
so You never felt the slackening of the life-lines as the years
  mounted.
But Your mother stood near the Cross, with tired face and
  greying hair.

And You loved her,
cared for her,
provided for her.
So You will be compassionate with those of us termed 'old
  fogies', won't You?

Even if we are slow on the up-take . . .
for the will to do still exists when the power to do departs.
The tenant remains youthful while the house decays.

It is Your own law, Master,
and You know best.

*Flora Larsson*


**771** Eternal God, who through the passing years remain ever the
same, be near to all who are aged or infirm. Though their
bodies fail let their spirits be strong in thee, that with patience
they may bear weariness and distress, and at the last may meet
death unafraid, through Jesus Christ our Lord.

*New Every Morning*


**772** O Lord Jesus Christ, who didst hear the prayer of thy two
disciples and didst abide with them at eventide: Abide, we
pray thee, with all thy people in the evening of life. Make
thyself known to them, and let thy light shine upon their path;
and whenever they shall pass through the valley of the shadow
of death, be with them unto the end; through Jesus Christ our
Lord.

*George Appleton*


**773** Jesus, who never grew old, it is not easy for any of us to face
old age. It is fine to be young, attractive, strong. Old age
reminds us of weakness and dependence upon others. But to
be your disciple means accepting weakness and interdepen-
dence. Because of you we can rejoice in weakness in ourselves, and be tender to it in others.

*Monica Furlong*

**774** May Christ-Omega keep me always young 'to the greater glory of God'.

For

old age comes from him,

old age leads on to him, and

old age will touch me only in so far as he wills.

To be 'young' means to be hopeful, energetic, smiling – and clear-sighted.

May I accept death in whatever guise it may come to me in Christ-Omega, that is within the process of the development of life.

A smile (inward and outward) means facing with sweetness and gentleness whatever befalls me.

Jesus-Omega, grant me to serve you, to proclaim you, to glorify you, to make you manifest, to the very end through all the time that remains to me of life, and above all through my death. Desperately, Lord Jesus, I commit to your care my last active years, and my death; do not let them impair or spoil my work I have so dreamed of achieving for you.

*Teilhard de Chardin*

**775** Lord, you know better than I know myself that I am growing older, and will some day be old. Keep me from getting talkative, and particularly from the fatal habit of thinking that I must say something on every subject and on every occasion.

Release me from craving to straighten out everybody's affairs. Make me thoughtful but not moody; helpful but not bossy. With my vast store of wisdom it seems a pity not to use it all, but you know, Lord, that I want a few friends at the end. Keep my mind from the recital of endless details – give me wings to come to the point.

I ask for grace enough to listen to the tales of others' pains. But seal my lips on my own aches and pains – they are increasing, and my love of rehearsing them is becoming sweeter as the years go by. Help me to endure them with patience.

I dare not ask for improved memory, but for a growing humility and a lessening cocksureness when my memory seems to clash with the memories of others. Teach me the glorious lesson that occasionally it is possible that I may be mistaken.

Keep me reasonably sweet. I do not want to be a saint – some of them are so hard to live with – but a sour old woman is one of the crowning works of the devil.

Give me the ability to see good things in unexpected places,
and talents in unexpected people. And give me, O Lord, the
grace to tell them so.

*Unknown Source*
*(Attributed to a seventeenth-century nun)*

# FRIENDS AND LOVED ONES

**776** O Lord our God, whose might is without compare and whose
glory surpasses understanding, whose mercy is without
measure and love of men beyond telling; look Thou Thyself,
O Master, according to Thy tenderness of heart, on us and all
whom we love; and deal with us, and all for whom we pray, in
the riches of Thy mercies and Thy compassions.

*Liturgy of St John Chrysostom\**

**777** Lord, I see clearly that any affection which I have ever had is
scarcely as one drop in the vast ocean of all the seas, when
compared with the tenderness of Thy divine Heart towards
those whom I love . . . Therefore I cannot even by one
thought wish anything other than that which Thy almighty
wisdom has appointed for each of them . . . Lord, bless Thy
special friends and mine, according to the good pleasure of
Thy divine goodness.

*St Gertrude and Mechthild of Magdeburg*

**778** O Dearest Lord, do not weary of my laziness and lack of
alacrity in serving you, but please help me by the indwelling of
your Holy Spirit.

Pour down, Lord, the fulness of your grace on all I love;
pour into their hearts your love and draw them to yourself. So
shall your name be glorified and your love perfected in them,
and for this your poor servant will praise you forever. Amen

*Maria Hare*

**779** Dear Lord! kind Lord!
Gracious Lord! I pray
Thou wilt look on all I love
Tenderly to-day!
Weed their hearts of weariness;
Scatter every care
Down a wake of angel-wings
Winnowing the air.

Bring unto the sorrowing
All release from pain;
Let the lips of laughter
Overflow again;
And with all the needy
O divide, I pray,
This vast treasure of content
That is mine to-day!

*James Whitcomb Riley*

**780** O God, our heavenly Father, who hast commanded us to love one another as thy children, and has ordained the highest friendship in the bond of thy Spirit, we beseech thee to maintain and preserve us always in the same bond, to thy glory, and our mutual comfort, with all those to whom we are bound by any special tie, either of nature or of choice; that we may be perfected together in that love which is from above, and which never faileth when all other things shall fail.

Send down the dew of thy heavenly grace upon us, that we may have joy in each other that passeth not away; and having lived together in love here, according to thy commandment, may live for ever together with thee, being made one in thee, in thy glorious kingdom hereafter, through Jesus Christ our Lord.

*George Hickes*

**781** O Fountain of Love, love Thou our friends and teach them to love thee with all their hearts, that they may think and speak and do only such things as are well pleasing to Thee; through Jesus Christ our Lord.

*St Anselm*

**782** Be pleased, O Lord, to remember my friends, all that have prayed for me, and all that have done me good.

Do good to them and return all their kindness a double time, rewarding them with blessings and sanctifying them with Thy graces.

Let all my family and kindred, my neighbours and acquaintances receive the benefit of my prayers, and the blessings of God; the comforts and supports of Thy providence, and the sanctification of Thy Spirit.

*Jeremy Taylor*

**783** I pray thee, good Lord Jesus, by the love thou hadst for thy young disciple John, to make me thankful for all thou hast given me in my friend. Bless him exceedingly above all that I can ask or think. Help us to be one in heart through all separations, and walk together in the path of thy service, and finally unite us in the place where love is perfect and immortal, even with thyself.

*William Bright*

**784** O God, who by the grace of thy Holy Spirit hast shed thy love abroad in the hearts of thy faithful people: Mercifully grant to those whom we love health of body and soul; that they may serve thee with all their strength and gladly fulfil all thy good pleasure; through Jesus Christ our Lord.

*Gregorian Sacramentary*

**785** O Lord of love, who art not far from any of thy children, watch with thy care those who are far away from us; be thou about their path; be thou within their hearts; give them unfailing trust in thee; grant them power against temptation; qualify them for whatever task thou givest them to do; make it their joy to do thy will. Let not distance break the bonds of love which bind them to us and to thee, but unite us closer in thy love; for the sake of Jesus Christ our Lord.

*W. Boyd Carpenter*

## DIGNITY OF THE INDIVIDUAL

**786** Lord, teach me to respect people, to accept each person as unique and created by you. Some people seem so unattractive that I find it extremely difficult to see you in them. Yet if I could see myself as others see me, perhaps I would be less critical and more understanding. Of your goodness give me compassion for myself and for others, and never let me give up trying for the sake of your Son, who genuinely loved and cared about sinners and outcasts.

*Michael Hollings and Etta Gullick*

**787** Eternal Father, source of life and light,
whose love extends to all people,
all creatures, all things:
grant us that reverence for life
which becomes those who believe in you,

lest we despise it, degrade it,
or come callously to destroy it.
Rather let us save it, secure it,
and sanctify it, after the example
of your Son, Jesus Christ our Lord.

*Robert Runcie*


**788** O God, you are the King of heaven:
you have called all who will listen
into your royal household,
and given them royal status.
And your call is something from which no-one is
  disqualified:
Jesus Himself sought out the despised and rejected,
the socially disgraced, and those of little account
in the world's eyes.
Please help your Church to raise people
in their estimation
by declaring the value
which your love has set upon us all
through Jesus Christ our Lord.

*Jamie Wallace*


## IN SICKNESS


**789** Almighty and everlasting God, who canst banish all affliction
both of soul and body; show forth the power of Thine aid upon
those who are sick, that by the help of Thy mercy they may be
restored to serve Thee afresh in holiness of living; through
Jesus Christ our Lord.

*Gelasian Sacramentary*


**790** Merciful Lord God, stretch out your hand and grant the sick
the grace of healing, fit them for health, free them from the
illness that now besets them. May they be healed in the name
of your only Son; may his holy name be their remedy, may it
make them sound and whole; for through him glory and
power are yours, in the Holy Spirit, and yours they will be age
after age. Amen

*Serapion of Thmuis*

**791** Father, your Son accepted our sufferings
to teach us the virtue of patience in human illness.
Hear the prayers we offer for our sick brothers and sisters.
May all who suffer pain, illness or disease
realise that they are chosen to be saints,
and know that they are joined in Christ
in his sufferings for the salvation of the world.

Lord, teach me the art of patience while I am well, and
give me the use of it when I am sick. In that day either
lighten my burden or strengthen my back. Make me,
who so often in my health have discovered my
weakness, to be strong in my sickness when I solely rely on
your assistance.

*Thomas Fuller*

**792** Father, lover of life, we pray for those suffering from disease
for which, at present, there is no known cure; give them
confidence in your love and never-failing support and a
stronger faith in the resurrection. Grant wisdom and
perseverance to all working to discover the causes of the
disease, so that they see in their labours the ministry of your
Son, who himself showed forth his divine power by healing
those who came to him.

*George Appleton*

**793** Lord, the one that I love is sick and in great pain; out of your
compassion heal him and take away his pain. It breaks my
heart to see him suffer; may I not share his pain if it is not your
will that he be healed? Lord, let him know that you are with
him; support and help him that he may come to know you
more deeply as a result of his suffering. Lord be our strength
and support in this time of darkness and give us that deep
peace which comes from trusting you.

*Etta Gullick*

**794** Lord, we pray
for all who are weighed down with the
mystery of suffering. Reveal yourself
to them as the God of love, who
yourself bear all our suffering.

*George Appleton*

**795** Lord of great compassion, we pray you for those who are
nervously ill, and too weak and anxious to lift themselves

above the fear and sadness that threaten to overwhelm them. Do you yourself, O Lord, lift them up and deliver them, as you delivered your disciples in the storm at sea, strengthening their faith and banishing their fear. Turning to you, O Lord, may they find you, and finding you may they find also all you have laid up for them within the fortress of your love.

*Elizabeth Goudge*

**796** Father, we pray for the mentally ill, for all who are of a disturbed and troubled mind. Be to them light in their darkness, their refuge and strength in time of fear. Give special skills and tender hearts to all who care for them, and show them how best to assist in your work of healing; through Jesus Christ our Lord.

*Timothy Dudley-Smith*

**797** Dearest Lord, may I see you today and every day in the person of your sick, and, whilst nursing them, minister unto you.

Though you hide yourself behind the unattractive disguise of the irritable, the exacting, the unreasonable, may I still recognize you, and say: 'Jesus, my patient, how sweet it is to serve you.'

Lord, give me this seeing faith, then my work will never be monotonous. I will ever find joy in humouring the fancies and gratifying the wishes of all poor sufferers.

O beloved sick, how doubly dear you are to me, when you personify Christ; and what a privilege is mine to be allowed to tend you.

Sweetest Lord, make me appreciative of the dignity of my high vocation, and its many responsibilities. Never permit me to disgrace it by giving way to coldness, unkindness, or impatience.

And O God, while you are Jesus my patient, deign also to be to me a patient Jesus, bearing with my faults, looking only to my intention, which is to love and serve you in the person of each one of your sick.

Lord, increase my faith, bless my efforts and work, now and for evermore. Amen

*Mother Teresa of Calcutta*

**798** Lord, you gave me health and I forgot you. You take it away and I come back to you. What infinite compassion that God, in order to give himself to me, takes away his gifts which I allowed to come between me and him. Lord, take away everything that is not you. All is yours. You are the Lord. Dispose everything, comforts, success, health. Take all the things that possess me instead of you that I may be wholly yours.

*François Fénelon*

**799** Father, the world is full of pain; each of us has a share; for some it is a slight burden, for others it is crushing. But every Christian can turn it into a blessing if he will seek the companionship of Christ in his sufferings; then the pain becomes a new point of fellowship with Christ; and even our suffering becomes part of the price of the world's redemption as we fill up what is left over of the suffering of Christ.

Pain does not then cease to be pain; but it ceases to be barren pain; and with fellowship with Christ upon the cross we find new strength for bearing it and even making it the means by which our hearts are more fully cleansed of selfishness and grow towards perfect love. Accomplish this in us through Christ our Lord.

*William Temple*

**800** Preserve my soul, O Lord, because it belongs to Thee, and preserve my body because it belongs to my soul. Thou alone dost steer my boat through all its voyage, but hast a more especial care of it, when it comes to a narrow current, or to a dangerous fall of waters. Thou hast a care of the preservation of my body in all the ways of my life; but, in the straits of death, open Thine eyes wider, and enlarge Thy Providence towards me so far that no illness or agony may shake and benumb the soul. Do Thou so make my bed in all my sickness that, being used to Thy hand, I may be content with any bed of Thy making.

*John Donne*

**801** I cannot tell why this day I am ill:
But I am unwell because it is thy will –
Which is to make me pure and right like thee.
Not yet I need escape – 'tis bearable
Because thou knowest. And when harder things
Shall rise and gather, and overshadow me,
I shall have comfort in thy strengthenings.

*George Macdonald*

**802** Grant, Lord, that as you sent this sickness to me, you will also send your Holy Spirit into my heart so that my present illness may be sanctified and used as a school in which I may learn to know the greatness of my misery and the riches of your mercy. May I be so humbled at my misery that I despair not of your mercy and thus renounce all confidence in myself and every other creature so that I may put the whole of my salvation in your all-sufficient merits.

*Lewis Bayley*

**803** Lord, let this sickness, like that of Lazarus, be unto the Father's glory and for the good of those who stand by. I must see to it that whatever I have to suffer is not wasted but is offered to the Father, and also that I do not give cause for disedification to those who have to wait on me. Inspire me during my illness at least to think of you occasionally: I do not want to make this time, so far as prayer is concerned, a blank. If my regular practices have to be abandoned, show me what new ones I may substitute. Give me, I pray you, a more vivid awareness of your presence, so as to make up for the kind of willed recollection which I try to maintain when I am well.

*Hubert van Zeller*

**804** My strength fails; I feel only weakness, irritation and depression. I am tempted to complain and to despair. What has become of the courage I was so proud of, and that gave me so much self-confidence? In addition to my pain, I have to bear the shame of my fretful feebleness. Lord, destroy my pride; leave it no resource. How happy I shall be if you can teach me by these terrible trials, that I am nothing, that I can do nothing, and that you are all!

*François Fénelon*

**805** Lord, bless all means that are used for my recovery, and restore me to my health in thy good time; but if otherwise thou hast appointed for me, thy blessed will be done. O draw me away from an affection for things below, and fill me with an ardent desire after heaven. Lord, fit me for thyself, and then call me to those joys unspeakable and full of glory, when thou pleasest, and that for the sake of thy only Son, Jesus, my Saviour. Amen

*Thomas Ken*

**806** Lord Jesus,
You know what pain is like.
You know
the torture of the scourge upon your back,
the sting of the thorns upon your brow,
the agony of the nails in your hands.
You know what I'm going through just now.
Help me
to bear my pain
gallantly, cheerfully and patiently,
And help me to remember
that I will never be tried
above what I am able to bear,
and that you are with me,
even in this valley of the deep dark shadow.
In ev'ry pang that rends the heart,
The Man of Sorrows had a part;
He sympathises with our grief,
And to the suff'rer sends relief.

*William Barclay*

**807** The worst of pain, O Lord, is that it makes it difficult to pray.
Yet, O Lord, I desire to pray, to have communion with you,
to draw strength and healing from you, to link to you those I
love and those who need your love, to thank you for those who
look after me, and those who wish me well.

*George Appleton*

**808** Lord, a whole long day of pain now, at last is o'er!
Ah, how much we can sustain, I have felt once more!
Felt how frail are all our powers, and how weak our trust;
If Thou help not, these dark hours crush us to the dust.
Could I face the coming night if Thou wert not near?
Nay, without Thy love and might I must sink with fear:
Round me falls the evening gloom, sights and sounds all
    cease,
But within his narrow room, Night will bring no peace!
O Lord, my God, do Thou Thy holy Will!
I will lie still!
I will not stir lest I forsake Thine arm,
And break the charm,
Which lulls me, clinging to my Father's breast
In perfect rest!

*John Keble*

**809** Lord, I thank you that in your love you have taken from me all earthly riches, and that you now clothe and feed me through the kindness of others. Lord, I thank you, that since you have taken from me the sight of my eyes, you serve me now with the eyes of others.

Lord I thank you that since you have taken away the power of my hands and my heart, you serve me by the hands and hearts of others. Lord, I pray for them. Reward them for it in your heavenly love, that they may faithfully serve and please you till they reach a happy end.

*Mechthild of Magdeburg*

## PREPARING FOR DEATH

**810** O best and first and truest of Teachers! Thou who art the Truth! I know and believe with my whole heart, that this very flesh of mine will rise again. I know, base and odious as it is at present, that it will one day, if I be worthy, be raised incorruptible and altogether beautiful and glorious. This I know, and this, by thy grace, I will ever keep before me.

*John Henry Newman*

**811** O God, who hast appointed unto men once to die, but hast hidden from them the time of their death: Help us so to live in this world that we may be ready to leave it; and that, being thine in death as in life, we may come to that rest that remaineth for thy people; through him who died and rose again for us, Jesus Christ our Lord.

*William Bright*

**812** Lord, God almighty, Jesus Christ, who came to call not the just but sinners to repentance. Your promise is clear. You were so good as to say that as soon as a sinner turned away from his evil deeds, you would forget his sins. Accept then, as a sign of my repentance, the sufferings I am now undergoing, and by this fire that is waiting to burn my body for a time, deliver me from the eternal fire that burns both soul and body.

Thanks be to you, Lord Jesus Christ: in your mercy you have chosen me to be a victim for the glory of your name – you who offered yourself on the cross as a victim for the salvation of the whole world, you the innocent for us the guilty, you the good for us the wicked, you the blessed for us the cursed, you the sinless for all us sinners.

To you I offer my sacrifice, to you who are one God with the Father and the Holy Spirit, with whom you live and reign, for ever and ever. Amen

*Afra of Augusta\**
*(before martyrdom)*

**813** Jesus, Mary and Joseph I give you my heart, my soul and my life.
Jesus, Mary and Joseph assist me in my last agony.
Jesus, Mary and Joseph may I breathe forth my soul in peace with you. Amen

*Traditional Prayer*

**814** Grant, Lord, that we may live in your fear, die in your favour, rest in your peace, rise in your power and reign in your glory; for your own beloved Son's sake, Jesus Christ our Lord.

*William Laud\**

**815** Lord, I am coming as fast as I can. I know I must pass through the shadow of death, before I can come to Thee. But it is but a mere shadow, a little darkness upon nature: but Thou, by Thy merits and passion, hast broken through the jaws of death. So, Lord, receive my soul, and have mercy upon me; and bless this kingdom with peace and plenty, and with brotherly love and charity, for Jesus Christ His sake, if it be Thy will.

*William Laud*
*(before execution)*

**816** O merciful God, be Thou unto me a strong tower of defence, I humbly entreat Thee. Give me grace to await Thy leisure, and patiently to bear what Thou doest unto me; nothing doubting or mistrusting Thy goodness towards me, for Thou knowest what is good for me better than I do. Therefore do with me in all things what Thou wilt; only arm me, I beseech Thee, with Thine armour, that I may stand fast; above all things, taking to me the shield of faith; praying always that I may refer myself wholly to Thy will, abiding Thy pleasure and comforting myself in those troubles which it shall please Thee to send me, seeing such troubles are profitable for me; and I am assuredly persuaded that all Thou doest cannot but be well; and unto Thee be all honour and glory.

*Lady Jane Grey*
*(before execution)*

**817** O sweet Jesus, abide with me because it draweth toward night. For the night of temptation, the night of tribulation, my last long night of death approacheth. O blessed Saviour, stay with me therefore now and ever. Go with me, and live with me, and let neither death nor life separate me from thee. Drive me from myself, draw me unto thee. Let me be sick, but sound in thee; and in my weakness let thy strength appear. Set me as a seal upon thine heart, and let thy seal be settled upon mine; that I may be out of love with all, that I may be only in love with thee.

*Lewis Bayley*

**818** Lord Jesus Christ, who willest that no man should perish, and to whom supplication is never made without the hope of mercy, for Thou saidst with Thine own holy and blessed lips: 'All things whatsoever ye shall ask in My name, shall be done unto you'; I ask to Thee, O Lord, for Thy holy Name's sake, to grant me at the hour of my death full consciousness and the power of speech, sincere contrition for my sins, true faith, firm hope and perfect charity, that I may be able to say unto Thee with a clean heart: Into Thy hands, O Lord, I commend my spirit: Thou hast redeemed me, O God of truth, who art blessed for ever and ever. Amen

*Vincent Ferrar*

**819** O blessed Jesu, most mighty lion, king immortal and victorious, have mind of the sorrow that thou sufferedst when all the powers of thine heart and body for feebleness failed thee utterly, and when thou saidst, inclining thine head thus: 'It is all done'. For mind of thine anguish and sorrow blessed Jesu, have mercy on me in my last end, when my soul shall be anguished and my spirit troubled. Amen

*St Bridget of Sweden*

**820** Lord, who said that at midnight, at an hour we least expect, the Bridegroom shall come; grant that the cry, 'the Bridegroom cometh', may sound continually in all ears so that we may never be unprepared to go out and meet our Lord and Saviour, Jesus Christ.

*Lancelot Andrewes*

**821** O Lord, support us all the day long, until the shadows lengthen and the evening comes, and the busy world is hushed, and the fever of life is over, and our work is done.

Then, Lord, in thy mercy grant us a safe lodging, and a holy rest, and peace at the last; through Jesus Christ our Lord.

*Attributed to John Henry Newman,*
*though probably earlier in origin*

**822** Lord Jesus, today we accept from your merciful hands what is to come. The times of trial in this world, the suffering of our death, the sorrow and loneliness of our last hours upon earth, the purifying, unknown pains of our purgatory. Into your hands, O Lord, into your hands, we commit our living and dying, knowing that you are the dawn of eternal day, the burning light of the morning star.

*Caryll Houselander*

**823** My Lord, give me to know Thee, to believe on Thee, to love Thee, to serve Thee, to live to and for Thee. Give me to die just at that time and in that way which is most for Thy glory.

*John Henry Newman*

**824** Heavenly and eternal Father, source of all being, from whom I spring, unto whom I shall return, thine I shall ever be. Thou wilt call me unto thyself when my hour comes. Blessed shall I then be if I can say: 'I have fought a good fight.' I fear not death, O Father of life; for death is not eternal sleep; it is the transition to a new life, a moment of glorious transformation, an ascension towards thee. How could that be an evil that cometh from thy hand, when thou art the all-good! Lord of life and death, I am in thy hand; do unto me as thou deemest fit; for what thou dost is well done. When thou didst call me from nothing into life, thou didst will my happiness; when thou callest me away from life, will my happiness be less thy care? No, no, thou art love, and whosoever dwells in love, dwells in thee, O Lord, and thou in him. Amen

*Heinrich Tschokke*

**825** Before the beginning Thou hast foreknown the end,
Before the birthday the death-bed was seen of Thee:
Cleanse what I cannot cleanse, mend what I cannot mend,
O Lord All-Merciful, be merciful to me.

While the end is drawing near I know not mine end;
Birth I recall not, my death I cannot foresee:
O God, wise to defend, wise to befriend,
O Lord All-Merciful, be merciful to me.

*Christina Rossetti*

**826** Bring us, O Lord God, at our last awakening into the house and gate of heaven, to enter into that gate and dwell in that house, where there shall be no darkness nor dazzling, but one equal light; no noise nor silence, but one equal music; no fears nor hopes, but one equal possession; no ends nor beginnings, but one equal eternity; in the habitations of Thy glory and dominion world without end.

*John Donne*

**827** O my most blessed and glorious creator, that hast fed me all my life long, and redeemed me from all evil; seeing it is thy merciful pleasure to take me out of this frail body, and to wipe away all tears from mine eyes, and all sorrows from my heart, I do with all humility and willingness consent and submit myself wholly unto thy sacred will. My most loving redeemer, into thy saving and everlasting arms I commend my spirit; I am ready, my dear Lord, and earnestly expect and long for thy good pleasure. Come quickly, and receive the soul of thy servant which trusteth in thee.

*Henry Vaughan*

**828** Lord God,
you have made us mortal and we must die.
Do not, we beseech you,
take our lives away for ever,
you who are a God of the living.
We ask you this for Jesus' sake,
today and every day,
for ever and ever.

*Huub Oosterhuis*

**829** Hear me, O Lord, and remember now that hour in which thou didst once commend thy blessed spirit into the hands of thy heavenly Father: when with a torn body and a broken heart, thou didst show forth the bounty of thy mercy, and die for us. I beseech thee, O thou Brightness and Image of God, so to assist me by this thy most precious death, that being dead unto the world, I may live only to thee; and at the last hour of my departing from this mortal life, I commend my soul into thy hands, and thou mayest receive me into life immortal, there to reign with thee for ever and ever. Amen

*John Cosin*

**830** O God, my Master, should I gain the grace
To see Thee face to face when life is ended,
Grant that a little dog, who once pretended
That I was God, may see me face to face!

*B. C. Boulter*

**831** Hold thou my hands!
    In grief and joy, in hope and fear,
Lord, let me *feel* that thou art near,
    Hold thou my hands.

If e'er by doubts
Of thy good fatherhood depressed,
I cannot find in thee my rest,
    Hold thou my hands.

    Hold thou my hands,
These passionate hands too quick to smite,
These hands so eager for delight,
    Hold thou my hands.

    And when at length,
With darkened eyes and fingers cold,
I seek some last loved hand to hold,
    Hold thou my hands.

*William Canton*

**832** O Father, thou art my eternity.
Not on the clasp of consciousness – on thee
My life depends; and I can well afford
All to forget, so thou remember, Lord.
In thee I rest; in sleep thou dost me fold;
In thee I labour; still in thee grow old;
And dying, shall I not in thee, my Life, be bold?

*George Macdonald*

**833** Forget me not, but come, O King,
And find me softly slumbering
    In dark and troubled dreams of thee,
Then, with one waft of thy bright wing,
    Awaken me!

*Robert W. Buchanan*

## FOR THOSE WHO MOURN

**834** Grant, O Lord, to all who are bereaved, the spirit of faith and courage, that they may have the strength to meet the days to come with steadfastness and patience; not sorrowing as those without hope, but in thankful remembrance of thy great goodness in past years, and in the sure expectation of a joyful reunion in the heavenly places; and this we ask in the name of Jesus Christ our Lord.

*Irish Prayer Book*

**835** O Lord Jesus Christ, God of all consolation, whose heart was moved to tears at the grave of Lazarus; look with compassion on your children in their loss. Strengthen in them the gift of faith, and give to their troubled hearts, and to the hearts of all men, the light of hope, that they may live as one day to be united again, where tears shall be wiped away, in the Kingdom of your love; for you died and were raised to life with the Father and the Holy Spirit, God, now and for ever.

*David Silk*

**836** Father of mercies and God of all comfort, look in thy tender love and pity, we beseech thee, on thy sorrowing servants. Be thou to them their refuge and strength, a very present help in trouble; make them to know the love of Christ, which passeth knowledge; who by death hath conquered death, and by rising again hath opened the gates of everlasting life, even Jesus Christ our Lord.

*Church of South India*

**837** O Lord God, Who knowest our frame and rememberest that we are dust, look in pity upon those who mourn. Make thy loving presence so real to them that they may feel round about them thine everlasting arms, upholding and strengthening them.

Grant them such a sense of certainty that their loved one is with thee, doing thy high service, unhindered by pain, that they may turn to life's tasks with brave hearts and steady nerves, consoled in the thought that they will meet their dear one again.

Teach us all to face death unafraid and take us at last in triumph through the shadows into thine everlasting light

where are reunion and never-ending joy. Through Jesus
Christ our Lord.

*Leslie D. Weatherhead*

**838** O Thou! who dry'st the mourner's tear,
How dark this world would be,
If, when deceiv'd and wounded here,
We could not fly to thee!
The friends, who in our sunshine live,
When winter comes are flown;
And he, who has but tears to give
Must weep those tears alone.
But thou wilt heal that broken heart,
Which, like the plants that throw
Their fragrance from the wounded part,
Breathes sweetness out of woe.

When joy no longer soothes nor cheers,
And e'en the hope that threw
A moment's sparkle o'er our tears
Is dimm'd and vanish'd too;
Oh! who would bear life's stormy doom,
Did not thy wing of love
Come, brightly wafting through the gloom,
Our Peace-branch from above?
Then sorrow, touch'd by thee, grows bright,
With more than rapture's ray,
As darkness shows us worlds of light
We never saw by day!

*Thomas Moore*

**839** O God, we pray for thy comforting spirit to bide this day upon
all who mourn. Some are bereaved because of the death of
loved ones. Some are sorry for sins and desire to be delivered
from their burden. Some are lonely and need companionship.
Some feel that life has tossed them aside and that all the major
blessings have been bestowed upon others. Some have been
hurt by the selfishness and carelessness of their fellow men. For
all of them we pray. Help them to put their trust in and to
wait upon the Lord. If they are of good courage thou wilt
strengthen their hearts. We would all faint, except we believed we shall yet see the goodness of the Lord in this land of
the living. Bless all who call upon thee, and even those who
know not upon whom to call. In Christ's name we pray.

*William H. Kadel*

**840** We remember, Lord, the slenderness of the thread which separates life from death, and the suddenness with which it can be broken. Help us also to remember that on both sides of that division we are surrounded by your love.

Persuade our hearts that when our dear ones die neither we nor they are parted from you.

In you may we find peace, and in you be united with them in the body of Christ, who has burst the bonds of death and is alive for evermore, our Saviour and theirs for ever and ever.

*Dick Williams*

**841** Almighty and everlasting God, the comfort of the sad, the strength of sufferers, let the prayers of them that cry out of any tribulation come unto thee. That all may rejoice to find that thy mercy is present with them in their affliction through Jesus Christ our Lord.

*Gelasian Sacramentary*

**842** Heavenly Father, hear our voice out of the deep sorrow which thou in thy mysterious wisdom hast brought upon us. We know that thou art with us, and that whatsoever cometh is a revelation of thine unchanging love. Thou knowest what is best for us. Thy will be done. Thou gavest and thou hast taken away, blessed be thy name. O keep our souls from all the temptations of this hour of mourning, that we may neither sorrow as those without hope, nor lose our trust in thee; but that the darker this earthly scene becomes the lighter may be our vision of that eternal world where all live before thee. And grant that the remnant of this our family, O Lord, still being upon earth, may be steadfast in faith, joyful through hope, and rooted in love, and so may pass the waves of this troublesome world, that finally we may come to the land of everlasting life, there to reign with thee world without end; through Jesus Christ our Lord.

*Laurence R. Tuttiett*

**843** Lord Christ, shine upon all who are in the darkness of suffering, or grief, that in your light they may receive hope and courage, and in your presence may find their rest and peace; for your love's sake.

*Alan Warren*

**844** Let the cry of widows, orphans and destitute children enter into thine ears, O most loving Saviour. Comfort them with a

mother's tenderness, shield them from the perils of this world,
and bring them at last to thy heavenly home.

*John Cosin*

**845** Almighty God, Father of mercies and giver of all comfort;
deal graciously, we pray Thee, with all those who mourn,
that, casting every care on Thee, they may know the consolation of Thy love; through Jesus Christ our Lord.

*Book of Common Prayer, 1928*

**846** Lord, my loved ones are near me.
I know that they live in the shadow.
My eyes can't see them because they have left for the
    moment their bodies as one leaves behind outmoded
    clothing.
Their souls, deprived of their disguise, no longer
    communicate with me.

But in you, Lord, I hear them calling me.
I see them beckoning to me.
I hear them giving me advice.
For they are now more vividly present.
Before, our bodies touched but not our souls.
Now I meet them when I meet you.
I receive them when I receive you.
I love them when I love you.
O, my loved ones, eternally alive, who live in me,
Help me to learn thoroughly in this short life how to live
    eternally.

Lord I love you, and I want to love you more.
It's you who make love eternal, and I want to love eternally.

*Michel Quoist*

## IN TIMES OF TROUBLE AND DIFFICULTY

**847** Lord give us grace
to hold to Thee
when all is weariness and fear
and sin abounds within, without,
when that which I would do I cannot do
and that I do I would not do,
when love itself is tested by the doubt

that love is false, or dead within the soul,
when every act brings new confusion, new distress,
new opportunities, new misunderstandings,
and every thought new accusation.

Lord give us grace
that we may know that in the darkness pressing round
it is the mist of sin that hides Thy face
that Thou art there
and Thou dost know we love Thee still . . .

*Gilbert Shaw*

**848**  Almighty God, the refuge of all that are distressed, grant unto
us that, in all trouble of this our mortal life, we may flee to the
knowledge of Thy loving kindness and tender mercy; that so,
sheltering ourselves therein, the storms of life may pass over
us, and not shake the peace of God that is within us. Whatsoever this life may bring us, grant that it may never take from
us the full faith that Thou art our Father. Grant us Thy light,
that we may have life, through Jesus Christ our Lord. Amen

*George Dawson*

**849**  Jesus, Deliverer!
Come thou to me:
Soothe thou my voyaging
Over Life's sea.
Thou, when the storm of Death
Roars, sweeping by,
Whisper, O Truth of Truth –
'Peace! It is I.'

*Anatolius*

**850**  Grant, O heavenly Father, that we may so faithfully believe in
Thee, and so fervently love one another, always living in Thy
fear, and in the obedience of Thy holy law and blessed will,
that we, being fruitful in all good works, may lead our life
according to Thy good pleasure in this transitory world and,
after this frail and short life, obtain the true and immortal life,
where thou livest and reignest, world without end. Amen

*Thomas Becon*

**851**  God of love, whose compassion never fails; we bring to you
the sufferings of all mankind; the needs of the homeless; the
cry of prisoners; the pains of the sick and injured; the sorrow

of the bereaved; the helplessness of the aged and weak. Strengthen and relieve them, Father, according to their various needs and your great mercy; for the sake of your Son our Saviour Jesus Christ.

*St Anselm\**

852 O God, by your mercy strengthen us who lie exposed to the rough storms of troubles and temptations. Help us against our own negligence and cowardice, and defend us from the treachery of our unfaithful hearts. Help us, we implore you, and bring us to your safe haven of peace and happiness.

*St Augustine of Hippo*

853 O holy and loving Father, Whose mercies are from everlasting to everlasting, we thank Thee that Thy children can flee for refuge in their afflictions to the blessed certainty of Thy love. From every grief that burdens our spirits, from the sense of solitude and loss, from the doubt and fainting of the soul in its trouble, we turn to Thee. Thou knowest our frame, Thou rememberest that we are dust. Be Thou our Strength and Deliverer; in our great need be Thou our Helper; pour Thy consolations into our hearts, and let the gospel of Thy beloved Son minister comfort and peace to our souls. Amen

*Henry W. Foote*

854 O God, the strength of the weak, the friend of sinners, and the comfort of the sorrowful: grant thy mighty protection to the tempted; reveal thy grace to the fallen; maintain the faith of those who are persecuted for righteousness' sake; and give the consolation of thy presence to those who are disappointed, embittered, lonely, or in despair; for thy mercies' sake.

*William E. Orchard*

855 Dear God, it is so hard for us not to be anxious,
we worry about work and money,
about food and health,
about weather and crops,
about war and politics,
about loving and being loved.
Show us how perfect love casts out fear.

*Monica Furlong*

856 O God, Creator of mankind, I do not aspire to comprehend You or Your creation, nor to understand pain or suffering. I

aspire only to relieve the pain and suffering of others, and I trust in doing so, I may understand more clearly Your nature, that You are the Father of all mankind, and that the hairs of my head are numbered.

*St Francis of Assisi*

**857** Father, you do not protect us against catastrophes but in them you come to our aid. It is in the very midst of the tempest and misfortune that a wonderful zone of peace, serenity and joy bursts in us if we dwell in your grace. You do not help us before we have helped ourselves, but when we are at the end of our resources you manifest yourself, and we begin to know that you have been there all the time.

*Louis Evely*

**858** I am silent, Lord, in my affliction. I am silent. In the stillness of a contrite and humble heart, I listen to you. Lord, see my wounds; you have made them. You have smitten me. I am silent; I suffer, I worship silently. Yet you hear my sighs, and the lamentations of my heart are not hidden from you. Let me not listen to myself. I long to hear your voice and to follow you.

*François Fénelon*

**859** Most merciful God, the helper of all men, so strengthen us by thy power, that our sorrows may be turned into joy, and we may continually glorify thy holy name; through Jesus Christ our Lord. Amen

*Sarum Breviary*

**860** God, Father of Mercies, save me from the hell within me. I acknowledge thee, I adore and bless thee, whose throne is in heaven, with thy Blessed Son and crucified Jesus, and thy Holy Spirit, and also, though thou slay me, yet will I trust in thee; I cannot think thou can hate and reject a poor soul that desires to love thee and cleave to thee, so long as I can hold by the skirts of thy garments, until thou violently shake me off; which I am confident thou wouldst not do, because thou art love and goodness itself and thy mercies endure for ever.

*Robert Leighton*

**861** O God, we cry out to Thee in the time of our trouble. For some sickness has taken hold, for others doubts have assailed them, others again have lost employment. Help us to remember the song of hope we would always sing in our days of prosperity and peace. Have Thine own way with our lives, teach us to see our troubles as hidden blessings. You are our changless God who loves us even when life tumbles in with all its problems and trials. Deepen our faith in that love, through Jesus Christ our Lord. Amen

*William H. Kadel\**

862 Almighty God, King of Kings, who hast called us into a Kingdom not of this world; send forth, we pray, Thy spirit unto the dark habitations of guilt and woe. Reach the heart of every oppression, and make arrogancy dumb before Thee. Still the noise of our strife and the tumult of the people. Put to shame the false idols of every heart. Carry faith to the doubting, hope to the fearful, strength to the weak, comfort to all who mourn. Commit Thy word, O Lord, to faithful witnesses, that Thy Kingdom may speedily come and Thy will be done on earth as it is in heaven.

*John Heuss*

863 Thou, O Lord, art the helper of the helpless; the hope of the hopeless; the saviour of them who are tossed with tempests; the haven of them who sail; be thou all to all. The glorious majesty of the Lord our God be upon us; prosper thou the work of our hands upon us; Oh, prosper thou our handy-work. Lord, be thou within me, to strengthen me; without me, to keep me; above me, to protect me; beneath me, to uphold me; before me, to direct me; behind me, to keep me from straying; round about me, to defend me. Blessed be thou, O Lord, our Father, for ever and ever. Amen

*Lancelot Andrewes*

864 Ah Lord, my prayers are dead, my affections dead, and my heart is dead: but thou art a living God and I bear myself upon thee.

*William Bridge*

865 Lord, ease my great affliction, or increase my patience; but, Lord, I do not complain, I am dumb, Lord, before You, because You permit it.

*George Herbert*

866 Bless and sanctify my soul with Thy heavenly blessings, that it may become Thy holy habitation, and let nothing be found in this temple of Thy Divinity, which shall offend the eyes of Thy

Majesty. According to the greatness of Thy goodness and multitude of Thy mercies, look upon me, and hear the prayer of Thy poor servant. Protect and keep my soul, amidst so many dangers of this life, and, by Thy grace accompanying me, direct it along the way of peace, to its home of everlasting brightness. Amen

*Thomas à Kempis*

**867** Almighty Lord, and everlasting God, vouchsafe, we beseech thee, to direct, sanctify, and govern, both our hearts and bodies, in the ways of thy laws, and in the works of thy commandments; that, through thy most mighty protection, both here and ever, we may be preserved in body and soul; through our Lord and Saviour Jesus Christ. Amen

*Gregorian Sacramentary*

**868** To all who are tossed by the sea; you are the calm of the harbour; you are the hope of the hopeful.
You are the health of the sick, the relief of the needy; the guide of the blind.
To those exposed to punishment on every count you are merciful, to the weary a wall, in darkness light.
You created the land, you rule the sea, you set every element in its place; a word from you and the heavens, the stars and all else was made, and made perfect.
You kept Noah safe and gave wealth to Abraham,
let Isaac go free and provided a victim in his place,
wrestled with Jacob, to his sweet confusion,
took Lot away from the accursed land of Sodom.
Moses you showed yourself to; to Jesus, son of Nun, you gave prudence.
In your mercy you went with Joseph on his way and brought your people out of the land of Egypt, leading them to the land they had been promised.
You protected the three children in the furnace.
You closed the lions' mouths, gave life to Daniel.
You did not allow Jonah to perish in the depths of the sea.
You gave Judith the weapons she needed; Susanna you saved from the unjust judges.
Esther had her triumph from you; you procured the downfall of Aman.
You brought us from darkness to eternal light, Father of our Lord and Saviour, Jesus Christ, light unquenchable, you who gave me the sign of the cross, the sign of Christ.

I beg you not to decide, Lord, that I am unworthy of these sufferings that my brethren have been allowed to undergo. Let me share the crown with them; let me be with them in glory.

*Severus of Thrace\**

869 Grant, we beseech thee, O Lord our God, that in whatever dangers we are placed we may call upon thy name, and that when deliverance is given us from on high we may never cease from thy praise; through Jesus Christ our Lord.

*Leonine Sacramentary*

870 O God our Father, hear me, who am trembling in this darkness, and stretch forth Thy hand unto me; hold forth Thy light before me; recall me from my wanderings; and, Thou being my guide, may I be restored to myself and to Thee.

*St Augustine of Hippo*

871 Blessed are all Thy saints, O God and King, who have travelled over the tempestuous sea of this life and have made the harbour of peace and felicity. Watch over us who are still on our dangerous voyage; and remember such as lie exposed to the rough storms of trouble and temptations.

Frail is our vessel, and the ocean is wide; but as in Thy mercy Thou hast set our course, so steer the vessel of our life towards the everlasting shore of peace, and bring us at length to the quiet haven of our heart's desire, where Thou, O God, art blessed and livest and reignest for ever.

*St Augustine of Hippo*

872 Almighty God, who knows we are powerless to help ourselves, keep us in your care, body and soul. May we be kept from all bodily danger and preserved from evil thoughts; through Jesus Christ our Lord. Amen

*Gregorian Sacramentary*

873 God, our Father, we are exceedingly frail and indisposed to every virtuous and gallant undertaking. Strengthen our weakness, we beseech you, that we may do valiantly in this spiritual war; help us against our own negligence and cowardice, and defend us from the treachery of our unfaithful hearts; for Jesus Christ's sake.

*Thomas à Kempis*

**874** O Lord our God, teach us to ask thee aright for the right blessings. Guide the vessel of our life toward thyself, thou tranquil haven of all storm-tossed souls. Show us the course wherein we should go. Renew a willing spirit within us. Let thy Spirit curb our wayward senses, and guide and enable us, unto that which is our true good, to keep thy laws and in all our works evermore to rejoice in thy glories and gladdening presence. For thine is the glory and praise of all thy saints for ever and ever.

*St Basil the Great*

**875** All-seeing light, and eternal life of all things, look upon my misery with thine eyes of mercy, and let thine infinite power vouchsafe to limit out some portion of deliverance unto me, as unto thee shall seem most convenient. But yet, O my God, I yield unto thy will, and joyfully embrace what sorrow thou wilt have me suffer. Only this much let me crave of thee (let my craving, O Lord, be accepted of thee, since even that proceeds from thee) – let me crave even by the noblest title, which in my great affliction I may give myself, that I am thy creature, and by thy goodness (which is thyself), that thou wilt suffer some beam of thy majesty so to shine into my mind, that it may still depend confidently on thee. Amen

*Sir Philip Sidney*

**876** Lord, do not permit my trials to be above my strength; and do thou vouchsafe to be my strength and comfort in the time of trial. Give me grace to take in good part whatever shall befall me, and let my heart acknowledge it to be the Lord's doing, and to come from thy providence, and not by chance. May I receive everything from thy hand with patience and with joy; through Jesus Christ our Lord.

*Thomas Wilson*

**877** Lord, my God! the amazing horrors of darkness were gathered round me, and covered me all over, and I saw no way to go forth; I felt the depth and extent of the misery of my fellow-creatures separated from the Divine harmony, and it was heavier than I could bear, and I was crushed down under it; I lifted up my hand, I stretched out my arm, but there was none to help me; I looked round about, and was amazed.

   In the depths of misery, O Lord, I remembered that thou art omnipotent; that I had called thee Father; and I felt that I loved thee, and I was made quiet in my will, and I waited for deliverance from thee. Thou hadst pity upon me, when no man could help me; I saw that meekness under suffering was showed to us in the most affecting example of thy Son, and thou taughtest me to follow him, and I said: 'Thy will, O Father, be done!'

*John Woolman*

**878** O God, the refuge of the poor, the strength of those who toil, and the Comforter of all who sorrow, we commend to your mercy the unfortunate and needy in whatever land they may be. You alone know the number and extent of their sufferings and trials. Look down, Father of mercies, at those unhappy families suffering from war and slaughter, from hunger and disease, and other severe trials. Spare them, O Lord, for it is truly a time for mercy.

*Peter Canisius*

**879** I humbly beg of thee, O merciful Father, that this present affliction may strengthen my faith, which thou sawest was growing weak; fix my hope which was staggering, quicken my devotion which was languishing, reunite me to my first love which I was forsaking, rekindle my charity which was cooling, revive my zeal which was dying, confirm my obedience which was wavering, recover my patience which was fainting, mortify my pride which was presuming; and perfect my repentance which was daily decaying: for all these and the like infirmities to which my soul is exposed, O make thy affliction my care. Amen

*Thomas Ken*

**880** O crucified Jesus, in giving me your cross give me too your spirit of love and self-abandonment; grant that I may think less of my suffering than of the happiness of suffering with you. What do I suffer that you have not suffered? Or rather what do I suffer at all, if I dare to compare myself with you? O Lord, grant that I may love you and then I shall no longer fear the cross.

*François Fénelon*

**881** O my Lord Jesus, I believe, and by thy grace will ever believe and hold, and I know that it is true, and will be true to the end of the world, that nothing great is done without suffering, without humiliation, and that all things are possible by means of it.

O my dear Lord, though I am so very weak that I am not fit to ask thee for suffering as a gift, and have not strength to do so, at least I will beg of thee grace to meet suffering well, when thou in thy love and wisdom dost bring it upon me. Let me bear pain, reproach, disappointment, slander, anxiety, suspense, as thou wouldest have me, O my Jesu, and, as thou by thy own suffering hast taught me, when it comes.

I wish to bear insult meekly, and to return good for evil. I wish to humble myself in all things, and to be silent when I am ill-used, and to be patient when sorrow or pain is prolonged, and all for the love of thee and thy cross.

*John Henry Newman*

**882** O God, animate us to cheerfulness. May we have a joyful sense of our blessings, learn to look on the bright circumstances of our lot, and maintain a perpetual contentedness. Preserve us from despondency and from yielding to dejection. Teach us that nothing can hurt us if, with true loyalty of affection, we keep Thy commandments and take refuge in Thee.

*William E. Channing*

**883** Thou knowest, good Lord, my tribulation, and now I am turned to thee; why sufferest thou me so long to be vexed with this trouble? Calm the winds, assuage the tempests, deliver my soul from these storms, for if thy meekness be turned to me, and thou look upon me, all the members of my body, and also my soul, shall be in rest and in peace. Therefore, good Lord, be thou turned to me, and deliver my soul from this tribulation wherewith it is troubled by reason of my sinfulness.

*John Fisher*

**884** O good Jesus, I offer and resign myself to you in perfect readiness of will to bear the affliction which I foresee coming upon me. I will accept it with unshaken will as from your hand and I will bear it with all the patience I can, in union with the love with which you bore all your afflictions as coming from your Father's hand and offered them in gratitude to him. I pray that you would grant me fortitude and patience to bear my suffering with gallantry to the praise of your eternal glory and the peace of all the world.

*St Gertrude*

**885** Grant us peace and establish Thy truth in us. Remember every faithful soul in trial; and comfort, if it be possible, every one in sorrow and distress.

O Helper of the helpless, bring the wanderer home, and give health to the sick, and deliverance to the captive.

Sustain the aged, comfort the weakhearted, set free those whose souls are bound in misery, remember all those that are in affliction, necessity, and emergency everywhere.

Let us dwell with Thee in peace, as children of light; and in Thy light, Lord, let us see the light. Amen

*Rowland Williams*

# THROUGH LIFE'S JOURNEY

**886** Teach us to know you, our God, and enable us to do your will as we ought to do. Give us hearts full of love for you, full of trust, full of faithfulness. May no temptations rock us, no tribulations drive us from you. May all that befalls us draw us closer in love and trust and fit us for your heavenly kingdom. Amen

*Benjamin Jenks*

**887** O God
 my God
  keep me from flinching/waning
   slumbering into that timeless rest
   that never is
 keep me from falling into a prison
  of egotistical habits
   where the bars
   are superficial friends
    and drinks
    and stupid laughter
    kisses without love
    business and organization
     without heart
    and gifts for self-flattery
   these bars that prevent life evolving
   towards that taste of the infinite
    open to your call . . .
 break down those barriers
  that prevent me living, my God.

*Jean Vanier*

**888** Teach us, good Lord, to serve you as you deserve; to give and not to count the cost; to fight and not to heed the wounds; to toil and not to seek for rest; to labour and not to ask for any reward, save that of knowing that we do your will; through Jesus Christ our Lord.

*Ignatius of Loyola*

**889** O Lord of life, and Lord of love! love us into life, and give us life to love Thee. Grant us life enough to put life into all things, that when we travel through this part of our life, and it seems but dust and barrenness, we may be full of hope in Thee. Touch this barrenness, till all things bloom. Lord, forgive us that our life is so poor, and grant us thoughts of God that we may be enabled for the time to come to make this very desert blossom. Grant that the Spirit of God may so come and so dwell, that the beauty of the Lord may be upon us: through Jesus Christ our Lord. Amen

*George Dawson*

**890** Lord Jesus, our Saviour, let us now come to you:
Our hearts are cold; Lord, warm them with your selfless
   love.
Our hearts are sinful; cleanse them with your precious
   blood.
Our hearts are weak; strengthen them with your joyous
   Spirit.
Our hearts are empty; fill them with your divine presence.
Lord Jesus, our hearts are yours; possess them always and
   only for yourself.

*St Augustine of Hippo\**

**891** Be thou, O Lord, our shield and defence as we travel along the perplexing path of life, with its many difficulties and dangers. So guide and protect us here on earth, that we may find eternal rest when our journey is finished and our work is done; through Jesus Christ our Lord.

*Unknown Source*

**892** Most merciful and gracious Father, I bless and magnify thy name that thou hast adopted me into the inheritance of sons, and hast given me a portion of my elder brother. Thou who art the God of patience and consolation, strengthen me that I may bear the yoke and burden of the Lord, without any uneasy and useless murmurs, and ineffective unwillingness.

Lord, I am unable to stand under the cross, unable of myself, but be thou pleased to ease this load by fortifying my spirit, that I may be strongest when I am weakest, and may be able to do and suffer every thing that thou pleasest, through Christ who strengtheneth me. Let me pass through the valley of tears, and the valley of the shadow of death with safety and peace, with a meek spirit, and a sense of the divine mercies, through Jesus Christ. Amen

*Jeremy Taylor*

893 Fix thou our steps, O Lord, that we stagger not at the uneven motions of the world, but steadily go on to our glorious home; neither censuring our journey by the weather we meet with, nor turning out of the way for anything that befalls us.

The winds are often rough, and our own weight presses us downwards. Reach forth, O Lord, thy hand, thy saving hand, and speedily deliver us.

Teach us, O Lord, to use this transitory life as pilgrims returning to their beloved home; that we may take what our journey requires, and not think of settling in a foreign country.

*John Wesley*

894 Go before us, O Lord, in all our doings with thy most gracious favour, and further us with thy continual help; that in all our works, begun, continued, and ended in thee, we may glorify thy holy name, and finally by thy mercy obtain everlasting life; through Jesus Christ our Lord.

*Book of Common Prayer, 1928*

895 O God, the protector of all that trust in Thee, without whom nothing is strong, nothing is holy, increase and multiply upon us Thy mercy; that, Thou being our Ruler and Guide, we may so pass through things temporal that we finally lose not the things eternal. Grant this, O heavenly Father, for Jesus Christ's sake.

*Book of Common Prayer, 1928*

896 Dear God, make me think about what I'm doing
with my mind
with my body
with my habits
with my study

with my friends
with my hopes
with my parents
with my faith
with life.

*Carl Burke*


**897** Lord, be with my spirit and dwell by faith in my heart. Oh make me as you would have me to be. Be with me everywhere and at all times, in all the events and circumstances of my life. Never leave me in my earthly pilgrimage, but bring me safe through all trials and dangers to be with you forever. Amen

*Benjamin Jenks*


**898** In the name of our Lord Jesus Christ, send me your Spirit; instil the wisdom of your Holy Spirit into my heart; protect my soul and body, every limb in my body, every fibre of my being, from all possible harm and all traps the Devil may set me and every temptation to sin. Teach me to give you thanks, O Father, Son and Holy Spirit.

*Euchologium Sinaiticium*


**899** We trust that you will bear us up, as tiny children and on to old age. When you are our strength it is strength indeed, but when our strength is our own it is only weakness. The good in us only grows and develops if you nourish it. Be our hope and our strength unto eternity.

*St Augustine of Hippo*


**900** O God, our Father, we are exceedingly frail, and indisposed to every virtuous and gallant undertaking: Strengthen our weakness, we beseech thee, that we may do valiantly in this spiritual war; help us against our own negligence and cowardice, and defend us from the treachery of our unfaithful hearts; for the sake of Jesus Christ our Lord.

*St Augustine of Hippo*


**901** I know, Lord, and humbly acknowledge that I am an object totally unworthy of your love. But I am sure that you are totally worthy of my love. I am not worthy to serve you, but you have a right to the best service I can give. Help me to rid my life of sin which stands in the way of me fulfilling my duty of service. Enable me so to organise and discipline myself that

when the race of life is run, I may sleep in peace and rest in
you.

*St Augustine of Hippo*

**902** Help of all who seek help from thee, can it be better to keep
silence about my necessities, hoping that thou wilt relieve
them? No, indeed; for thou, my Lord and my joy, knowing
how many they must be, and how it will alleviate them if we
speak to thee of them, dost bid us pray to thee of them, and
say that thou wilt not fail to give.

*St Teresa of Avila*

**903** I stand before thee, O Lord, as thy servant, trusting not
wholly in myself, nor in any created thing, but in thee. Since
thou art my God and all my hope, save me from all perils; give
me the victory over all carnal desires. When even the truly
devout are not free from conflict, I may not ask complete
freedom from these desires in my body, but that sin may not
reign there. Save me, O Lord, from these dangers, that my
soul may command and my body obey.

*Tenth-century Prayer*

## DISSATISFACTION WITH SELF

**904** To thee, O Jesus, thou peace of the troubled heart, I come!
Save me from myself. Shine into my heart with thy life and
love. Melt away all cold distrust. Take away all sin; and
make me like to thyself, for thy love and kindness' sake, O
Lord!

*W. Boyd Carpenter*

**905** O Christ, my Lord, again and again I have said with Mary
Magdalene, 'They have taken away my Lord and I know not
where they have laid him'. I have been desolate and alone.
And thou hast found me again, and I know that what has died
is not thou, my Lord, but only my idea of thee, the image
which I have made to preserve what I have found, and to
be my security. I shall make another image, O Lord, better
than the last. That too must go, and all successive images,
until I come to the blessed vision of thyself, O Christ, my
Lord.

*George Appleton*

**906** O my Father, I have moments of deep unrest – moments when I know not what to ask by reason of the very excess of my wants. I have in these hours no words for Thee, no conscious prayers for Thee.

My cry seems purely worldly; I want only the wings of a dove that I may flee away. Yet all the time Thou hast accepted my unrest as a prayer. Thou hast interpreted its cry for a dove's wings as a cry for Thee, Thou hast received the nameless longings of my heart as the intercessions of Thy Spirit.

They are not yet the intercessions of my spirit; I know not what I ask. But Thou knowest what I ask, O my God. Thou knowest the name of that need which lies beneath my speechless groan. Thou knowest that, because I am made in Thine image, I can find rest only in what gives rest to Thee; therefore Thou hast counted my unrest unto me for righteousness, and hast called my groaning Thy Spirit's prayer.

*George Matheson*

**907** I am tired, Lord,
too tired to think,
too tired to pray,
too tired to do anything.
Too tired,
drained of resources,
'labouring at the oars against a head wind',
pressed down by a force as strong as the sea.
Lord of all power and might,
'your way was through the sea,
your path through the great waters',
calm my soul,
take control,
Lord of all power and might.

*Rex Chapman*

**908** If I am to complain, let me complain to Jesus fastened on his cross. But in thy presence, my Saviour, what have I to complain of? What are my sufferings compared with those thou bearest without complaining? I might perhaps convince my fellow-man that I am unjustly afflicted, but in thy presence, Lord, I cannot, for my sins are known to thee. Thou knowest my sufferings are far less than I deserve. And since all my afflictions proceed from thee, reproach not my afflictions, not my wrongs, but myself and my own want of patience. To

thee I come; give me strength, and hearten me to suffer in
silence; as once thou didst thyself.

*Claude de la Colombière*

# IN JOY

**909** Give us, Lord, a bit o' sun,
a bit o' work and a bit o' fun;
give us all in the struggle and sputter
our daily bread and a bit o' butter;
give us health, our keep to make,
an' a bit to spare for others' sake;
give us sense, for we're some of us duffers,
an' a heart to feel for all that suffers;
give us, too, a bit of a song
and a tale, and a book to help us along.
An' give us our share o' sorrow's lesson
that we may prove how grief's a blessin'.
Give us, Lord, a chance to be
our goodly best, brave, wise, and free,
our goodly best for ourself, and others,
till all men learn to live as brothers.

*From the wall of an old inn, Lancaster*

**910** O Thou, who art the sun of righteousness and the light
eternal, giving gladness to all things, shine upon us both now
and ever, that we may be glad and cheerful in thee; for thy
Name's sake.

*Ancient Collect*

**911** Lord, you have sent me joy! I leap . . . I skip . . . it is good to
be alive. You give life; you give the spirit of gladness to feed it.
I love you. My sins are forgiven. It is good to be alive . . . and
you have made it so.

*Hubert van Zeller*

**912** Today my heart sings, Lord;
Everything within me rejoices.

Joy bubbles up in my soul,
overflows and cascades like a stream leaping all barriers;
the joy of knowing You,
the joy of union with You.

One with You, Creator of the world,
and my Creator,
one with You, Saviour of the world,
and my Saviour.
One with You, Spirit of the eternal God,
and my God,
one with You, almighty King of kings
and my Lord and King.

Joy, joy at the heart of living,
joy in doing, joy in being;
sing for joy, my heart,
for sheer joy, my soul.

The joy of loving You,
the joy of following You,
the joy of serving You;
all the way 'long it is glory.

Today my heart sings, Lord;
everything within me rejoices,
joy bubbles up in my soul,
glory . . . glory!

*Flora Larsson*

**913** Thank you, Lord Jesus,
for all our happiness.
Thank you especially
for the happiness which takes us by surprise.
Above all we ask you
to lead us toward the surprising discovery
that what most pleases you
will bring the greatest joy to us.

*Jamie Wallace*

# VII   INTERCESSORY PRAYERS

## FOR NEW CHRISTIANS

**914** God the all-powerful, Father of Christ, who is your only Son, give me a clean body, a pure heart, a watchful mind and knowledge free from error. May your Holy Spirit come to me and bring me truth, yes and the fulness of truth, through your Christ.

Through him may glory be yours, in the Holy Spirit, throughout the ages. Amen

*Third-century Prayer*

**915** O God, by whose Spirit the whole body of the Church is multiplied and governed: Preserve in the new-born children of thy family the fullness of thy grace; that, being renewed in body and soul, they may be fervent in the faith, and be enabled to serve thee all the days of their life; through Jesus Christ our Lord.

*Gelasian Sacramentary*

**916** Keep us, O Lord, from the vain strife of words, and grant us a constant profession of our faith. Preserve us in the way of truth, so that we may ever hold fast that which we professed when we were baptised into the name of the Father, and of the Son, and of the Holy Ghost, and may give glory to thee, our Creator, Redeemer and Sanctifier, now and for evermore.

*St Hilary of Poitiers\**

**917** Lord God, by our baptism into the death and resurrection of your Son Jesus Christ we have been born again to be your children and heirs of eternal life; strengthen us by your Spirit to live in newness of life all our days; through the same Christ our Lord.

*David Silk*

# FOR USE BY GOD

**918** Use me, my Saviour, for whatever purpose and in whatever way thou mayest require. Here is my poor heart, an empty vessel; fill it with thy grace. Here is my sinful, troubled soul; quicken it and refresh it with thy love. Take my heart for thine abode; my mouth to spread abroad the glory of thy name; my love and all my powers for the advancement of thy believing people, and never suffer the steadfastness and confidence of my faith to abate.

*Dwight L. Moody*

**919** Good Lord, Who alone orderest all things well, I cast myself wholly upon Thine infinite mercy; I trust Thee with my all, myself, and all whom I love, and all which I desire; my present and my future, my hopes and my fears, my time and my eternity, my joys and my sorrows. Deal with me as Thou willest, and knowest best, only bind me safe to Thine everlasting love. Amen

*Treasury of Devotion*

**920** O Lord, you order and arrange all things for us in your infinite wisdom and love. You know my weakness and every beat and ache of my heart is known to you. Blindly I give myself to your tender loving heart. Only give me grace to think, speak, act, feel according to your loving purposes. Amen

*E. B. Pusey*

**921** Lord Jesus,
I give you my hands to do your work.
I give you my feet to go your way.
I give you my eyes to see as you do.
I give you my tongue to speak your words.
I give you my mind that you may think in me.
I give you my spirit that you may pray in me.

Above all,
I give you my heart that you may love in me,
your Father, and all mankind.
I give you my whole self that you may grow in me,
so that it is you, Lord Jesus,
who live and work and pray in me.

I hand over to your care, Lord,
my soul and body,
my mind and thoughts,
my prayers and my hopes,
my health and my work,
my life and my death,
my parents and my family,
my friends and my neighbours,
my country and all men.
Today
and always.

*Lancelot Andrewes*

922 Sever me from myself that I may be grateful unto thee;
May I perish to myself that I may be safe in thee;
May I die to myself that I may live in thee;
May I wither to myself that I may blossom in thee;
May I be emptied of myself that I may abound in thee;
May I be nothing to myself that I may be all to thee.

*Erasmus*

## FOR CHRISTIAN UNITY

923 O Lord God, the one God, make thy people one. Whatever our differences, even in matters essential, may we ever realise that we are one in Christ Jesus. Let not Satan break the blessed bond of union between believers, but may it be increasingly strengthened in our own experience, and in all thy people everywhere, for the sake of Jesus Christ our Redeemer.

*Benjamin Jenks*

924 Almighty and everliving God, lover of peace and unity, you have called us, in Christ, to the same love and unity. We pray that your Holy Spirit will so guide and direct our hearts that being released from human pride and fears we may serve you in mercy, humility and gentleness united with our brothers and sisters, through your dear Son, Jesus Christ.

*Christian K. J. Bunsen*

925 Lord Jesus Christ, who prayed for your disciples that they might be one, even as you are one with the Father; draw us to

yourself, that in common love and obedience to you we may be united to one another, in the fellowship of the one Spirit, that the world may believe that you are Lord, to the glory of God the Father.

*William Temple*

**926** O God, the physician of men and nations, the restorer of the years that have been destroyed: look upon the distractions of the world, and be pleased to complete the work of thy healing hand; draw all men unto thee and one to another by the bands of thy love; make thy Church one, and fill it with thy Spirit, that by thy power it may unite the world in a sacred brotherhood of nations, wherein justice, mercy and faith, truth and freedom may flourish, and thou mayst be ever glorified; through Jesus Christ our Lord.

*Acts of Devotion*

**927** O Thou who art the light of the world, the desire of all nations, and the shepherd of our souls: let thy light shine in the darkness, that all the ends of the earth may see the salvation of our God; by the lifting up of thy cross gather the peoples to thine obedience, to whom alone belongeth the sceptre and the crown; let thy sheep hear thy voice and be brought home to thy fold; so that there may be one flock, one shepherd; one holy kingdom of righteousness and peace; one God and Father of us all, above all, and through all, and in all.

*William E. Orchard*

**928** O God, whose will it is that all your children should be one in Christ; we pray for the unity of your Church. Pardon all our pride and our lack of faith, of understanding and of charity, which are the causes of our divisions. Deliver us from narrow-mindedness, from our bitterness, from our prejudices. Save us from considering as normal that which is a scandal to the world and an offence to your love. Teach us to recognise the gifts of grace among all those who call upon you and confess the faith of Jesus Christ our Lord.

*Liturgy of the French Reformed Church*

**929** O God the Father, Origin of Divinity, Good that is beyond all that is good, Fair beyond all that is fair, in whom is calmness, peace and concord; do thou make up the dissensions which divide us from each other, and bring us back to a unity of love, which may bear some likeness to thy divine nature. And as

thou art above all things, make us one by the unanimity of a
good mind, that through the embrace of charity and the bonds
of affection, we may be spiritually one, as well in ourselves as
in each other; through that peace of thine which maketh all
things peaceful, and through the grace, the mercy, and
tenderness of thy Son, Jesus Christ.

*Dionysius Telmaharensis*

**930** Eternal God, look mercifully upon the broken body of thy
Church. Draw its members unto thee and one to another by
the bands of thy love; that its restored unity may bring healing
to the nations, and the life of mankind may glorify thee;
through Jesus Christ our Lord.

*New Every Morning*

**931** Jesus, Saviour of human activity to which You have given
meaning, Saviour of human suffering to which You have given
living value, be also the Saviour of human unity; compel us to
discard our pettinesses, and to venture forth, resting upon
You, into the undaunted ocean of charity.

*Teilhard de Chardin*

**932** O Christ, may all that is part of today's encounter be born of
the Spirit of truth and be made fruitful through love.
Behold before us: the past and the future.
Behold before us: the desires of so many hearts.
You, who are the Lord of history and the Lord of human
hearts, be with us. Christ Jesus, eternal Son of God, be
with us. Amen

*Prayed by Pope John Paul II in Canterbury
Cathedral, 29th June 1982*

# FOR THE GOVERNMENT

**933** Sovereign Lord of men and nations, we pray for rulers and
statesmen who are called to leadership among their fellow
countrymen; give them vision to see far into the issues of their
time, courage to uphold what they believe to be right, and
integrity in their words and motives; and may their service to
their people promote the welfare and peace of mankind;
through Jesus Christ our Lord.

*Basil Naylor*

**934** Almighty God, who hast given us this good land for our heritage, we humbly beseech thee to bless us with honourable industry, sound learning, and good manners. Save us from violence, discord, and confusion; from pride and arrogance and every evil way. Defend our liberties, preserve our unity. Endue with the spirit of wisdom, prudence, and fortitude our rulers and all those entrusted with the authority in government. May there be justice and peace at home, and obedience to thy law among the nations of the earth; through Jesus Christ our Lord.

*Acts of Devotion*

**935** O God, almighty Father, King of kings and Lord of lords, grant that the hearts and minds of all who go out as leaders before us, the statesmen, the judges, the men of learning and the men of wealth, may be so filled with the love of thy laws, and of that which is righteous and life-giving, that they may be worthy stewards of thy good and perfect gifts; through Jesus Christ our Lord.

*Knights of the Garter Prayer*

**936** Grant and continue unto us a succession of legislators and rulers who have been taught the wisdom of the kingdom of Christ. Endow all members of Parliament with a right understanding, a pure purpose, and sound speech; enable them to rise above all self-seeking and party zeal into the larger sentiments of public good and human brotherhood. Purge our political life of every evil; subdue in the nation all unhallowed thirst for conquest or vainglory. Inspire us with calmness and self-restraint and the endeavour to get thy will done everywhere upon the earth.

*John Hunter*

**937** O righteous Lord, that lovest righteousness, may thy Holy Spirit be with our rulers, with our sovereign and all in authority under her, that they may govern in thy faith and fear, striving to put down all that is evil and to encourage all that is good. Give thy spirit of wisdom to those who make our laws, grant that they may understand how great a work thou hast given them to do; that they may not do it lightly, but gravely and soberly, to the putting away of all wrong and oppression and to the advancement of the true welfare of thy people.

*Thomas Arnold*

**938** Almighty God, by whom alone kings reign and princes decree justice, and from whom alone cometh all counsel, wisdom, and understanding:

We, Thine unworthy servants, here gathered together in Thy name, do most humbly beseech Thee to send down the heavenly wisdom from above, to direct and guide us in all our consultations:

And grant that, we having Thy fear always before our eyes, and laying aside all private interests, prejudices, and partial affections, the result of all our counsels may be the glory of Thy blessed name, the maintenance of true religion and justice, and the safety, honour and happiness of the Queen, the public welfare, peace, and tranquillity of the realm, and the uniting and knitting together of the hearts of all persons and estates within the same in true Christian love and charity one towards another, through Jesus Christ our Lord and Saviour. Amen

*House of Commons Prayer*

**939** O let Thine enemies know that Thou hast received England . . . into Thine own protection. Set a wall about it, O Lord, and ever more mightily defend it. Let it be a comfort to the afflicted, a help to the oppressed, and a defence to Thy church and people persecuted abroad . . . Direct and go before our armies both by sea and land. Bless them and prosper them, and grant unto them Thy honourable success and victory.

*Queen Elizabeth I*
*(National Prayer at the time of the Armada)*

**940** O Lord God everlasting, Which reignest over the kingdoms of men . . . so teach me, I humbly beseech Thee, Thy word, and so strengthen me with Thy grace that I may feed Thy people with a faithful and a true heart, and rule them prudently with power. O Lord, Thou hast set me on high. My flesh is frail and weak. If I therefore at any time forget Thee, touch my heart, O Lord, that I may again remember Thee. If I swell against Thee, pluck me down in my own conceit . . . I acknowledge, O my King, without Thee my throne is unstable, my seat unsure, my kingdom tottering, my life uncertain. I see all things in this life subject to mutability, nothing to continue still at one stay . . . Create therefore in me, O Lord, a new heart, and so renew my spirit that Thy law may be my study. Thy truth my delight, Thy church my care, Thy people my crown, Thy righteousness my pleasure, Thy service my

government; so shall this my kingdom through Thee be
established with peace.

*Queen Elizabeth I*

**941** Grant, O Lord,
  that we may approach every question of foreign policy from
    the point of sight of our creed;
  that we may check in ourselves and in others every temper
    which makes for war, all ungenerous judgements, all
    presumptuous claims, all promptings of self-assertion, the
    growth of ignorance and passion;
  that we may endeavour to understand the needs, the
    feelings, the endowments, the traditional aspirations of
    other countries;
  that we may do gladly, unweariedly, patiently, what lies in us
    to remove suspicions and misunderstandings; that we may
    honour all men. Amen

*Brooke Foss Westcott*

## FOR SOCIETY

**942** O God, grant us a vision of our city, fair as she might be; a city
of justice, where none shall prey on others; a city of plenty,
where vice and poverty shall cease to fester; a city of brotherhood, where all success shall be founded on service, and
honour shall be given to nobleness alone; a city of peace,
where order shall not rest on force, but on the love of all for
the city, the great mother of the common life and weal. Hear
thou, O Lord, the silent prayer of all our hearts as we each
pledge our time and strength and thought to speed the day of
her coming beauty and righteousness. Amen

*Walter Rauschenbusch*

**943** Christ, look upon us in this city,
And keep our sympathy and pity
Fresh, and our faces heavenward;
Lest we grow hard.

*Thomas Ashe*

**944** We who stand in the world offer ourselves and our society
    for your blessed healing.
  We confess we have failed to love as you did.

We have been socially unjust, and our society is imperfect,
  fragmented, and sometimes sick to death.
Teach us your ways in the world and in this life which we
  share together.
Don't let us restrict you to a narrow ghetto labelled
  'religion', but lead us to worship you in the fulness of life
  as the lord of politics, economics and the arts.
Give us light to seek true morality, not in narrow legalisms
  but in sacrifice and open responsibility. Show us how to
  express our love for you in very specific, human service to
  other men.
Lord, change our hearts from hearts of stone to hearts of
  flesh, and let us give thanks to you for all of life.

*Malcolm Boyd*

**945** In the name of Jesus Christ, who was never in a hurry, we
pray, O God, that Thou wilt slow us down, for we know that
we live too fast. With all of eternity before us, make us take
time to live – time to get acquainted with Thee, time to enjoy
Thy blessings, and time to know each other.

*Peter Marshall*

# FOR ENEMIES

**946** Almighty God, have mercy on all that bear me evil will, and
would me harm, and their faults and mine together, by such
easy, tender, merciful means as Thine infinite wisdom can
divine, vouchsafe to amend and redress. Make us saved souls
in heaven together where we may ever live and love together
with Thee and Thy blessed saints, O glorious Trinity, for the
bitter passion of our sweet Saviour Christ.

*Thomas More*

**947** Merciful and loving Father, we beseech Thee most humbly,
  even with all our hearts, to pour out upon our enemies
  with bountiful hand, whatsoever things Thou knowest will
  do them good.
And chiefly a sound and uncorrupt mind so that they may
  know Thee and love Thee in true charity and with their
  whole heart, and love us, Thy children, for Thy sake.
Let not their first hating of us turn to their harm, seeing that
  we cannot do them good for want of ability.
Lord we desire their amendment and our own. Separate

them not from us by punishing them, but join and knit
them to us by Thy favourable dealing with them.
And seeing that we be all ordained to be citizens of one
everlasting City, let us begin to enter into that way here
already by mutual love which may bring us right forth
thither.

*Old English Prayer*

# FOR THE HOMELESS

**948** O God, who wouldst not that any should live without comfort
and hope, have compassion on the multitudes in our day who
have no homes, or who are overcrowded in wretched dwell-
ings. Bless and inspire those who are labouring for their good.
Stir the conscience of the whole nation, O Lord, and both
break the bonds of covetousness and make plain the way of
deliverance for the sake of Jesus Christ, our Saviour.

*Frank Colquhoun*

**949** O God, the Father of our Lord Jesus Christ, who in perfect
love for man chose to live as one who had nowhere to lay his
head; we pray for all who are homeless, all refugees, all who
must live in exile or in a strange land; grant them human
friendship in their need and loneliness, the chance of a new
beginning, and the courage to take it, and, above all, an
abiding faith in your sure love and care; through Jesus Christ
our Lord.

*Christian Aid*

# FOR THE HUNGRY

**950** Bless, O God, all who dedicate their powers today to the
making of peace in the world;
Bless all who give their training and experience to feed and
clothe and house the destitute;
Bless all who lend their energies and skills to teach
impoverished people to till their land, to water it, and
harvest it.
And give us all a lively concern for the underprivileged, and
show us practical ways of helping. For Christ's sake.
Amen

*Rita Snowden*

**951** As thou, Lord, hast lived for others
so may we for others live;
freely have thy gifts been granted,
freely may thy servants give.
Thine the gold and thine the silver,
thine the wealth of land and sea,
we but stewards of thy bounty,
held in solemn trust for thee.

*S. C. Lowry*

**952** O God our Father, in the name of him who gave bread to the
hungry we remember all who, through our human ignorance,
folly, selfishness and sin, are condemned to live in want; and
we pray that all endeavours for the overcoming of world
poverty and hunger may be so prospered that there may be
found food sufficient for all. We ask this through Jesus Christ
our Lord.

*Christian Aid*

**953** O Lord, who though thou wast rich yet for our sakes didst
become poor, and hast promised in thy holy gospel that
whatsoever is done to the least of thy brethren thou wilt
receive as done to thee: Give us grace, we humbly beseech
thee, to be ever willing and ready to minister, as thou enablest
us, to the needs of others, and to extend the blessings of thy
kingdom over all the world; to thy praise and glory, who art
God over all, blessed for ever.

*St Augustine of Hippo*

**954** Make us worthy, Lord, to serve our fellow men throughout
the world who live and die in poverty and hunger. Give them
through our hands this day their daily bread, and by our
understanding love, give peace and joy.

*Mother Teresa of Calcutta*

**955** O Merciful and loving Father, look in thy mercy, we pray
thee, on the many millions who are hungry in the world of
today and are at the mercy of disease. Grant that we who have
lived so comfortably and gently all our lives may have true
sympathy with them and do all in our power, as individuals
and as a nation, to help them to that abundant life which is thy
will for them; through Jesus Christ our Lord.

*George Appleton*

**956** O God, Father of the forsaken, the help of the weak, the supplier of the needy; who teachest us that love towards the race of man is the bond of perfectness, and the imitation of Thy blessed Self; open and touch our hearts that we may see and do, both for this world and that which is to come, the things which belong to our peace.

*Seventh Earl of Shaftesbury*

## FOR HELP IN LIFE'S DUTIES

**957** O Lord God, the Almighty who gives strength to the weak, conscious that I can do nothing without your help, I pray for your gracious assistance in all my duties. I come to you, Lord of all power and love, trusting completely that you will supply what is wanting in me. My God, may your grace be sufficient for me and always with me that I may do everything faithfully and well, through Jesus Christ. Amen

*Benjamin Jenks*

**958** Grant us, we beseech thee, O Lord, grace to follow thee whithersoever thou goest. In little daily duties to which thou callest us, bow down our wills to simple obedience, patience under pain or provocation, strict truthfulness of word or manner, humility and kindness. In great acts of duty or perfection, if thou shouldst call us to them, uplift us to sacrifice and heroic courage; that in all things, both small and great, we may be imitators of thy dear Son, even Jesus Christ our Lord.

*Christina Rossetti**

**959** Keep us, Lord, so awake in the duties of our calling that we may sleep in Thy peace and wake in Thy glory.

*John Donne*

**960** O Lord, my Maker and Protector, who hast graciously sent me into this world to work out my salvation, enable me to drive from me all such unquiet and perplexing thoughts as may mislead or hinder me in the practice of those duties which Thou hast required.

When I behold the works of thy hands, and consider the course of thy providence, give me grace always to remember that thy thoughts are not my thoughts, nor thy ways my ways.

And while it shall please thee for me to continue in this world, where much is to be done, and little to be known, teach me by thy Holy Spirit, to withdraw my mind from unprofitable and dangerous enquiries, from difficulties vainly curious, and doubts impossible to be solved.

Let me rejoice in the light which Thou hast imparted, let me serve Thee with active zeal and humble confidence, and wait with patient expectation for the time in which the soul which Thou receivest shall be satisfied with knowledge. Grant this, O Lord, for Jesus Christ's sake.

*Dr Johnson*

**961** O Eternal God, who hast created me to do the work of God after the manner of men, give me Thy grace that I may be a prudent spender of my time, so that I may be profitable to the Christian commonwealth; and by discharging all my duty, may glorify Thee.

*Jeremy Taylor*

# FOR TRUTH

**962** God almighty, Father of our Lord Jesus Christ, by the gift of your Spirit establish and ground us in your truth. Reveal to us what we do not know; perfect in us what is lacking; strengthen in us what we know; and keep us in your service without fault; through the same Jesus Christ our Lord.

*Clement of Rome*

**963** God of truth, who hast guided men in knowledge throughout the ages, and from whom every good thought cometh, help us in our study to use thy gifts of wisdom and knowledge. Let us read good books carefully, and listen to wise teaching humbly, that we may be led into all truth, and strengthened in all goodness of life, to the praise of thy holy Name.

*Rowland Williams*

**964** Almighty God, who hast sent the Spirit of truth unto us to guide us into all truth, so rule our lives by thy power, that we may be truthful in word, deed, and thought. O keep us, most merciful Saviour, with thy gracious protection, that no fear or hope may ever make us false in act or speech. Cast out from us whatsoever loveth or maketh a lie, and bring us all to the perfect freedom of thy truth; through Jesus Christ thy Son our Lord.

*Brooke Foss Westcott*

**965** We beseech thee, O God, the God of Truth
That what we know not of things we ought to know, thou
    wilt teach us.
That what we know of Truth, thou wilt keep us therein.
That what we are mistaken in, as men must be, thou wilt
    correct.
That at whatsoever truths we stumble, thou wilt yet establish
    us.
And from all things that are false and from all knowledge
    that would be hurtful, thou wilt evermore deliver us,
Through Jesus Christ our Lord. Amen

*St Fulgentius of Ruspe*

**966** Make our hearts to burn within us, O Christ, as we walk with Thee in the way and listen to Thy words; that we may go in the strength of Thy presence and Thy truth all our journey through, and at its end behold Thee, in the glory of the Eternal Trinity, God for ever and ever.

*Eric Milner-White*

# FOR FREEDOM

**967** O God, who has taught us that we are most truly free when we find our wills in thine; Help us to gain this liberty by continual surrender to thee, that we may walk in the way which thou hast ordained for us, and in doing thy will we may find our life.

*Gelasian Sacramentary*

**968** Set me free, Lord, from faith and hope in lesser things.
Set me free from commitment to my own blue-prints for my
    own future.
Set me free for faith and hope in you.
Set me free for commitment to your plans for my future.
Set me free to live and work and serve, building your future.
Set me free, Lord, to be a man.

*Rex Chapman*

**969** From all my lame defeats and oh! much more
From all the victories that I seemed to score;
From cleverness shot forth on thy behalf,
At which, while angels weep, the audience laugh;
From all my proofs of thy divinity,
Thou, who wouldst give no sign, deliver me.
Thoughts are but coins. Let me not trust instead
Of thee, their thin-worn image of thy head.
From all my thoughts, even from my thoughts of thee,
O thou fair silence, fall, and set me free.
Lord of the narrow gate and needle's eye,
Take from me all my trumpery, lest I die.

*C. S. Lewis*

**970** O Lord my God, I hope in Thee;
My dear Lord Jesus, set me free;
In chains, in pains,
I long for Thee.
On bended knee
I adore Thee, implore Thee
To set me free.

*Mary Queen of Scots*

**971** Lord, who alone art God, the gracious and merciful; who commandest them that love thy name to cast away all fear and care, and to lay their burden upon thee: Receive us under thy protection, and give us now and evermore that everlasting rest which thou hast promised to them that obey thy Word; through Jesus Christ our Lord.

*Primer of 1555*

**972** Our heavenly Father, we commend to your mercy those for whom life does not spell freedom: prisoners of conscience, the homeless and the handicapped, the sick in body and mind, the elderly who are confined to their homes, those who are enslaved by their passions, and those who are addicted to drugs. Grant that, whatever their outward circumstances, they may find inward freedom, through him who proclaimed release to captives, Jesus Christ our Saviour.

*John R. W. Stott*

**973** O Almighty God, eternal treasure of all good things, never let my desires of this world be greedy, nor my thoughts intemperate, nor my cares vexatious and distracting; but moderate, holy, subordinate to Thy will, the measure Thou hast appointed me.

*Jeremy Taylor*

**974** O my God, give me thy grace so that the things of this earth and things more naturally pleasing to me, may not be as close as thou art to me. Keep thou my eyes, my ears, my heart from clinging to the things of this world. Break my bonds, raise my heart. Keep my whole being fixed on thee. Let me never lose sight of thee; and while I gaze on thee, let my love of thee grow more and more every day.

*John Henry Newman*

## FOR PEACE

**975** O God of peace, who hast taught us that in returning and in rest we shall be saved, and in quietness and in confidence shall be our strength: by the might of thy spirit lift us, we pray thee, to thy presence, where we may be still and know that thou art God; through Jesus Christ our Lord.

*John W. Suter*

**976** O Lord, who art the shadow of a great rock in a weary land, who beholdest thy weak creatures, weary of labour, weary of pleasures, weary of heart from hope deferred, and weary of self. In thine abundant compassion and unutterable tenderness bring us we pray thee, unto thy rest, through Jesus Christ, thy Son, our Saviour.

*Christina Rossetti*

**977** Most loving Father, who willest us to give thanks for all things, to dread nothing but the loss of thee, and to cast all our care on thee who carest for us: preserve us from faithless fears and worldly anxieties, and grant that no clouds of this mortal life may hide us from the light of thy love which is immortal, and which thou hast manifested to us in thy Son, Jesus Christ our Lord.

*William Bright*

**978** To be there before you, Lord, that's all.
To shut the eyes of my body,
To shut the eyes of my soul,
And to be still and silent,

To expose myself to you who are there, exposed to me.
To be there before you, the Eternal Presence.
I am willing to feel nothing, Lord,
 to see nothing
 to hear nothing.
Empty of all ideas,
 of all images,
In the darkness.
Here I am, simply,
To meet you without obstacles,
In the silence of faith,
Before you, Lord.
But Lord, I am not alone
I can no longer be alone.
I am a crowd, Lord,
For men live within me.
I have met them,
They have come in,
They have settled down,
They have worried me,
They have tormented me,
They have devoured me.
And I have allowed it, Lord, that they might be nourished
 and refreshed.
I bring them to you, too, as I come before you.
I expose them to you in exposing myself to you.
Here I am,
Here they are,
Before you, Lord.

*Michel Quoist*

**979** O Lord, calm the waves of this heart; calm its tempest! Calm
thyself, O my soul, so that the divine can act in thee! Calm
thyself, O my soul, so that God is able to repose in thee, so
that his peace may cover thee! Yes, Father in heaven, often
have we found that the world cannot give us peace. O but
make us feel that thou art able to give peace; let us know the
truth of thy promise: that the whole world may not be able to
take away thy peace.

*Søren Kierkegaard*

**980** In peace, let us beseech the Lord
for the peace that is from above
and the salvation of our souls;

for the peace of the whole world
and of the holy churches of God
and of all men.
For our homes, that they may be holy,
and for all our pastors, teachers and governors;
for our city (township, village) and country
and all who dwell therein;
for all that travel by land, by air, by water;
for the sick and all who need your pity and protection.
On all, have mercy, and preserve all, O God, by your grace:
for to you, O Lord, is due glory, honour, and worship;
world without end.

*Liturgy of St John Chrysostom*

**981** Deep and silent and cool as a broad, still, tree-shaded river
Is the peace of thy presence, thou rest of our souls.
From the thousand problems of this our hurrying life
We turn, with silent joy, to plunge in thee,
To steep our souls in thy quiet depths
Where no clamour of earth disturbs our perfect content.
Thou art our home and refuge;
In thee we are safe and at peace:
Ever in the din and hurry of the world
We know that thou art near,
We know that close at hand – closer than our little life –
Floweth that silent river of thy presence and love.
In a moment we may be with thee and in thee,
In a moment be surrounded and soaked in thy peace:
In a moment, as this loud world clangs round us,
We may rest secure in the bliss of thine eternity.

*John S. Hoyland*

**982** Deep peace of the Running Wave to you.
Deep peace of the Flowing Air to you.
Deep peace of the Quiet Earth to you.
Deep peace of the Shining Stars to you.
Deep peace of the Son of Peace to you.

*Celtic Benediction*

**983** O Lord, whose way is perfect: Help us, we pray thee, always
to trust in thy goodness; that walking with thee in faith, and
following thee in all simplicity, we may possess quiet and
contented minds, and cast all our care on thee, because thou
carest for us; for the sake of Jesus Christ our Lord.

*Christina Rossetti*

**984** O my Lord, abide with me, I beseech Thee, and in Thee let my soul find rest, and let it delight itself in Thee, for what is there that can be compared with that peace which is in Thee, seeing that it passeth all understanding? Nothing can bring me any good if I lack Thy peace. And what can I lack if I have Thee, Who art all Good? I will rejoice in Thee, and Thou, I hope and pray most humbly, wilt disperse this cloud, and wilt show me the light of Thy will and wilt cause Thy peace and serenity to fill and gladden my heart. Truly the heart is ever restless, until it rest in Thee alone. Amen

*The Way of Eternal Life*

**985** O Lord God, my soul is sorrowful, sometimes, even unto tears; sometimes also my spirit is disquieted, by reason of impending sufferings. I long after the joy of thy peace, the peace of thy children I earnestly crave. If thou give peace, if thou pour into me holy joy, the soul of thy servant shall be full of melody, and shall become devout in thy praise. Amen

*Thomas à Kempis*

**986** O God, who art peace everlasting, whose chosen reward is the gift of peace, and who hast taught us that the peacemakers are thy children: Pour thy peace into our hearts, that everything discordant may utterly vanish, and all that makes for peace be loved and sought by us always: through Jesus Christ our Lord.

*Mozarabic Sacramentary*

**987** Hallowed be Thy name,
not mine,
thy kingdom come,
not mine,
Give us peace with Thee,
peace with men,
peace with ourselves,
And free us from all fear.

*Dag Hammarskjöld*

**988** Lord, make me an instrument of your peace;
where there is hatred let me sow love,
where there is injury let me sow pardon,
where there is doubt let me sow faith,
where there is despair let me give hope,
where there is darkness let me give light,
where there is sadness let me give joy.

O divine master, grant that I may
not try to be comforted but to comfort,
not try to be understood but to understand,
not try to be loved but to love.

Because it is in giving that we are received,
it is in forgiving that we are forgiven,
and it is in dying that we are born to eternal life.

*Unknown Source*
*(Attributed to St Francis of Assisi,*
*first appeared 1913)*

**989** Lead me from death
To life, from falsehood to truth.

Lead me from despair
To hope, from fear to trust.

Lead me from hate
To love, from war to peace.

Let peace fill our heart,
Our world, our universe.

*International Prayer for Peace*

**990** We beseech thee to teach mankind to live together in peace;
no man exploiting the weak, no man hating the strong, each
race working out its own destiny, unfettered, self-respecting,
fearless.

Teach us to be worthy of freedom, free from social wrong,
free from individual oppression and contempt, pure of heart
and hand, despising none, defrauding none, giving to all
men – in all dealings of life – the honour we owe to those who
are thy children, whatever their colour, their race or their
caste.

*John S. Hoyland*

**991** God, I am travelling out to death's sea,
I, who exulted in sunshine and laughter,
Thought not of dying – death is such waste of me! –
Grant me one prayer: Doom not the hereafter
Of mankind to war, as though I had died not –
I, who in battle, my comrade's arm linking,
Shouted and sang – life in my pulses hot
Throbbing and dancing! Let not my sinking
In dark be for naught, my death a vain thing!

God, let me know it the end of man's fever!
Make my last breath a bugle call, carrying
Peace o'er the valleys and cold hills for ever!

*John Galsworthy*

992 God, the king of righteousness, lead us, we pray, in ways of
justice and peace; inspire us to break down all tyranny and
oppression, to gain for every man his due reward, and from
every man his due service; that each may live for all, and all
may care for each, in the name of Jesus Christ our Lord.

*William Temple**

993 Give us courage, O Lord, to stand up and be counted,
to stand up for those who cannot stand up for themselves,
to stand up for ourselves when it is needful for us to do so.
Let us fear nothing more than we fear you.
Let us love nothing more than we love you,
for thus we shall fear nothing also.
Let us have no other God before you,
whether nation or party or state or church.
Let us seek no other peace but the peace which is yours,
and make us its instruments,
opening our eyes and our ears and our hearts,
so that we should know always what work of peace we may
do for you.

*Alan Paton*

994 Almighty God, from whom all thoughts of truth and peace
proceed, kindle, we pray thee, in the hearts of all men the true
love of peace; and guide with thy pure and peaceable wisdom
those who take counsel for the nations of the earth; that in
tranquillity thy kingdom may go forward, till the earth be
filled with the knowledge of thy love: through Jesus Christ our
Lord.

*Francis Paget*

## FOR RECONCILIATION

995 O God the Father of all
you ask every one of us to spread
love where the poor are humiliated
joy where the church is brought low

and reconciliation where people are divided
father against son, mother against daughter,
husband against wife,
believers against those who cannot believe,
Christians against their unloved fellow Christians.
You open this way for us,
so that the wounded body of Jesus Christ, your church,
may be leaven of communion for the poor of the earth
and in the whole human family.

*Brother Roger of Taizé and*
*Mother Teresa of Calcutta*

**996** Heavenly Father, who hast reconciled us to thyself through
the cross of thy Son, and hast committed to us the ministry of
reconciliation: Grant that we who bear witness to thy reconciling word with our lips may also demonstrate thy reconciling
power in our lives; through the same, thy Son Jesus Christ our
Lord.

*Frank Colquhoun*

**997** May I be no man's enemy, and may I be the friend of that
which is eternal and abides.
May I never quarrel with those nearest me; and if I do, may I
be reconciled quickly.
May I love, seek, and attain only that which is good.
May I wish for all men's happiness and envy none.
May I never rejoice in the ill-fortune of one who has
wronged me.
May I win no victory that harms either me or my opponent.
May I reconcile friends who are angry with one another.
May I, to the extent of my power, give all needful help to my
friends and all who are in want.
May I never fail a friend who is in danger.
May I respect myself.

*Eusebius of Caesarea*

## FOR RACIAL HARMONY

**998** Grant us, O Lord, to see in our coloured countrymen, our
nearest neighbours to love as ourselves, equally with us the
brothers and sisters for whom Christ was born. Give us grace
to welcome them into our national life, to help them to find a

satisfactory place in it, and to receive from them gifts which we may have lost. Save us from racial pride, colour prejudice, personal indifference, and desire for apartness. And grant that we may all become a new race in Christ Jesus, the Lord and Saviour of all, born as a stranger far from home.

*George Appleton*

**999** God, the Father of mankind, who in your great love made all the peoples of the world to be one family; help those of different races and religions to love, understand and accept one another. Take away all hatred, jealousy and prejudice so that all may work together for the coming of your kingdom of righteousness and peace; through Jesus Christ our Lord.

*Evelyn Underhill\**

**1000** I see white and black, Lord
I see white teeth in a black face,
I see black eyes in a white face.
Help me to see persons, Jesus, not a black person,
or a white person, a red person or a yellow person,
but human persons.

*Malcolm Boyd*

**1001** O God, who hast made of one blood all nations to dwell upon the face of the earth, and who by thy Son Jesus Christ hast broken down the wall of partition between the races of men: Break down, we beseech thee, all that divides us one from another. Shame our jealousies and lay low our pride; do away with all race-prejudice, that the bonds of fellowship and mutual service may unite all peoples, and we may live in peace together, to the glory of thy great name; through the same Jesus Christ our Lord.

*G. C. Binyon\**

# FOR COURAGE

**1002** Make us, O blessed Master, strong in heart, full of courage, fearless of danger, holding pain and danger cheap when they lie in the path of duty. May we be strengthened with all might by thy Spirit in our hearts.

*F. B. Meyer*

**1003** O Lord and heavenly Father, be unto us this day, we beseech thee, our refuge and our strength. Mark out the path in life in which we shall walk. Shield us from danger on the right hand and on the left. And grant us, of thy good grace, both nerve and courage, that we may not shrink from needful conflict but in every encounter may have victory over evil. Let thy mercy rest this day upon the homes from which we come and upon the country to which we belong, and upon all the nations of the earth; through Jesus Christ our Lord.

*H. Bisseker*

**1004** God grant me the courage to change the things I can change, the serenity to accept those I cannot change, and the wisdom to know the difference – but God grant me the courage not to give up on what I think is right even though I think it is hopeless. Amen

*Chester W. Nimitz*
*(based upon Niebuhr's prayer)*

**1005** Almighty God, give us grace to contend always for what is true and right, and to be ready if need be to suffer for it. Give us not over to any death of the soul, but rather lift us into newness of life, and let us glorify and enjoy thee for ever; through Jesus Christ our Lord.

*Book of Prayers for Students*

**1006** Take from us, O Lord God, all pride and vanity, all boasting and self-assertion, and give us the true courage that shows itself in gentleness; the true wisdom that shows itself in simplicity; and the true power that shows itself in modesty; through Jesus Christ our Lord.

*Charles Kingsley*

**1007** Lord Jesus Christ, light shining in our darkness; have mercy on our tired and doubting hearts. Renew in us the courage we need, to bring to completion the work your calling has begun in us.

*Taizé prayer*

**1008** Lord and King, we pray thee for courage to face unpopularity for the sake of truth; for courage to declare boldly our convictions, though they make us despised; for courage to break with evil custom and evil opinions. Give us strong hearts that will not fear what any man may do to us. Give us, O

Lord, the spirit of boldness, that being delivered from all fears of our fellows, we may be strong in thee, and very courageous.

*John S. Hoyland*

1009 Help me, O Lord, so to strive and so to act, that those things which cloud my own way may not darken the path which others have to tread. Give me unselfish courage so that I am ready always to share my bread and wine yet able to hide my hunger and my thirst.

*Leslie D. Weatherhead*

## FOR HUMILITY

1010 O God, who by the example of your Son, our Saviour Jesus Christ, has taught us the greatness of true humility, and dost call us to watch with him in his passion. Give us the grace to serve one another in all lowliness, and to enter into the fellowship of his sufferings; who lives and reigns with you and the Holy Spirit, one God, world without end.

*William E. Orchard*

1011 Teach my endeavours so Thy works to read,
That learning them, in Thee I may proceed.
Give Thou my reason that instructive flight,
Whose weary wings may on Thy hands still light.
Teach me to soar aloft, yet ever so
When near the Sun, to stoop again below.
Thus shall my humble Feathers safely hover,
And, though near Earth, more than the Heavens discover.

*Sir Thomas Browne*

1012 O Lord, who made me and gave me so many gifts, both of soul and body and personal ability, I beseech thee, give me grace to use all of them in thy service to the end for which thou gavest them to me that, through thy gifts, I may worship thee. Grant me grace to be always modest about my talents, to be content with, and never presumptuous of thy gifts, but ever acknowledge myself for what I am, a sinful creature.

*Richard Rolle*

1013 O Lord God, we pray thee to keep us from all self-confidence and vainglory, and to bestow upon us thy great grace of humility and self-forgetfulness: To thee may we look up, in all that we do, alike for the will and for the power; and to thee may we ascribe with a sincere heart all the praise; through Jesus Christ our Lord.

*Charles J. Vaughan*

**1014** O Lord Jesus Christ, in all the fullness of thy power most gentle, in thine exceeding greatness most humble: Bestow thy mind and spirit upon us, who have nothing whereof to boast; that clothed in true humility, we may be exalted to true greatness. Grant this, O Lord, who livest and reignest with the Father and the Spirit, one God for evermore.

*Primer of 1559\**

# FOR SINCERITY

**1015** Grant, Lord, that what we have said with our lips we may believe in our hearts and practise in our lives; and of thy mercy keep us faithful unto the end.

*John Hunter*

**1016** Lift up our hearts, we beseech thee, O Christ, above the false show of things, above fear, above laziness, above selfishness and covetousness, above custom and fashion, up to the everlasting truth and order that thou art; that so we may live joyfully and freely, in faithful trust that thou art our Saviour, our example, and our friend, both now and for evermore.

*Charles Kingsley*

**1017** O Lord, the Lord whose ways are right, keep us in Thy mercy from lip-service and empty forms; from having a name that we live, but being dead.

Help us to worship Thee by righteous deeds and lives of holiness; that our prayer also may be set forth in Thy sight as the incense, and the lifting up of our hands be as an evening sacrifice.

*Christina Rossetti*

# FOR PATIENCE AND PERSEVERANCE

**1018** Grant me strength, merciful Father, that I may suffer and endure; patience alone I ask. Lord, give me this, and behold my heart is ready. O God, my heart is ready to receive whatsoever shall be laid upon me. Grant that in my patience I may possess my soul; to that end, may I often look upon the face of Christ Thy Son, that, as He hath suffered such terrible things in the flesh, I may endeavour to be armed with the same mind. I commit my strength unto Thee, O Lord; for Thou art my Strength and my Refuge. Amen

*Treasury of Devotion*

**1019** When many are coming and going and there is little leisure, give us grace, O heavenly Father, to follow the example of our Lord Jesus Christ, who knew neither impatience of spirit nor confusion of work, but in the midst of his labours held communion with thee, and even upon earth was still in heaven; where he now reigneth with thee and the Holy Spirit world without end.

*Charles J. Vaughan*

**1020** O God, who makest cheerfulness the companion of strength, but apt to take wings in time of sorrow, we humbly beseech thee that if, in thy sovereign wisdom, thou sendest weakness, yet for thy mercy's sake deny us not the comfort of patience. Lay not more upon us, O heavenly Father, than thou wilt enable us to bear; and, since the fretfulness of our spirit is more hurtful than the heaviness of our burden, grant us that heavenly calmness which comes of owning thy hand in all things, and patience in the trust that thou doest all things well. Amen

*Rowland Williams*

**1021** Help us this day, O God, to run with patience the race that is set before us. May neither opposition without nor discouragement within divert us from our goal. Inspire in us both strength of mind and steadfastness of purpose, that we may meet all fears and difficulties with unswerving courage, and may fulfil with quiet fidelity the tasks committed to our charge, through Jesus Christ our Lord.

*H. Bisseker*

**1022** O God, who hast in thy great wisdom prepared for each one of us our task to do for thee, give us, we beseech thee, honesty and patience, that we may seek to know thy will for ourselves, and may dedicate our lives to serve thee where we are needed. Enlighten the perplexed, strengthen the faint-hearted, rouse the indifferent, and kindle in us all the fire of true devotion; through Jesus Christ our Lord.

*Book of Prayers for Students*

**1023** Give us, O God, the power to go on,
To carry our share of Thy burden through to the end,
To live all the years of our life
Faithful to the highest we have seen,
With no pandering to the second best,
No leniency to our own lower selves;
No looking backward,
No cowardice. Give us the power to give ourselves,
To break the bread of our lives unto starving humanity;
In humble self-subjection to serve others,
As Thou, O God, dost serve Thy world. Amen

*John S. Hoyland*

**1024** O Lord God, when thou givest to thy servants to endeavour any great matter, grant us also to know that it is not the beginning, but the continuing of the same to the end, until it be thoroughly finished, which yieldeth the true glory; through him who for the finishing of thy work laid down his life, our Redeemer, Jesus Christ.

*Sir Francis Drake*

**1025** O God, give us patience when those who are wicked hurt us. O how impatient and angry we are when we think ourselves unjustly slandered, reviled and hurt! Christ suffers blows upon his cheek, the innocent for the guilty; yet we may not abide one rough word for his sake. O Lord, grant us virtue and patience, power and strength, that we may take all adversity with good will, and with a gentle mind overcome it. And if necessity and your honour require us to speak, grant that we may do so with meekness and patience, that the truth and your glory may be defended, and our patience and steadfast continuance perceived.

*Miles Coverdale*

**1026** O God our Father, let us not be content to wait and see what will happen, but give us the determination to make the right things happen.

While time is running out, save us from patience which is akin to cowardice.

Give us the courage to be either hot or cold, to stand for something, lest we fall for anything. In Jesus' name. Amen

*Peter Marshall*

**1027** O Lord, our God, grant us, we beseech you, patience in troubles, humility in comforts, constancy in temptations, and victory over all our spiritual foes. Grant us sorrow for our sins, thankfulness for your benefits, fear of your judgment, love of your mercies, and mindfulness of your presence; now and for ever.

*John Cosin*

**1028** To me, Lord Jesus, thou art the model of patience and its reward. Urgently thou dost ask it of me, and powerfully grant it. Thy own example strengthens me in every conflict, and the reward of my endurance is the royal gift of thy presence. Either way, thou dost in a wonderful way win me to thyself, as it were, compelling me. Beckon me on, then; gladly will I follow, and yet more gladly take joy in thy presence; for if thou art so good to those who seek, what wilt thou not be to those who find?

*St Bernard of Clairvaux*

**1029** Lord, Who hast suffered all for me
My peace and pardon to procure,
The lighter cross I bear for Thee,
Help me with patience to endure!

*William Cowper*

**1030** O Holy Spirit,
give me faith that will protect me
from despair, from passions, and from vice;
Give me such love for God and men
as will blot out all hatred and bitterness;
Give me the hope that will deliver me
from fear and faint-heartedness.
O holy and merciful God,
my Creator and Redeemer,
my Judge and Saviour,

thou knowest me and all that I do.
Thou dost hate and punish evil without respect of persons
in this world and the next;
Thou forgivest the sins of those
who sincerely pray for forgiveness;
Thou lovest goodness, and rewardest it on this earth
with a clear conscience,
and, in the world to come,
with a crown of righteousness.
I remember in thy presence all my loved ones,
my fellow-prisoners, and all who in this house
perform their hard service;
Lord, have mercy.
Restore me to liberty
and enable me to so live now
that I may answer before thee and before men.
Lord, whatever this day may bring,
thy name be praised. Amen

*Dietrich Bonhoeffer*

## FOR HELP IN TEMPTATION

1031 Lord, help us in times of temptation. May nothing induce us to distrust your care of us, nor use your gifts, denying knowledge of you as their Giver. May we never presume upon your protection, or be disloyal to your service. So support us, we pray, that when we have been tried and tested we may receive the crown of life, which you have prepared for those that love you. Amen

*Henry Alford*

1032 O Father, calm the turbulence of our passions; quiet the throbbing of our hopes; repress the waywardness of our wills; direct the motions of our affections; and sanctify the varieties of our lot.

Be Thou all in all to us; and may all things earthly, while we bend them to our growth in grace, and to the work of blessing, dwell lightly in our hearts, so that we may readily, or even joyfully, give up whatever Thou dost ask for.

May we seek first Thy kingdom and righteousness; resting assured that then all things needful shall be added unto us.

Father, pardon our past ingratitude and disobedience; and purify us, whether by Thy gentler or Thy sterner dealings, till we have done Thy will on earth, and Thou removest us to Thine own presence with the redeemed in heaven.

*Mary Carpenter*

1033 O God, we ask thee not to lift us out of life, but to prove thy power within it; not for tasks more suited to our strength, but for strength more suited to our tasks. Give us the vision that moves, the strength that endures, the grace of Jesus Christ, who wore our flesh like a monarch's robe, and walked our earthly life like a conqueror in triumph; we ask it for his sake.

*William E. Orchard*

1034 O Lord, grant us grace never to parley with temptation, never to tamper with conscience; never to spare the right eye, or hand, or foot that is a snare to us; never to lose our souls, though in exchange we should gain the whole world.

*Christina Rossetti*

1035 Let us beg the Lord with all our hearts that we may fight for the truth body and soul to the very end. If circumstances arise that put our faith to the test, and even if persecution breaks out, may he find us ready. Otherwise, our houses might fall in that winter; the building might be blown down by the storms, as though it had been built on sand.

When the Devil, the worst of the wicked spirits, blows with his winds, may our conduct stand up to him, as it has until now – unless it has been covertly undermined – and by preparing ourselves for the campaign, may we show what love we have for God and Christ Jesus, to whom glory and power belong and will belong for ever and ever. Amen

*Origen*

1036 Lord God Almighty, strengthen me against the temptations of the devil, and put far from me every unrighteousness. Shield me against my foes, seen and unseen; and teach me to do Thy will, that I may inwardly love Thee before all things with a clean mind and a clean body. For Thou art my maker and redeemer, my help, my comfort, my trust and my hope. Praise and glory be to Thee, now, ever and ever, world without end. Amen

*King Alfred**

**1037** Almighty and most merciful Father give us, we pray, the grace to examine our inmost hearts and our secret thoughts. May we never be drawn to do anything to dishonour your name; may we, on the contrary, persevere in all good purposes, and in your faithful service.

*George Hickes*

**1038** Remember, O Lord, of what I am made, that I am but human. Take pity on my weakness, support my frail nature. Thou knowest the temptations I suffer, how they surge within me, and the storms they raise in me. Thou knowest well.

*St Isidore*

**1039** O Christ, do not abandon me in the midst of this world,
for I love you alone, even if as yet I have not known you;
I look to you alone for strength to keep your precepts;
I, who am completely in the power of my passions; I, who do
   not know you;
would the one who has known you seek the pleasures of the
   world?
Would the one who loves you search out other pleasures?
Or feel the urge to seek another friend?
God, creator of the universe, giver of all that is good in me,
in your kindness have compassion on my poor soul;
give me the gift of true discernment, that I may be drawn
by the treasures of eternity and only those.
I will love you with my whole heart, seeking only your glory,
not that which comes from man,
so that I may become entirely one with you
even now, and after death, thus attaining,
O Christ, to reign with you,
who for my sake accepted the most infamous of deaths.
Then I will be the happiest among all men.
Amen, so be it, O Lord, now and for all ages.

*Simeon, the New Theologian*

**1040** Good Jesu, God's Son, knower of all things, help me in wicked thoughts, that I displease Thee not. Courteous Jesu, when Thy will is, put them away and take me to Thy grace.

Jesu Christ, God's Son, who stood still before the judge nothing answering, withdraw my tongue till I think what and how I shall speak that may be to Thy worship.

Jesu Christ, God's Son, whose hands were bound for my love full sore, govern and teach mine hands and all mine other limbs that all my works may begin and graciously end to Thy most pleasing.

*Priest's Prayer*

**1041** Lord Jesus, you were a man; you had my eyes, my ears, my sense of touch and smell; you know my feelings of body and heart; you were like me in everything – except sin. But, Lord, were you never tempted by human beauty, the beauty you had created? Surely, anyhow, you understand how I feel now. How I long for what I should not have! Tempted as I am, help me not to sin.

*Michael Hollings*

**1042** O Lord, who alone canst cast out the evil passions and desires of the soul: Come among us, we pray thee, and by thy mighty power subdue our spiritual enemies, and set us free from the tyranny of sin. We ask it in thy name and for thy glory.

*Henry Alford*

**1043** Blessed Lord, who wast tempted in all things like as we are, have mercy on our frailty. Out of weakness give us strength. Grant to us thy fear that we may fear thee only. Support us in time of temptation. Embolden us in time of danger. Help us to do thy work with good courage, and to continue thy faithful soldiers and servants unto our life's end. Amen

*Brooke Foss Westcott*

# VIII  OCCASIONAL PRAYERS

## AT THE NEW YEAR

**1044**  O Lord Christ, who art both Alpha and Omega, the beginning and the end, and whose years shall not fail: Grant us so to pass through the coming year with faithful hearts, that in all things we may please thee and glorify thy name; who livest and reignest with the Father and the Holy Ghost, ever one God, world without end.

*Mozarabic Sacramentary**

**1045**  O Lord God of time and eternity, who makest us creatures of time that, when time is over, we may attain thy blessed eternity: With time, thy gift, give us also wisdom to redeem the time, lest our day of grace be lost; for our Lord Jesus' sake.

*Christina Rossetti*

**1046**  O Thou whose patient ways with us and whose unfailing love for us, surprise and humble us, go with us along the unknown paths of this New Year. Forgive the sins of the year that has gone; keeping near to Thee may we do better; live more worthily and serve more faithfully, so that our lives may show forth a new beauty and a deeper harmony and Thy holy name be glorified. Through Jesus Christ our Lord. Amen

*Leslie D. Weatherhead*

**1047**  Grant, O Lord, that as the years change, we may find rest in your eternal changelessness. May we meet this new year bravely, sure in the faith that, while men come and go, and life changes around us, you are always the same, guiding us with your wisdom, and protecting us with your love; through our Saviour Jesus Christ.

*William Temple**

**1048**  Eternal God, who makest all things new, and abidest for ever the same: grant us to begin this year in thy faith, and to continue it in thy favour; that, being guided in all our doings, and guarded all our days, we may spend our lives in thy service, and finally, by thy grace, attain the glory of everlasting life; through Jesus Christ our Lord.

*William E. Orchard*

**1049** Father,
We pray thee for the vision which sees beyond the things of
    time and sense.
Beyond the vain attractions of this world, where we abide for
    but a few days,
To the eternal realities –
To the deathless truth and beauty of love
For whose sake Thou hast given us being.

*John S. Hoyland*

# BEFORE WORSHIP

**1050** Almighty God, from whom every good prayer cometh, deliver us, when we draw nigh to thee, from coldness of heart and wanderings of mind, that with steadfast thought and kindled desire we may worship thee in the faith and spirit of Jesus Christ our Lord.

*William Bright*

**1051** Almighty God, the fountain of all wisdom, who knowest our necessities before we ask, and our ignorance in asking: we beseech thee to have compassion upon our infirmities; and those things, which for our unworthiness we dare not, and for our blindness we cannot ask, vouchsafe to give us, for the worthiness of thy Son, Jesus Christ our Lord.

*Book of Common Prayer, 1549*

**1052** O Lord, our God, great, eternal, wonderful in glory, who keepest thy promise for those that love thee with their whole heart, the life of all who love thee, the help of those that flee unto thee, the hope of those who cry unto thee: cleanse from sin, and from every thought displeasing to thee, our souls and bodies, our hearts and consciences, that with a pure heart and a clear mind, with perfect love and calm hope, we may venture confidently and fearlessly to pray unto thee.

*Fourth-century Prayer*

**1053** Almighty God, the Father of our Lord Jesus Christ, and our Father: help us as we seek through our prayers to draw near unto thee; to bow our wills to thine, and to yield our spirits to the influence of thy Holy Spirit. Help us as we would worship thine eternal goodness; meditate on the unwearied mercy of which we are constant partakers; confess our shortcomings and sins, and give ourselves up to be led by thee in the ways of purity and peace.

*John Hunter*

**1054** Eternal God, we come, we come again,
seeking, hoping, wanting to hear your word.

We come because, despite our best efforts,
we have failed to live by bread alone.

We come impelled by a desire too deep for words,
with longings that are too infinite to express.

We come yearning for meaning in our existence
and purpose for our life.

We come acknowledging our need for each other's
affirmation and encouragement, understanding and love.

We come confessing our dependence on you.
Lord, embrace us with your forgiveness, and claim us
by the mystery and depths of your love. Amen

*Terry Falla*

**1055** O heavenly Father, forasmuch as none can come to receive thy word, except thou draw them by thy gracious inspiration, we beseech thee to pour out thy Holy Spirit upon those who worship today in thy house of prayer, that their hearts may be inclined favourably to receive, steadfastly to retain, and obediently to perform, whatsoever shall be taught them in thy Name; and that they may manifest, in the dedication to thee of their lives and substance, that thankfulness which they owe to thee for thy redeeming love; through Jesus Christ our Lord.

*Richard M. Benson*

**1056** Holy Spirit, you make alive;
bless also this our gathering,
the speaker and the hearer;
fresh from the heart it shall come,
by your aid,
let it also go to the heart.

*Søren Kierkegaard*

**1057** On thee we cast our care; we live
through thee, who know'st our every need:
O feed us with thy grace, and give
our souls this day the living bread. Amen

*John Wesley*

**1058** We thank Thee, our Father, for the life and knowledge which
Thou hast made known unto us through Jesus Thy Servant.
To Thee be glory for ever. As this broken bread, once
scattered upon the mountains, has been gathered together
and been made one, so may Thy Church be gathered together
from the ends of the earth into Thy Kingdom; for Thine is the
glory and the power through Jesus Christ for ever.

*Didache*

**1059** My God, and is thy table spread,
and does thy cup with love o'erflow?
Thither be all thy children led,
and let them all thy sweetness know.

Hail, sacred feast, which Jesus makes!
Rich banquet of his flesh and blood!
Thrice happy he, who here partakes
that sacred stream, that heavenly food.

O let thy table honoured be,
and furnished well with joyful guests;
and may each soul salvation see,
that here its sacred pledges tastes.

*Philip Dodderidge*

**1060** Draw nigh and take the body of the Lord,
and drink the holy blood for you outpoured.
Saved by that body and that holy blood,
with souls refreshed, we render thanks to God.
Mankind is ransomed from eternal loss
by flesh and blood offered upon the cross.
Salvation's giver, Christ, the only Son,
by his dear cross and blood the victory won.
Offered was he for greatest and for least,
himself the victim, and himself the priest.
Victims are offered by the law of old,
which in a type this heavenly mystery told.
He, ransomer from death, and light from shade,
now gives his holy grace his saints to aid.

Approach ye then with faithful hearts sincere,
and take the safeguard of salvation here.
He, that his saints in this world rules and shields,
to all believers life eternal yields;
With heavenly bread makes them that hunger whole,
gives living waters to the thirsting soul. Amen.

*Bangor Antiphonary*

**1061** Lord Jesus Christ,
I approach your banquet table
in fear and trembling,
for I am a sinner,
and dare not rely on my own worth,
but only on your goodness and mercy.
I am defiled by many sins in body and soul,
and by my unguarded thoughts and words.
Gracious God of majesty and awe,
I seek your protection,
I look for your healing.
Poor troubled sinner that I am,
I appeal to you, the fountain of all mercy.
I cannot bear your judgment,
but I trust in your salvation.
Lord, I show my wounds to you
and uncover my shame before you.
I know my sins are many and great,
and they fill me with fear,
but I hope in your mercies,
for they cannot be numbered.

Lord Jesus Christ, eternal king, God and man,
crucified for mankind,
look upon me with mercy and hear my prayer,
for I trust in you.
Have mercy on me,
full of sorrow and sin,
for the depth of your compassion never ends.
Praise to you, saving sacrifice,
offered on the wood of the cross for me and for all mankind.
Praise to the noble and precious blood,
flowing from the wounds of my crucified Lord Jesus Christ
and washing away the sins of the whole world.
Remember, Lord, your creature,
whom you have redeemed with your blood.
I repeat my sins,

and I long to put right what I have done.
Merciful Lord, take away all my offences and sins;
purify me in body and soul,
and make me worthy to taste the holy of holies.
May your body and blood,
which I intend to receive, although I am unworthy,
be for me the remission of my sins.

*St Ambrose of Milan*

1062 O God, who makest us glad with the weekly remembrance of
the glorious resurrection of thy Son our Lord, vouchsafe us
this day such a blessing through thy worship, that the days
which follow it may be spent in thy favour; through the same
Jesus Christ our Lord. Amen

*William Bright*

1063 O God, the world is so much with me, late and soon. Every
day brings its tasks, its trials, its temptations. I may sometimes
resent the rush and clamour of everyday life; but if the world
was suddenly to be stilled, to an unbroken and deathly silence,
I should be distressed far more.

I am glad, though, for the stillness of Sunday morning; for
the anticipation of the day's work and worship; for the chance
it will give of rich enjoyment, true recreation, of body, mind
and spirit; for the so welcome change from the everyday run of
things.

*Leonard Barnett*

# BEFORE READING THE BIBLE

1064 O Gracious God and most merciful Father, who hast vouchsafed us the rich and precious jewel of thy holy Word: Assist
us with thy Spirit that it may be written in our hearts to our
everlasting comfort, to reform us, to renew us according to
thine own image, to build us up into the perfect building of thy
Christ, and to increase us in all heavenly virtues. Grant this, O
heavenly Father, for the same Jesus Christ's sake.

*Geneva Bible, 1560*

1065 O Lord, you have given us your word for a light to shine upon
our path; grant us so to meditate on that word, and to follow
its teaching, that we may find in it the light that shines more

and more until the perfect day; through Jesus Christ our Lord.

*St Jerome*

**1066** Let us keep the Scriptures in mind and meditate upon them day and night, persevering in prayer, always on the watch. Let us beg the Lord to give us real knowledge of what we read and to show us not only how to understand it but how to put it into practice, so that we may deserve to obtain spiritual grace, enlightened by the law of the Holy Spirit, through Jesus Christ our Lord, whose power and glory will endure throughout the ages. Amen

*Origen*

**1067** All-seeing Father of Christ, hear these prayers. Let your servant hear the wonderful song of Scripture. Guide my feet along God's path; and may the royal Christ, who wards off ills from mortal man, lead me to the Father's will.

*St Gregory of Nazianzus*

**1068** Lord, who can grasp all the wealth of just one of your words? What we understand in the Bible is much less than what we leave behind, like thirsty people who drink from a fountain. For your word has many shades of meaning, just as those who study it have many different points of view. You have coloured your words with many hues so that each person who studies it can see in it what he loves. You have hidden many treasures in your word so that each of us is enriched as we meditate on it.

*Ephrem Syrus*

**1069** Let not thy Word, O Lord, become a judgment upon us, that we hear it and do it not, that we know it and love it not, that we believe it and obey it not: O thou, who with the Father and the Holy Spirit livest and reignest, world without end. Amen

*Thomas à Kempis*

**1070** Almighty, everlasting God, Lord, heavenly Father, whose Word is a lamp to our feet and a light on our way: Open and enlighten my mind that I may understand thy Word purely, clearly, and devoutly, and then, having understood it aright, fashion my life in accord with it, in order that I may never displease thy majesty; through Jesus Christ, thy Son, our dear

Lord, who liveth and reigneth with thee and the Holy Ghost, ever one God, world without end. Amen

*Johannes Bugenhagen*

**1071** Almighty and most merciful God, who hast given the Bible to be the revelation of thy great love to man, and of thy power and will to save him; grant that our study of it may not be made vain by the callousness or the carelessness of our hearts, but that by it we may be confirmed in penitence, lifted to hope, made strong for service, and, above all, filled with true knowledge of thee and of thy Son Jesus Christ.

*George Adam Smith*

**1072** O Lord, heavenly Father, in whom is the fullness of light and wisdom, enlighten our minds by your Holy Spirit, and give us grace to receive your Word with reverence and humility, without which no one can understand your truth. For Christ's sake. Amen

*John Calvin*

**1073** Blessed Lord, who hast caused all holy scriptures to be written for our learning: grant that we may in such wise hear, read, mark, learn, and inwardly digest them, that by patience and comfort of thy holy Word, we may embrace and ever hold fast the blessed hope of everlasting life, which thou hast given us in our Saviour Jesus Christ.

*Book of Common Prayer, 1549*

**1074** O Almighty God, we pray thee, sow the seed of thy Word in our hearts, and send down upon us thy heavenly grace; that we may bring forth the fruits of the Spirit, and at the great day of harvest may be gathered by thy holy angels into thy garner; through Jesus Christ our Lord.

*Canterbury Convocation, 1862*

**1075** Blessed Lord, by whose providence all holy scriptures were written and preserved for our instruction, give us grace to study them this and every day with patience and love. Strengthen our souls with the fullness of their divine teaching. Keep from us all pride and irreverence. Guide us in the deep things of thy heavenly wisdom, and of thy great mercy lead us by thy Word unto everlasting life; through Jesus Christ our Lord and Saviour.

*Brooke Foss Westcott*

**1076** Lord Jesus Christ, open the ears and eyes of my heart, that I may hear and understand thy Word and do thy will. I am a pilgrim on earth; hide not thy commandments from me. Take away the covering from mine eyes, that I may see wonderful things in thy law.

*Ephrem Syrus*

**1077** Eternal Light, shine into our hearts;
Eternal Goodness, deliver us from evil;
Eternal Power, be our support;
Eternal Wisdom, scatter the darkness of our ignorance;
Eternal Pity, have mercy upon us;
that with all our heart and mind and soul and strength we
   may seek thy face and be brought by thine infinite mercy
   to the holy presence; through Jesus Christ our Lord.

*Alcuin*

**1078** O Lord Jesus Christ, who art the Truth incarnate and the Teacher of the faithful; let thy Spirit overshadow us in the reading of thy Word, and conform our thoughts to thy revelation; that learning of thee with honest hearts, we may be rooted and built up in thee, who livest and reignest with the Father and the Holy Spirit, world without end.

*William Bright*

**1079** O God, we thank you on this day for the sacred scriptures; for the comfort the Bible has brought to the sorrowful, for guidance offered to the bewildered, for its gracious promises to the uncertain, for its strength given to the weak, and for its progressive revelation of yourself.

We thank you for the men of God who speak to us still from its pages, and for the men of God whose learning has made those pages live.

We thank you most of all that it reveals to us your Son, the Word made flesh.

Help us to ponder this record of your ways with men, that your Word may be indeed a lamp to our feet and a light to our path; through Jesus Christ our Lord.

*Leslie D. Weatherhead*

# BEFORE STUDY

**1080** God of Truth, who hast guided men in knowledge throughout the ages, and from whom every good thought cometh, help us in our study to use thy gifts of wisdom and knowledge. Let us read good books carefully, and listen to all wise teaching humbly that we may be led into all truth, and strengthened in all the goodness of life, to the praise of thy holy name. Amen

*Rowland Williams*

**1081** Grant us the knowledge that we need
To solve the questions of the mind;
Light Thou our candles while we read,
To keep our hearts from going blind;
Enlarge our vision to behold
The wonders Thou hast wrought of old;
Reveal Thyself in every law,
And gild the towers of truth with holy awe.

*Henry van Dyke*

**1082** O God, who hast ordained that whatever is to be desired, should be sought by labour, and who, by thy blessing, bringest honest labour to good effect, look with mercy upon my studies and endeavours. Grant me, O Lord, to desire only what is lawful and right; and afford me calmness of mind, and steadiness of purpose, that I may so do thy will in this short life, as to obtain happiness in the world to come; for the sake of Jesus Christ our Lord.

*Dr Johnson*

**1083** Almighty God, the giver of wisdom, without whose help resolutions are vain, without whose blessing study is ineffectual; enable me, if it be Thy will, to attain such knowledge as may qualify me to direct the doubtful, and instruct the ignorant; to prevent wrongs and terminate contentions; and grant that I may use that knowledge which I shall attain, to Thy glory and my own salvation, for Jesus Christ's sake.

*Dr Johnson*

**1084** Grant, Lord, to all students, to love that which is worth loving, to know that which is worth knowing, to praise that which pleases you most, to esteem that which is most precious to you, and to dislike that which is evil in your eyes. Grant that with true judgment they may distinguish between things that differ, and above all, may search out and do what is well-pleasing to you; through Jesus Christ our Lord.

*Thomas à Kempis*

**1085** Good Jesus, you have deigned to refresh our souls with the sweet streams of knowledge; grant that one day we may come to you, its source and spring.

*Alcuin*

**1086** Hear our prayers, Lord Jesus, the everlasting Wisdom of God the Father. You give us, in our youth, aptness to learn. Add, we pray, the furtherance of your grace, so to learn knowledge and the liberal sciences that, by their help, we may attain to a fuller knowledge of you, whom to know is the height of blessedness; and by the example of your boyhood, may duly increase in age, wisdom and favour with God and man.

*Erasmus*

**1087** I beseech thee, my God, very Truth, that what it is well for me to know and I do not know, this thou wouldst teach me. That what I rightly know thou wouldst keep in my memory. Where my human intellect may fail, do thou correct me. When I would hesitate in the truth, do thou strengthen me, and from all false and harmful ways of thought do thou protect me.

*St Fulgentius of Ruspe*

**1088** I pray Thee, good Jesus, that to him whom Thou hast graciously given to drink in with delight the words of Thy knowledge, Thou wouldest mercifully grant to come one day unto Thee, the fountain of all wisdom, and to appear for ever before Thy face.

*The Venerable Bede*

## DAILY WORK

**1089** O Lord, give me grace and strength to do thy will, to begin the day and to end it with prayer and searching of my own heart, and with reading of thy word. Make me to understand it, to understand thee; to bring home to my heart the reality of thy perfect Godhead and perfect humanity, and, above all, of my entire need of a Saviour; of my utter inability to do anything that is right by my own strength; make me humble, reasonable, contented, thankful, just, and considerate. Restrain my tongue and my thoughts; may I act as ever in thy sight, as if I may die this day. May I not fear man nor man's opinions, but remember that thou knowest my motives and my thoughts, and that thou wilt be my Judge. Let me do to-day's work as well as I can today; so living in humility, thankfulness, and contentment.

*Sir Henry Lawrence*

**1090** Lord, I desire that, at all times, those who profit by my labour may be not only refreshed in body, but may be also drawn to Thy love and strengthened in every good.

*St Gertrude and Mechthild of Magdeburg*

**1091** Take from me Lord, all slothfulness, and give me a diligent and active spirit, and wisdom to choose my employment, that I may do works suitable to my person, and to the dignity of a Christian. Fill up the spaces of my time with actions of religion and charity; that when the Devil assaults me, he may not find me idle, and my dearest Lord at His sudden coming may find me busy in lawful, necessary, and pious actions. May I improve my talent entrusted to me by Thee, my Lord; that I may enter into the joy of my Lord.

*Jeremy Taylor*

**1092** Teach me, my God and King
In all things thee to see;
And what I do in anything,
to do it as for thee.

All may of thee partake;
Nothing can be so mean,
which with this tincture 'for thy sake'
will not grow bright and clean.

A servant with this clause,
makes drudgery divine;
Who sweeps a room, as for thy laws,
makes that and the action fine.

*George Herbert*

**1093** Lord temper with tranquillity
Our manifold activity
That we may do our work for Thee
With very great simplicity.

*Sixteenth-century Prayer*

**1094** O Lord, renew our spirits and draw our hearts unto thyself, that our work may not be to us a burden, but a delight; and give us such a mighty love for thee as may sweeten all our obedience. Let us not serve thee with the spirit of bondage as slaves, but with cheerfulness and gladness, delighting ourselves in thee, and rejoicing in thy work, for the sake of Jesus Christ.

*Benjamin Jenks*

**1095** O Eternal God, Fountain of justice, mercy and benediction, who by my education and other effects of Thy Providence hast called me to this profession, that by hard work I may in some small proportion work together for the good of myself and others. I humbly beg Thy grace to guide me in my affairs, so that I may be diligent, just, and faithful; and give me Thy favour, that this my work may be accepted by Thee as part of my necessary duty. Be pleased to let Thy Holy Spirit be for ever present with me, that I may never be given to covetousness and sordid greed, to lying and falsehood, or any other base dishonesty; but give me prudence, honesty, and Christian sincerity. May my Trade be sanctified by my Religion, my labour by my intention and Thy blessing; that, when I have done my portion of work Thou hast allotted me, and improved the talent Thou hast entrusted to me, I may receive the reward of my high calling, which I expect and beg, in the portion and inheritance of the ever-blessed Saviour and Redeemer Jesus.

*Jeremy Taylor*

**1096** Lord, as we go to our work this day, help us to take pleasure therein. Show us clearly what our duty is, help us to be faithful in doing it. May all we do be well done, fit for thine eye to see. Give us enthusiasm to attempt, patience to perform. When we cannot love our work, may we think of it as thy task, and make what is unlovely beautiful through loving service; for thy Name's sake.

*George Dawson*

**1097** Lord, teach us to work with love, knowing that work is love made visible.

Teach us to weave the cloth with threads drawn from our heart, even as if you our beloved were to wear that cloth.

To build a house with affection, even as if you were to dwell in that house.

To sow seeds with tenderness and reap the harvest with joy,
   even as if you were to eat the fruit.

To charge all things we fashion with a breath of our own
   spirit,

And to know that all the blessed dead are standing about us
   and watching.

*Kahlil Gibran*

**1098** Lord, our attitude to work changes with our moods;
we are as variable as the weather.
Some days we enjoy every moment of our work;
other days we feel tired and resentful of it.
There are mornings when we dread the thought of getting
      up;
but there are also times when we go to work gladly.

Lord, some of us get paid for doing the things we enjoy;
others must work at distasteful tasks for their living.
Some of us work with kind and interesting people;
others must work with sour and ugly characters.
Some who long for company must work alone;
others who yearn for privacy must work with a crowd.

Lord, whether we work for love or pleasure,
or whether it is only for duty or money,
we thank you for the privilege of daily work,
for the rewards of labour in whatever form.
In a world where millions are unemployed,
we count ourselves as richly blessed.

As products of the work of a loving Creator,
we thank you for skills of eye, brain, and hand.
As friends of the carpenter's Son of Nazareth,
we offer to you our work as an act of praise.
As children of the Spirit who has never ceased to work,
we seek to honour you in everything we do.

*Bruce Prewer*

**1099** Lord Christ, you said to your disciples, 'My Father has
worked till now, and I work': we pray for those who through
no fault of their own have been deprived of the work that leads
towards the fulfilment of their lives.
   Inspire and guide those who bear the responsibility of
finding the answer to our industrial problems.

Open their minds to the truth, that they may discern in the
events of our time the direction of your will; and give them
the courage to declare what they believe to be right, and the
power to carry it through.

*Basil Naylor*

## GENERAL INTERCESSIONS

**1100** Almighty God, you have taught us to make prayers and
intercessions for all men:
We pray for the clergy, and for all who guide the thoughts of
the people; for artists, authors, musicians, and journalists;
that our common life may be crowned with truth and
beauty;
For all who heal the body, guard the health of the nation,
and tend the sick; that they may follow the footsteps of
Christ, the great physician;
For all on whose labour we depend for the necessities of life;
for all who carry on the commerce of the world, that they
may seek no private gain which would hinder the good of
all;
For parents and children; that purity, love, and honour may
dwell in our homes, and duty and affection may be the
bond of our family life;
For all who draw near to death, that they may know your
presence with them through the valley of the shadow and
may wake to the vision of your glory; through Jesus Christ
our Lord.

*John Hunter\**

**1101** Be mindful, O Lord, of thy people present here before thee,
and of those who are absent through age, sickness or infirmity.
Care for the infants, guide the young, support the aged,
encourage the faint-hearted, collect the scattered, and bring
the wandering to thy fold. Travel with the voyagers, defend
the widows, shield the orphans, deliver the captives, heal the
sick. Succour all who are in tribulation, necessity, or distress.
Remember for good all those that love us, and those that hate
us; and those that have desired us, unworthy as we are, to pray
for them. And those whom we have forgotten, do thou, O
Lord, remember. For thou art the Helper of the helpless, the
Saviour of the lost, the Refuge of the wanderer, the Healer of

the sick. Thou, who knowest each man's need, and hast heard his prayer, grant unto each according to thy merciful loving-kindness and thy eternal love; through Jesus Christ our Lord.

*Eastern Orthodox Prayer*

1102 God the Father, and the eternal High Priest Jesus Christ, build us up in faith and love, and grant us part among the saints with all those who believe in our Lord Jesus Christ. We pray for all Christian people, for rulers and leaders, for the enemies of the cross of Christ; and for ourselves we pray that our fruit may be abundant, and that we may be made perfect in Christ our Lord.

*Polycarp of Smyrna*

1103 O, You who are love, and see all the suffering, injustice, and misery, which reign in this world. Have pity, we implore you, on the work of your hands. Look mercifully on the poor, the oppressed, and all who are heavy laden with error, labour and sorrow. Fill our hearts with deep compassion for those who suffer, and hasten the coming of your kingdom of justice and truth.

*Eugène Bersier*

1104 O God, those whom we, through ignorance or forgetfulness have not remembered, do thou, remember them, who knowest the age and the name of each one, who knowest each from his mother's womb. For thou, O God, are the help of the helpless, the hope of the hopeless, the saviour of the tempest-tossed, the harbour of mariners, the physician of the sick. Be yourself all things to all men, who know each and his petition and his dwelling and his need.

*Coptic Liturgy of St Basil*

1105 Almighty God and Father, who hast taught us to offer prayer to thee for all men, help us now with brotherly kindness to remember the sorrows and sins of our lost world, so that with pitiful hearts we may make intercession with thee for our brothers and sisters of the whole human race.

Have mercy, O God, on all mankind; convert the heathen nations to the Cross of Christ; increase the liberality and holy living of Christian peoples; let Christ's kingdom come, and let us and ours be found in Him in that great day when He shall judge the World.

Defend, O Lord, by thy mighty power, and with thy counsel

guide all Christian kings and righteous rulers of men; especially our Sovereign and all who, under her, direct the order and administer the government of this great nation.

Bless with light and life from on high the whole Church of Christ; dispel darkness and superstition, worldliness and unbelief; unite all good men in loyalty to thee and love to one another and let the truth ever be more fully known and the Master more faithfully served.

Guard our homes from hurt and harm; console friends that mourn; recover any that are sick; bless the little children; cheer the aged, the lonely, and careworn; fulfil the hopes of youth; strengthen those who bear the burdens of maturer years, and bring us all at last to thy Heavenly home.

Accept these petitions, and the unspoken prayers of our hearts, which we offer one for another for the sake of our Lord Jesus Christ.

*W. Gray Elmslie*

**1106** O God of infinite mercy, who hast compassion on all men, hear the prayers of thy servants, who are unworthy to ask any petition for themselves, yet are in duty bound to pray for others.

Let thy mercy descend upon thy Church; preserve her in peace and truth, in unity and service; that her sacrifice of prayer and thanksgiving may ever ascend to thy throne.

In mercy remember the Queen; keep her perpetually in thy fear and favour; and grant that all who bear office under her may serve with a single eye to thy glory.

Remember our friends, all that have done us good; return all their kindness double unto their own bosom. Forgive our enemies; and help us to forgive, as we hope to be forgiven.

Comfort the afflicted; speak peace to troubled consciences; strengthen the weak; confirm the strong; instruct the ignorant; deliver the oppressed; relieve the needy; and bring us all by the waters of comfort and in the ways of righteousness to thy eternal kingdom; through Jesus Christ our Lord.

*After Jeremy Taylor*

# INDEX OF SUBJECTS

# INDEX OF SOURCES

# BIOGRAPHICAL INDEX

**Abelard, Peter** (1079–1144)
Theologian, moral philosopher, poet and logician; the most controversial teacher of his time.

**Acts of Peter**
A small book which was written between 180 and 190 by an unknown writer in Palestine or Syria. Like the apocryphal gospels it belongs to that vast quantity of Christian literature which abounded in the first centuries claiming connection with the apostles.

**Aelred of Rievaulx, St** (1110–1167)
An English writer, historian and outspoken Cistercian abbot.

**Afra of Augusta** (d.c.302)
A martyr of the Diocletian persecution. It seems she was arrested while still preparing to become a Christian and her prayer was heard as she burnt to death.

**Alcuin** (c.732–804)
Of noble Anglo-Saxon family, he became headmaster of the renowned York Cathedral School. Meeting the Emperor Charlemagne in 781, he was persuaded to be his educational counsellor. He is famous for revising the liturgy of the Frankish church.

**Alford, Henry** (1810–1871)
Dean of Canterbury, writer and the editor of the Greek Testament.

**King Alfred** (849–901)
Enlightened Saxon king of Wessex who saved England from conquest by the Danes and promoted Christianity and a great revival of learning.

**Ambrose of Milan, St** (339–397)
While still governor of the province of Milan, Ambrose was chosen by popular acclaim as their new bishop. He is thought to be the first

to introduce the singing of hymns into Christian worship. Beyond his hymn writing and scriptural studies he is famous for converting the great Augustine of Hippo.

**Anatolius**
Fifth-century Christian writer.

**Andrewes, Lancelot** (1555–1626)
Theologian and court preacher who energetically defended and advanced Anglican doctrines.

**Anselm, St** (1033–1109)
Archbishop of Canterbury, monk and philosopher, founder of Scholasticism.

**Appleton, George** (b.1902)
Writer, formerly Archbishop of Perth, Australia and Archbishop of Jerusalem, now retired.

**Aquinas, St Thomas** (1224–1274)
Eminent monk, theologian and philosopher whose major works form the classical systematisation of Latin theology.

**Arndt, Johann** (1555–1621)
Pastor and Lutheran theologian, author of mystical writings.

**Arnold, Thomas, Dr** (1795–1842)
Educator, influential Headmaster of Rugby Public School

**Ashe, Thomas** (1836–1889)
English poet and man of letters.

**Augustine of Hippo, St** (354–430)
Converted late in life, Augustine brought the education and cultural values of his time to his appointment as Bishop of Hippo. Philosopher, theologian and defender of orthodoxy against various heresies. His literary activity was the most copious of all Roman antiquity.

**Baillie, John** (1886–1960)
Sometime Professor of Divinity at the University of Edinburgh and principal of New College; author of *A Diary of Private Prayer*.

**Baldwin of Canterbury** (d.1190)
Archbishop of Canterbury. Scripture scholar and writer. Helped to lead a crusade to the Holy Land where he died.

**Bangor Antiphonary**
The Irish Abbey of Bangor was founded in 557 by St Comgall. It became a celebrated seat of learning. Its book of hymns, the Bangor Antiphonary, which dates from seventh century, is the oldest and most notable document of Celtic liturgy.

**Barclay, William** (1907–1978)
New Testament scholar, prolific writer of over 60 books and spiritual mentor to millions.

**Barnett, Leonard** (b.1919)
Methodist minister, religious writer, journalist and playwright.

**Barth, Karl** (1886–1968)
Influential theologian who initiated a radical change in Protestant thought.

**Basil the Great, St** (329–379)
One of the great Fathers of the early church, Basil defended the orthodox faith against Arianism. He became bishop and wrote many works on monasticism, theology and canon law.

**Baxter, Richard** (1615–1691)
Very productive writer and Puritan minister who profoundly influenced seventeenth-century English Protestantism.

**Becon, Thomas** (1511–1567)
English Protestant divine and religious writer.

**Bede, The Venerable** (673–735)
Considered one of the most learned Englishmen of the Middle Ages, Bede was offered to a monastery at the age of 7 and remained there until his death. Although most of his work consists of biblical exegesis, he is famous for his history of the Anglo-Saxon church.

**Beethoven, Ludwig van** (1770–1827)
One of the greatest composers in the history of Western music.

**Benedict of Nursia, St** (480–547)
Conditions of his time drove Benedict to seek a solitary life. Later

he founded the Benedictine monastery at Monte Cassino. He is acknowledged as the father of Western monasticism. His rule of life has been widely adopted.

**Benson, Edward White** (1829–1896)
Educator and Archbishop of Canterbury responsible for liturgical reform in the Anglican church.

**Benson, Richard Meux** (1824–1915)
Founder and first superior of the Society of St John the Evangelist, commonly called the Cowley Fathers.

**Bernard of Clairvaux, St** (860–1090)
Cistercian monk and mystic, founder abbot of the Abbey of Clairvaux; one of the most influential churchmen of his time.

**Bernardine of Siena, St** (1380–1444)
Franciscan friar who preached with great eloquence, called 'the people's preacher'.

**Bersier, Eugène** (1831–1889)
Writer and minister of a congregation of the Free Reformed Church in Paris; Eugène worked for Church unity and wrote on Church history and liturgy.

**Bisseker, Harry** (1878–1965)
Anglican priest, theologian, writer and Scripture scholar; headmaster of Leys School, Cambridge, for fifteen years.

**Blake, William** (1757–1827)
Poet, painter, engraver and visionary creator of an emotionally direct method of thought and artistic expression.

**Bloom, Anthony** (b.1914)
Former doctor of medicine and soldier, now the Russian Orthodox Metropolitan Archbishop for Western Europe.

**Boehme, Jacob** (1575–1624)
Shoemaker of Silesia who imparted his mystical experiences through writings, most of which were published posthumously.

**Boethius** (480–524)
Scholar, theologian, statesman and philosopher, transmitted classical texts to the Middle Ages.

**Bonar, Horatius** (1808–1889)
Scottish Presbyterian minister whose poems, hymns, etc., were popular during the nineteenth century.

**Bonaventure, St** (1217–1274)
Theologian, Minister General of the Franciscan Order and Cardinal.

**Bonhoeffer, Dietrich** (1906–1945)
Protestant theologian who supported ecumenism but died for his opposition to the Nazis.

**Book of Common Prayer, 1928**
Liturgical book of the churches of the Anglican Communion. First authorised in 1549, radically revised in 1552, minor revisions being made in 1559, 1604 and 1662. A proposed revision of 1928 was rejected by Parliament; however this revision was accepted and used by the Protestant Episcopal Church of the USA.

**Botting, Michael** (b.1925)
Rector of Aldford with Bruera, Chester; writer and joint Director of Training for the Diocese of Chester.

**Boyd Carpenter, W.** (1841–1918)
Bishop of Ripon, Royal chaplain, prolific writer and notable preacher.

**Boyd, Malcolm**
Episcopalian priest well known for his book of 1965 *Are you running with me, Jesus?*

**Bradwardine, Thomas** (1290–1349)
Chaplain to King Edward III, theologian and mathematician, called 'the profound doctor'; elected Archbishop of Canterbury, but died before being enthroned.

**Brent, Charles H.** (1862–1929)
American Bishop of the Protestant Episcopal Church in the Philippines.

**Bridge, William** (1600–1670)
Puritan divine, frequently preached before the Long Parliament; one of the writers of *Apologetical Narration*.

**Bridget of Sweden, St** (1303–1373)
Founder of the Brigittine Order, influential mystic of Middle Ages, patron saint of Sweden.

**Bright, William** (1824–1901)
Theologian, scholar and writer; Canon of Christ Church, Oxford.

**Brooks, Phillips** (1835–1893)
Bishop of Massachusetts who won an international reputation for his sermons; composer of 'O Little Town of Bethlehem'.

**Browne, Sir Thomas** (1605–1682)
Physician and author best known for his book of reflections, *Religio Medici*.

**Browning, Elizabeth Barrett** (1806–1861)
English poet whose reputation rests chiefly upon her love poems.

**Browning, Robert** (1812–1889)
One of the Victorian period's greatest poets, noted for his mastery of dramatic monologue and portraiture.

**Buchanan, Robert Williams** (1841–1901)
English poet and novelist who used the pseudonym Thomas Maitland.

**Buckley, Michael** (b.1924)
Catholic theologian, writer, liturgist and former director of Woodhall Pastoral Centre; well-known for his peace work in Northern Ireland.

**Bugenhagen, Johannes** (1485–1558)
A priest colleague of Martin Luther who organised the Lutheran Church in northern Germany.

**Bunsen, Christian K. J.** (1791–1860)
Liberal Prussian diplomat, scholar and theologian.

**Burke, Carl** (b.1917)
A Baptist minister and one-time chaplain to Eire County Gaol NY; author of the best-selling *God is for real, man* and subsequent books.

**Caedmon** (flourished 657–680)
The Venerable Bede tells how Caedmon, an illiterate herdsman, had a dream in which he was told to sing of 'the beginning of things'. By virtue of his hymn of creation, Caedmon has the distinction of being the first Old English Christian poet.

**Calvin, John** (1509–1564)
Theologian, ecclesiastical statesman and one of the most important figures of the Protestant Reformation.

**Camara, Helder** (b.1909)
Archbishop of Olinda and Recife in Brazil, champion of the poor and human rights.

**Campion, Thomas** (1567–1620)
Composer, poet, physician and one of the outstanding songwriters of sixteenth to seventeenth-century England.

**Campling, Christopher**
Educationalist, writer and former Chaplain of King's School, Ely; and then Lancing College. Latterly vicar of Pershore, Worcestershire.

**Canisius, Peter** (1521–1597)
Jesuit scholar who has been called 'the second Apostle of Germany'.

**Canton, William** (1845–1926)
English poet.

**Carmichael, Amy** (1868–1951)
Missionary in South India who founded the Dohnavur Fellowship.

**Carpenter, Mary** (1807–1887)
English philanthropist, social reformer and founder of free schools for poor children.

**Catherine of Siena, St** (1347–1380)
Tertiary sister of the Dominican Order, mystic, patron saint of Italy; Catherine drew a spiritual 'family' around her and worked tirelessly in public affairs.

**Celtic Prayers/Benediction**
The Celtic Church was founded in the second or third century, one

of the first peoples outside the Roman Empire to embrace Christianity. Highly ascetic in character, it contributed to the conversion of the Anglo-Saxons in the seventh century. Cut off for centuries from the rest of the church, they developed their own distinctive forms of life and worship.

**Cennick, John** (1718–1755)
An evangelist and writer who worked with the Wesleys in the West Country of England and in Ireland; later joined the Moravian Church.

**Chamberlain, Elsie** (Rev.)
Minister and broadcaster, producer in 1950s of BBC feature 'Lift up your hearts'.

**Channing, William** (1780–1842)
American Congregationalist, later Unitarian, minister, author and moralist, known as the 'apostle of Unitarianism'.

**Chapman, George** (1550–1634)
Poet and dramatist, translator of the classics.

**Chapman, Rex** (b.1938)
Writer and prayer-book compiler; former school chaplain, now canon of Aberdeen cathedral, currently the bishop's adviser for Education.

**Charlemagne, Emperor** (742–814)
King of the Franks, Charles the Great united by conquest nearly all the Christian lands of Western Europe. His reign was characterised by a unity unrivalled for centuries.

**King Charles I** (1600–1649)
King of Great Britain and Ireland whose authoritarian rule in a period of political and religious unrest led to the Civil War and his execution.

**Clement of Rome** (dates uncertain)
One of the earliest successors of Peter in the see of Rome. The letter he wrote to the Christian community at Corinth, about the year 96, contains the oldest Christian prayer known outside scripture.

**Clough, Arthur Hugh** (1819–1861)
Friend of Matthew Arnold; educationalist and popular poet whose

work reflects the religious doubt of mid-nineteenth-century England.

### Coleridge, Samuel Taylor (1772–1834)
A leading English Romantic poet and one of the most profound literary theorists of his day.

### Colonna, Lady Vittoria (1508–1572)
Marchioness of Pescara, and a supporter of Juan Valdez, one of the leaders of the Reformation in Italy.

### Colquhoun, Frank (b.1909)
Anglican Canon Emeritus of Norwich Cathedral and former editor of *The Churchman*, well known for his books of prayers.

### Columba of Iona, St (521–597)
With twelve disciples, the Abbot Columba erected a church and monastery on the island of Iona. This was their springboard for the conversion of Scotland to Christianity. He and his associates spread the gospel in Britain more than any other contemporary group. Many poems and some hymns are ascribed to Columba.

### Columbanus, St (543–615)
One of the greatest missionaries of the Celtic church, Columbanus was an abbot of great learning. He initiated a revival of monastic and lay spirituality. His calls for renewal brought him persecution from the powerful.

### Coptic Liturgy of St Basil/Coptic Liturgy of St Cyril
The ancient church of Egypt, later known as 'Coptic' has a simpler liturgy than other Eastern churches. It goes back to the traditions of early Egyptian Christianity and comes in several forms – the most used is that of Basil, the least used is under the name of Cyril.

### Cosin, John (1594–1672)
Bishop of Durham, a liturgist whose scholarly promotion of traditional worship and doctrine established him as one of the fathers of Anglo-Catholicism.

### Cotton, George Edward (1813–1866)
Educationalist and Anglican bishop of Calcutta.

### Coverdale, Miles (1488–1569)
Bishop of Exeter and supporter of the Reformation, who translated the first printed English Bible.

**Cowper, William** (1731–1800)
English poet, one of the most widely read of his time. His popularity sprang from the simple directness of his work.

**Cranmer, Thomas** (1489–1556)
Archbishop of Canterbury in the reign of Henry VIII who compiled the Book of Common Prayer, and died for his beliefs under Mary Tudor.

**Craven, Countess of, Elizabeth** (1750–1828)
Writer and dramatist.

**Cumings, Llewellyn** (b.1929)
Writer and contributor to compilations of prayers; rector of Denver in the Diocese of Ely, England.

**Cyprian of Carthage** (d.258)
He led the church of Carthage as bishop during the Decian persecution. He wrote to fulfil his pastoral leadership with particular charity and concern for those who fell away from the church.

**Dearmer, Percy** (1867–1936)
Theologian, prolific writer, sought-after lecturer and finally Canon of Westminster Abbey.

**de Castre, Richard** (died 1401)
A little known medieval English devotional writer, probably a contemporary of Richard Rolle.

**de Chantal, Jane** (1572–1641)
Married to a baron, but widowed with four children after eight happy years; Jane met St Francis de Sales and their friendship led to the foundation of a new order of religious sisters, under Francis' guidance. There were eighty houses of Visitation sisters at her death. Honoured in the Roman Catholic Church as a saint.

**de Foucauld, Charles-Eugène** (1858–1916)
French soldier and explorer who after conversion became a Trappist monk then later a hermit, first in Palestine, then in Algeria, where he worked among the Tuareg tribemen and was murdered.

**de la Colombiere, Claude** (1641–1682)
French Jesuit, court preacher to Mary, James II of England's

queen; spiritual director of Margaret Mary Alacoque. Falsely accused of complicity in the Titus Oates plot.

**De la Mare, Walter** (John) (1873–1956)
Novelist and eminent poet, who wrote of children, spirits and time. Decorated twice for his contribution to literature.

**Dickens, Charles** (1812–1870)
Regarded by many as the greatest English novelist. Noted for imaginative comic writing and social criticism.

**Didache** (or 'The Teaching of the Apostles')
The oldest surviving Christian church order, probably written in Egypt or Syria in the second century. Its sixteen chapters were quoted in the fourth century by Eusebius in his *Church History*.

**Dionysius, Telmaharensis** (d.845)
Patriarch of the Syrian Jacobite church and author of *The Chronicles*, an important source document on Eastern Christianity between 582 and 842. After some years as a monk, Dionysius was chosen as patriarch.

**Dodderidge, Philip**
Eighteenth-century British nonconformist minister and hymnist.

**Donne, John** (1572–1631)
Famous preacher at St Paul's, London, where he was Dean, a leading poet of the seventeenth century.

**Dostoevsky, Fydor** (1821–1881)
Russian novelist whose penetration into the recesses of the human heart has had a profound influence on the twentieth-century novel.

**Dowden, John** (1840–1910)
Scholar, writer and Bishop of Edinburgh.

**Drake, Sir Francis** (1543–1596)
English admiral who circumnavigated the world, the most renowned seaman of the Elizabethan age.

**Dudley-Smith, Timothy** (b.1926)
Archdeacon of Norwich, writer of popular religious books and modern hymns.

**Duncan, Mary L.** (1814–1840)
Hymnwriter.

**Edmund of Abingdon, St** (1175–1240)
Distinguished scholar and outspoken Archbishop of Canterbury. His virtue and literary works strongly influenced the English church.

**Eliot, T. S.** (1888–1965)
Poet, playwright and critic, a leader of the modernist movement in poetry, literary doyen of his age.

**Queen Elizabeth I** (1533–1603)
Daughter of Henry VIII and Queen of England in a period in which England began to assert itself as a major European power.

**Madame Elizabeth of France** (1764–1794)
Sister of King Louis XVI, praised for her charity work.

**Elliott, Charlotte** (1789–1871)
Hymnwriter who wrote many religious poems.

**Elmslie, W. Gray** (1848–1889)
Doctor of Divinity and in his time a well-known and popular Scottish nonconformist preacher.

**Ephrem Syrus** (306–373)
(Also known as Ephraem of Edessa or Ephrem the Syrian). Born at Nisibis (in modern Turkey), he moved to Edessa (Syria) and founded 'the Persian school', for Christians of Persian origin. He taught these until his death. A contemplative soul, Ephrem's prolific theological and poetic writings earned him the title of 'lyre of the Holy Spirit'.

**Erasmus, Desiderius** (1466–1536)
The greatest patristic and classical scholar of the Northern Humanist Renaissance.

**Euchologium Sinaiticum**
A very ancient collection of prayers from the Slavonic liturgy discovered at the monastery of St Catherine on Mount Sinai in 1880.

**Eusebius of Caesarea** (d.c.340)
Fourth-century bishop of Caesarea; exegete, and historian whose accounts of the first centuries of Christianity have been invaluable.

**Evely, Louis** (b.1910)
Belgian Catholic spiritual writer.

**Faber, Frederick** (1814–1863)
Originally a Calvinist, he became a follower of John Henry Newman; priest, noted hymnwriter and devotional writer.

**Falla, Terry**
Australian Baptist Minister; married with a family. Author and compiler of collections of prayers, presently working as a University chaplain.

**Fénelon, François** (1651–1715)
Archbishop, mystical theologian and man of letters whose liberal views exerted a lasting influence on French culture.

**Ferrar, St Vincent** (1350–1419)
Revivalist Dominican preacher of English/Spanish parentage who drew huge crowds and worked as a missionary to the Moslems.

**Fisher, John** (1469–1535)
Distinguished scholar, Bishop of Rochester, England, and martyr who resisted King Henry VIII by refusing to recognise the royal supremacy over the church.

**Fortunatus, Venantius** (540–640)
As a court poet Fortunatus won acclaim and after ordination wrote prose lives of saints, poems and hymns. Of his six poems on the cross, two, 'Pange lingua' and 'Vexilla Regis', are still in regular use. He ended his days as Bishop of Poitiers.

**Francis of Assisi, St** (1181/82–1226)
Founder of the Franciscan orders of men and women, leader of the religious movements of the early thirteenth-century reform of the church.

**Francis of Sales** (1567–1622)
Roman Catholic bishop of Geneva who was active in the struggle against Calvinism; founder of the order of Visitation Sisters. Honoured by the title of *Saint* by the Roman Catholic Church.

**Fulgentius of Ruspe, St** (467–533)
A monk who defended orthodoxy against the heresy of Arianism, Fulgentius then accepted the African bishopric of Ruspe; he was a fervent disciple of St Augustine, being like him a prolific writer.

**Fuller, Thomas** (1608–1661)
Scholar, preacher and one of the most witty and prolific authors of the seventeenth century.

**Furlong, Monica** (b.1930)
Convert to Christianity, former journalist, now an established novelist, poet and spiritual writer.

**Gaelic Prayers**
(See Celtic Prayers)

**Gallican Formularies**
For use in their worship, Christians of the first few centuries followed the classical literary form of collections of prose and verse, called 'patchwork'. In this way compilations or formulae of prayers, homilies and treatises were composed and used in the community's assembly. This material probably dates from ninth-century France.

**Gallican Sacramentary**
In the Gaul of the Franks, between the fifth and ninth centuries, the Latin liturgy was different from the rest of Europe. This collection of prayers was used in that liturgy. Charlemagne suppressed the Gallican Rite in favour of the Roman.

**Galsworthy, John** (1867–1933)
Novelist and playwright; winner of the Nobel Prize for Literature in 1932.

**Gasztold, Carmen Bernos de**
Teacher, who wrote the celebrated *Prayers from the Ark*, during the German occupation of France. After a breakdown she was taken in by the nuns of the Abbaye at Limon-par-Igny, where she still lives.

**Gelasian Sacramentary**
A number of books of prayers (or collects) for use in the liturgical assembly have survived and are usually associated with the reforming spirit of one person; this collection is linked with St Gelasius, pope from 492–496. However, the material is probably later, dating from around the seventh or eighth century.

**Gertrude the Great, St** (1256–1302)
In the thirteenth century a Cistercian convent at Helfta, in Thuringia, was a remarkable community and centre of mystical activity under the influence of two visionaries, Mechthild of Magdeburg and Gertrude the Great. (See Mechthild.)

**Gibran, Kahlil** (1883–1931)
Philosophical essayist, novelist, mystic, poet and artist originally of the Maronite Christian community of Lebanon, but settled in the USA.

**Gordon, General Charles George** (1833–1885)
British general who became a national hero for his exploits in China and his ill-fated defence of Khartoum.

**Goudge, Elizabeth** (1900–1984)
Writer of novels, children's stories, and plays, as well as religious biographies and anthologies.

**Gray, A. Herbert** (1868–1956)
Writer and Presbyterian minister on staff of the Student Christian Movement and involved in pastoral work in several London churches.

**Greet, Dr Kenneth** (b.1918)
Theologian, secretary general of the Methodist Conference and writer on religious and social questions.

**Gregorian Sacramentary**
A number of books, or parts of books, providing prayers for use in the liturgy have come down to us. They are usually associated with some great name, this one with Pope Gregory the Great (540–604) who reformed the church's liturgy.

**Gregory of Nazianzus, St** (d.390)
Ordained priest by his father, the Bishop of Nazianzus, he later resigned a bishopric because he could not face the practical daily problems. A sensitive and prolific writer, with Basil and Gregory of Nyssa, he bought Arianism to an end.

**Grey, Lady Jane** (1537–1554)
Manipulated by unscrupulous politicians and made Queen of England for nine days in 1553 at the age of sixteen. Her subsequent execution aroused universal sympathy.

**Grou, John Nicholas** (1731–1803)
Preacher and spiritual director. At the time of the French Revolution, John, a Jesuit, fled to England.

**Guardini, Romano** (1885–1968)
Italian-born German Roman Catholic theologian and writer.

**Gullick, Etta**
Former Anglican lecturer in Spirituality at St Stephen's, Oxford; compiler, with Michael Hollings, of a number of popular collections of prayers.

**Hall, Joseph** (1574–1656)
Bishop of Norwich, moral philosopher and successful satirist; pleaded for unity and tolerance in the literary campaign between Anglicans and Puritans.

**Hammarskjöld, Dag** (1905–1961)
Economist, statesman and second General Secretary of the United Nations; his leadership enhanced the prestige and effectiveness of the UN.

**Harries, Richard** (b.1936)
Dean of King's College, London; lecturer, broadcaster and writer, particularly on prayer and spirituality.

**Harvey, Christopher** (1597–1663)
Anglican clergyman, poet and friend of Isaak Walton.

**Harvey, F. W.** (b.1912)
Playwright and script-writer.

**Havergal, Frances R.** (1836–1879)
Hymnwriter and writer of religious verse.

**Heber, Reginald** (1783–1826)
Hymnwriter and poet; widely travelled Bishop of Calcutta.

**King Henry VI** (1421–1471)
King of England and a pious and studious recluse whose incapacity for government was the chief cause of the Wars of the Roses.

**Herbert, George** (1593–1633)
Devotional poet of the metaphysical school of John Donne, ended his days as a saintly country parson.

**Herrick, Robert** (1591–1674)
English cleric and poet, most original of the 'sons of Ben Jonson'. He held the living of Dean Prior, Devonshire.

**Hickes, George** (1642–1715)
Bishop, author of *Hickes Devotions* published in 1700.

**Hilary of Poitiers, St** (315–367)
Converted to Christianity through studying Holy Scripture; although married, the people of Poitiers chose him as their bishop. Profound thinker and brilliant theologian, Hilary's greatest treatise was *On the Trinity* from which his prayers spring.

**Hippolytus of Rome** (d.235)
A bishop and vigorous opponent of heresy. He opposed church authority but after his condemnation to hard labour in mines, he was reconciled to the church and died a martyr.

**Hollings, Michael** (b.1921)
English Roman Catholic parish priest, author and compiler of a number of books of prayer.

**Hopkins, Gerard Manley** (1844–1889)
Jesuit priest and one of the most individual of Victorian poets; his poetry combined perception, force of intellect and religious feelings.

**Horneck, Anthony**
Chaplain to King Charles II and author of *The Crucified Jesus*.

**Houselander, Caryll** (1901–1954)
English writer and poet, worked with child victims of World War II.

**How, W. Walsham** (1823–1897)
Bishop of Wakefield, remembered for his books of sermons and prayers.

**Howard, Philip** (d.1595)
Thirteenth Earl of Arundel; embraced Catholicism and as a result was imprisoned in the Tower of London where he died.

**Hoyland, John S.** (1887–1957)
Writer and lecturer at Woodbrooke College, Birmingham; decorated for public service in India.

**Hunt, Leigh** (1784–1859)
Essayist, critic, journalist, poet and editor of influential journals.

**Hunter, John** (1849–1917)
Congregational minister, speaker, hymn-writer and compiler of *Devotional Services*.

**Idle, Christopher** (b.1938)
Anglican Rector of the parish of Limehouse, London, part-time journalist and hymn-writer.

**Ignatius, of Loyola** (1491–1556)
Founder of the Society of Jesus (Jesuits) and one of the most influential figures in the Catholic Reformation of the sixteenth century. Honoured as a saint by the Roman Catholic Church.

**Irenaeus of Lyons, St** (d.202)
Born at Smyrna, and taught by Polycarp, a friend of John the Evangelist, he became Bishop of Lyons. He fought the spread of Gnosticism.

**Isidore of Seville, St** (c.560–636)
Theologian Archbishop of Seville, Spain, and last of the Western Labin Fathers of the church.

**Jacopone da Todi** (1230–1306)
Author and religious poet of mystical poems of great power and originality.

**James, Walter** (1828–1910)
Writer, rector of Fleet, Hampshire, England; later canon of Lincoln Cathedral.

**Jarrett, Bede** (1881–1934)
Dominican priest, historian, scholar, lecturer; at the time of his death was the prior of Blackfriars, Oxford.

**Jenks, Benjamin** (1647–1724)
Non-conformist clergyman, speaker and writer.

**Jerome, St** (347–420)
One of the most learned of the Fathers of the church, Jerome became a hermit for a short period, before becoming a priest and founding a monastery at Bethlehem. A prolific writer, he is best

remembered for his Latin translation of the Bible which profoundly influenced the early Middle Ages.

**John XXIII, Pope** (1881–1963)
Angelo Roncalli, one of the most popular popes of all time, inaugurating a new era for the Roman Catholic Church by convoking the Second Vatican Council.

**John Chrysostom, St** (347–407)
A renowned preacher (hence the name Chrysostom – 'golden-mouthed'), John was appointed Archbishop of Constantinople. His reforming zeal offended the rich and powerful. He was deposed and banished. Recognised as a biblical interpreter and Father of the church.

**John Paul II, Pope** (b.1920)
Karol Wojtyla, the first Polish pope, elected on 16th October 1978. In his own right a poet, dramatist, philosopher and theologian.

**Johnson, Samuel (Dr),** (1709–1784)
Poet, essayist, critic, journalist, Doctor Johnson is regarded as one of the outstanding figures of English eighteenth-century life.

**Johnson, Samuel (Rev.)** (1696–1772)
Nonconformist clergyman, speaker and writer; author of the influential *Father, in Thy Presence Kneeling*.

**Jowett, J. H.** (1864–1923)
Celebrated American preacher of his time, lecturer and writer; author of the popular *The Preacher, His Life and Work*.

**Julian of Norwich, Lady** (1342–died after 1416)
Celebrated mystic and recluse whose *Revelations of Divine Love* is considered one of the most remarkable documents of medieval religious experience.

**Julian of Toledo, St** (d.690)
Archbishop of Toledo, Spain, responsible for revising the Mozarabic liturgy.

**Kadel, William H.**
Presbyterian pastor, first president of Florida Presbyterian College, later president of Pittsburgh Theological Seminary.

**Keble, John** (1792–1866)
Anglican priest, theologian and poet who originated and helped lead the Oxford Movement.

**Kempis, Thomas à** (1379–1471)
Reputed author of *The Imitation of Christ*, written between 1390 and 1440. He was a representative of the 'devotio moderna'.

**Ken, Thomas** (1637–1711)
Anglican bishop, hymnwriter, royal chaplain to King Charles II. Deprived of his see in 1691 for opposing William of Orange.

**Kentigern, St** (d.612)
Also, in Scotland, known as St Mungo; abbot, missionary and traditionally known as the first bishop of Glasgow.

**Kierkegaard, Søren** (1813–1855)
Religious philosopher and critic of Rationalism, regarded as the founder of Existentialist philosophy.

**Kingsley, Charles** (1819–1875)
Anglican clergyman, teacher and writer whose novels influenced social developments in Victorian Britain.

**Knowles, Frederic Lawrence** (1869–1905)
American poet, whose copious works return repeatedly to the themes of Nature and death.

**Langton, Stephen** (1150–1228)
English cardinal whose appointment as Archbishop of Canterbury precipitated King John's quarrel with the pope.

**Larsson, Flora**
Married to a Swedish Salvation Army officer, Flora is British, and as a Salvationist has worked in many countries round the world.

**Laud, William** (1573–1645)
Archbishop of Canterbury, religious adviser to King Charles I, his policies towards religious dissidents contributed to the outbreak of the English Civil War.

**Law, William** (1686–1761)
Author of influential works on Christian ethics and mysticism.

**Lawrence, Brother** (1611–1691)
Originally known as Nicholas Herman of Loraine, who after being a footman and a soldier, joined the barefooted Carmelites as a lay brother. His letters, *The Practice of the Presence of God*, are spiritual classics.

**Lawrence, Sir Henry Montgomery** (1806–1857)
English general and political administrator; lived all his life in India where he was involved in the Sikh wars and mortally wounded at the siege of Lucknow.

**Leighton, Robert** (1611–1684)
Scottish Presbyterian minister and devotional writer, who successively accepted two Anglican bishoprics in an effort at reconciliation between the Presbyterian and Episcopal concepts of the church.

**Leonine Sacramentary**
This compilation of texts for the liturgy was associated with St Leo I, called 'the Great' and pope from 440–461. He was a staunch defender of orthodoxy and the unity of the church. He has left us 432 letters and 96 sermons.

**Lessius, Leonard** (1554–1623)
Belgian Jesuit theologian and lecturer.

**Lewis, C. S.** (1898–1963)
Scholar, novelist and author of many books on Christian apologetics, also famous for his classic stories for children.

**Liturgy of St James**
A eucharistic service based on the Antiochene Liturgy, said to be the most ancient Christian liturgy. Modified forms are used today by Maronite and Jacobite Christians.

**Liturgy of St John Chrysostom**
A shortened version of the Liturgy of St Basil associated with John Chrysostom, but more likely composed in the sixth century.

**Longfellow, Henry** (1807–1882)
The most popular of US poets in the nineteenth century. After his death a memorial was unveiled to him in Westminster Abbey.

**Luther, Martin** (1483–1546)
Biblical scholar, Augustinian monk, linguist and a prolific writer, who posted his 95 theses and precipitated the Protestant Reformation.

**Macarius of Egypt** (d.390)
A large number of writings are attributed to Macarius (also called 'the great' or 'the Elder') who lived for sixty years in the desert. However, much of what is attributed to him is now believed to be by a number of contemporary monks.

**Macdonald, George** (1824–1905)
Congregational minister, then a freelance preacher, novelist, poet and writer of Christian allegories, best remembered for his children's stories.

**Macnutt, Frederick B.** (1873–1949)
Canon of Canterbury Cathedral and chaplain to King George V (1931).

**Mansfield, Katherine** (1888–1923)
Pseudonym of Kathleen Mansfield Beauchamp, a New Zealand-born writer, considered a master of the short story.

**Margaret of Scotland, St** (1045–1093)
Queen, consort of Malcolm III (Canmore) and patroness of Scotland.

**Markham, Edwin** (1852–1940)
Lecturer and poet, best known for his social protest poems.

**Marmion, Columba** (1858–1923)
Irish Benedictine Abbot of Maredsous Abbey, Belgium, eloquent preacher with a special ministry to fellow priests.

**Marshall, Peter** (1902–1949)
Writer, preacher and chaplain to US Congress.

**Martineau, James** (1805–1900)
Unitarian theologian and philosopher whose writings emphasised the primacy of the individual conscience.

**Mary Queen of Scots** (1542–1587)
Mary Stuart, controversial Scottish queen, put to death by her cousin Queen Elizabeth I who considered her a threat.

**Matheson, George** (1842–1906)
Blind clergyman, lecturer and prolific writer.

**Mechthild of Magdeburg** (1210–1297)
Also known as Mechtilde of Helfta. A medieval mystic whose writings are ardent and romantic, the principal collection being *The Flowing Light of the Godhead.* (See St Gertrude the Great.)

**Melancthon, Philip** (1497–1560)
Humanist, theologian and reformer; author of the *Augsburg Confession* of the Lutheran Church.

**Merton, Thomas** (1915–1968)
US journalist who joined the Cistercian Order (Trappist monk) and became a celebrated counsellor and spiritual writer.

**Meyer, F. B.** (b.1927)
Lecturer in theology; American writer on history and religious subjects.

**Micklem, Caryl**
United Reformed Church minister and spiritual writer.

**Milner-White, Eric** (1884–1963)
Former Dean of York; lecturer in history and spiritual writer.

**Milton, John** (1608–1674)
One of the greatest poets of the English language, best known for his epic poem, *Paradise Lost.*

**Monod, Adolphe**
Rev. Monod became the first Protestant pastor of the French colony in Naples, where his prayer was written in 1826.

**Moody, Dwight L.** (1837–1899)
Prominent American evangelist who set the pattern for later evangelism in large cities.

**Moore, Thomas** (1779–1852)
English writer and poet.

**More, Gertrude** (1606–1633)
An English Benedictine nun who was under the spiritual guidance of Augustine Baker OSB.

**More, Thomas** (1477–1535)
Eminent scholar, humanist and statesman, chancellor of England, who died for refusing to accept Henry VIII's Act of Succession. Honoured with the title *saint* by the Roman Catholic Church.

**Mozarabic Sacramentary**
By the fifth century, the Christians of Spain had their own traditions of worship which reached a full flowering in the sixth and seventh centuries. This collection of texts for worship dates from this period, although the term 'Mozarab' for Christians under Muslim rule did not come into use until after the Muslim invasion of 711. (The Psalter is of eleventh-century origin.)

**Nairne, Alexander** (1863–1936)
Theologian, Scripture scholar and writer, finally Canon of St George's Chapel, Windsor.

**Nakatenus**
Seventeenth-century Jesuit priest and preacher, author of *Coeleste Palmetium.*

**Naylor, Basil** (b.1911)
Canon Charles B. Naylor, Anglican chancellor and canon of Liverpool Cathedral.

**Neri, Philip** (1515–1595)
Priest-reformer in a demoralised time (called the apostle of the city of Rome) and unconventional founder of the Congregation of the Oratory; honoured for his sanctity.

**Newman, John Henry** (1801–1890)
Eminent churchman and man of letters, led the Oxford Movement in the Church of England, later became a cardinal of the Roman Catholic Church.

**Nicholas of Flue** (1417–1487)
Married man and father of ten children who at fifty became a hermit and a spiritual counsellor.

**Niebuhr, Reinhold** (1892–1971)
One of most important American theologians of the twentieth century, who had extensive influence on political thought.

**Nimitz, Chester W.** (1885–1966)
After the Pearl Harbor attack, Admiral Nimitz was appointed Commander-in-Chief of the US Pacific Fleet: the Japanese capitulation was signed aboard his flagship, the *USS Missouri*.

**Nouwen, Henri** (b.1932)
Roman Catholic theologian, lecturer and writer in Pastoral Theology, now a Trappist monk of the Abbey of Genesee, New York.

**Oldham, John H.** (1653–1683)
Poet and educator, pioneer of the imitation of classical satire in English.

**Olier, Jean-Jacques** (1608–1657)
Founder of the Sulpicians, a group of secular priests dedicated to training candidates for the Roman Catholic priesthood.

**Oosterhuis, Huub** (b. 1933)
Ordained a Jesuit priest, his pastoral work has revolved around the student community of Amsterdam, where he participated in the renewal of the Dutch Liturgy.

**Orchard, William E.** (1877–1955)
A Presbyterian minister, preacher and lecturer who strove for better ecumenical relations between the churches; became a Roman Catholic priest.

**Origen** (185–254)
Brilliant head of the Alexandrian school, and prolific writer who is acknowledged as the greatest theologian the Greek church has produced. His father died a martyr and he himself died as a result of the torture endured during the Decian persecution.

**Osgood, Samuel** (1808–1885)
American portrait painter, painted famous figures like Edgar Allan Poe.

**Oxenden, Ashton** (1808–1892)
Anglican Bishop of Montreal, Canada, prolific writer of short popular religious works.

**Oxenham, John** (1852–1941)
Pseudonym of William Dunkerley, businessman turned novelist and poet, co-edited *The Idler* with Jerome K. Jerome.

**Paget, Francis** (1851–1911)
Anglican bishop of Oxford, theologian and writer.

**Parker, Mathew** (1504–1575)
Scholar, Archbishop of Canterbury and moderate reformer under Queen Elizabeth I.

**Parker, Theodore** (1810–1860)
American Unitarian theologian, pastor and social reformer active in the anti-slavery movement.

**Pascal, Blaise** (1623–1662)
Mathematician, physicist, religious philosopher and writer; he defended Jansenism and is famous for his *Pensées*.

**Paton, Alan** (b.1903)
One of South Africa's foremost writers who through circumstances became a reluctant but eminent politician.

**Patrick, St** (385–461)
Missionary-bishop credited with bringing Christianity to Ireland and probably in part responsible for the christianization of the Picts and Anglo-Saxons.

**Paulinus of Nola, St** (352–431)
Baptised late in life he gave away all his money and lived an austere life. He was consecrated Bishop of Nola. Paulinus left many important poetic works.

**Polycarp of Smyrna** (70–156)
Bishop of Smyrna and disciple of the Apostle John, who was burnt to death at the age of 86. His martyrdom is reliably described in a letter to the Christians at Philomelium. In his final prayer he remembers his priestly functions.

**Pope, Alexander** (1688–1744)
English satirist and poet of outstanding ability.

**Prewer, Bruce** (b.1931)
Minister of the Uniting Church in Australia at Pilgrim Church, central Adelaide. Bruce, married with a family, has a special interest in social justice issues.

**Pseudo-Athanasius**
St Athanasius (c.295–c.373) was a staunch opponent of Arianism; some ancient writings, in his style and ascribed to him, are not from his pen. For want of a better title these are attributed to 'Pseudo-Athanasius'.

**Pusey, Edward Bouverie** (1800–1882)
Anglican theologian, scholar and a leader of the Oxford Movement, helped found the first Anglican sisterhood.

**Quoist, Michel** (b.1921)
Sociologist and Roman Catholic parish priest, his popular book *Prayer of Life*, published in 1963, was responsible for a new realism in prayer.

**Rabbula of Edessa** (d.436)
Bishop of Edessa, Rabbula was a great opponent of Nestorianism. He is said to be the author of a Syriac translation of the New Testament.

**Rahner, Hugo**
Brother of Karl Rahner, and like him a Jesuit scholar and priest.

**Rahner, Karl** (1904–1984)
Renowned German Roman Catholic theologian, lecturer and writer.

**Raleigh, Sir Walter** (1554–1618)
English adventurer, favourite of Queen Elizabeth I and an early coloniser of America.

**Rauschenbusch, Walter** (1861–1918)
Baptist clergyman and theology professor who led the Social Gospel movement in the United States.

**Richard of Chichester, St** (1198–1253)
Bishop of Chichester and friend of St Edmund of Canterbury. His great love and concern for the poor won him the title of the 'model diocesan bishop'.

**Ridley, Nicholas** (1503–1555)
Protestant reformer and Bishop of London, considered one of the finest academics of the English Reformation; died for his beliefs under Queen Mary Tudor.

**Riley, James Whitcomb** (1849–1916)
American poet famous for nostalgic dialect verse; often called 'the poet of the common people'.

**Ritter, Karl Bernhard** (1890–1976)
German Reform minister, theologian and compiler of collections of prayers.

**King Robert I** (865–923)
Briefly King of the Franks, his decisive victory at Chartres in 911 halted the advances of the Normans.

**Rolle, Richard** (1300–1349)
The hermit of Hampole and early English mystic, author of several mystical writings, probably died a victim of the Black Death.

**Rossetti, Christina** (1830–1894)
Youngest member of an illustrious family, Christina was a devout Anglican who wrote sacred poetry of a high standard.

**Runcie, Robert** (b.1921)
Archbishop of Canterbury, enthroned 1980; former Guardsman during the Second World War, University chaplain and later principal of Cuddesdon College.

**Sarum Breviary/Missal/Primer**
These books were compiled for the use of the community that centred round the English medieval cathedral town of Salisbury ('Sarum' is derived from the Latin for Salisbury). The first bishop, Norman St Osmund (1078) compiled a breviary, missal and primer, but these prayers are probably later additions.

**Schuetz, Roger** (b.1915)
Protestant Prior of Taizé (France), and ecumenical community, especially working with young people, his life totally dedicated to unity, of the church and mankind.

**Seager, Ralph W.** (b.1911)
American poet and lecturer in English Studies.

**Serapion of Thmuis** (d. after 339)
At the end of the last century an important collection of prayers was found on Mount Athos. These bear the name of Serapion, abbot of the monastery of Thmuis, Egypt, from the year 339.

**Severus of Thrace** (d.304)
A priest of Heradea in Thrace (Greece). He was martyred in c.304.

**Shaftesbury, seventh Earl of** (1801–1885)
Anthony Ashley Cooper, one of most effective social reformers of nineteenth-century England, also a leader of the evangelical movement within the Church of England.

**Shakespeare, William** (1564–1616)
Poet and dramatist, considered the greatest writer of all time.

**Shaw, Gilbert**
Writer of spiritual books, *The Face of Love* and others.

**Sidney, Sir Philip** (1554–1586)
Military leader, writer, idealistic politician and considered the ideal gentleman of his age.

**Silk, David** (b.1936)
Archdeacon of Leicester, pastoral minister and liturgist.

**Sill, Edward Rowland** (1841–1887)
American poet.

**Simeon, the New Theologian** (949–1022)
After many years as the superior of a monastery, Simeon was deposed for rigorism. Recalled after a year's exile he preferred to found a small monastery near Constantinople where he wrote many short treatises. His title was for his particular interpretation of mysticism.

**Smith, Sir George Adam** (1856–1942)
Scottish Free Church preacher and Semitic scholar who helped make higher criticism of the Old Testament acceptable.

**Snowden, Rita**
Prolific writer of inspirational books; deaconess and first elected woman Vice-President of Methodist Church, New Zealand.

**Solzhenitsyn, Alexander** (b.1918)
Soviet novelist and Nobel Prize winner, who exposed the Soviet labour camp system and was exiled in 1974.

**Southey, Robert** (1774–1843)
Poet and prose writer, associated with the leaders of the early Romantic movement, Coleridge and Wordsworth.

**Spencer, George** (1799–1864)
Youngest son of 2nd Earl Spencer, ordained to Anglican ministry, later became a Roman Catholic; better known as Father Ignatius Spencer, he was the companion of the famous Passionist preacher, Dominic Barberi and great, great uncle of Diana, Princess of Wales.

**Spenser, Edmund** (1552–1599)
Poet, best remembered for his long allegorical poem, *The Faerie Queene.*

**Spurgeon, Charles Haddon** (1834–1892)
Gifted and popular Baptist minister and preacher who weekly drew thousands to the Metropolitan Tabernacle, London; his collected sermons fill 50 volumes.

**Stevenson, Robert Louis** (1850–1894)
Poet, literary critic, author of travel books, but best remembered for his romantic adventure stories.

**Stitch, Wilhelmina**
Writer of popular religious verse in 1930s.

**Stobart, Hugh** (1883–1952)
A Lieutant Colonel who obtained a DSO in First World War; later a business man involved in food production companies.

**Stott, John R. W.** (b.1921)
Scholar, theologian, writer, honorary chaplain to Queen Elizabeth II and rector emeritus of All Souls church, Langham Place, London.

**Tallis, Thomas** (1510–1585)
Considered the most important English composer of sacred music before William Byrd.

**Tauler, Johann** (1300–1361)
Dominican preacher who with Meister Eckhart and Heinrich Suso, was one of the chief Rhineland mystics.

**Taylor, Jeremy** (1613–1667)
Theologian and writer who held post of chaplain to Archbishop Laud and later King Charles I. After the Restoration he was appointed Bishop of Down and Connor.

**Teilhard de Chardin, Pierre** (1881–1955)
Jesuit priest, philosopher and palaeontologist, famous for his theory that man is presently evolving to a final spiritual unity.

**Temple, Frederick** (1821–1902)
Archbishop of Canterbury and educational reformer.

**Temple, William** (1881–1944)
Archbishop of Canterbury, leader in the ecumenical movement and in educational and labour reforms.

**Teresa of Avila, St** (1515–1582)
Mystic and spiritual writer who was influential in reforming the Carmelite Order to its original austerity.

**Mother Teresa of Calcutta** (b.1910)
Founder of the Order of the Missionaries of Charity dedicated to serving the poor and abandoned, particularly in India. Awarded the Nobel Peace Prize in 1979.

**Tertullian** (155–220)
A Roman jurist who was converted to Christianity, Tertullian emerged as leader of the African church, primarily as a theologian and teacher. He left the orthodox church to found his own rigorous sect.

**Traherne, Thomas** (1637–1674)
Writer and last of the mystical poets of the Anglican clergy with a temperament inclined to Celtic mysticism.

**Trench, Richard Chenevix** (1807–1886)
Scholar, writer; Archbishop of Dublin, opposed disestablishment of the church.

**Underhill, Evelyn** (1875–1941)
Mystical writer and sought-after religious counsellor who helped establish mystical theology as a respectable discipline.

**van Dyke, Henry** (1852–1933)
Presbyterian minister, poet, short-story writer and essayist who was popular in the early twentieth century.

**van Zeller, Hubert** (1905–1983)
Benedictine priest, writer and retreat-giver.

**Vanier, Jean** (b.1928)
Son of a former Governor General of Canada, philosophy lecturer, now member of a French lay institute; famous for the foundation of L'Arche, an association of small groups that care for the handicapped.

**Vaughan, Charles J.** (1816–1897)
Writer, preacher and Dean of Llandaff, often simply known as 'Dean Vaughan'.

**Vaughan, Henry** (1621–1695)
One of the most original poets of his day and a mystic of remarkable intuition.

**Verlaine, Paul** (1844–1896)
Among the most gifted of the French lyric poets of nineteenth century.

**Vives, Johannes Ludovicus** (1492–1540)
Spanish scholar at the English court, humanist and student of Erasmus.

**Wallace, Jamie** (b.1929)
A Baptist minister and honorary pastor of Earls Barton Baptist Church, Northamptonshire.

**Warren, Alan** (b.1932)
Anglican canon and Provost of Leicester.

**Weatherhead, Leslie D.** (1893–1976)
Theologian, eminent preacher and pastor at City Temple, London; president of methodist conference 1955–1956; prolific writer of a wide range of Christian books.

**Wells, H. G.** (1866–1946)
Journalist, novelist and popular historian who had a powerful influence on early twentieth-century thought.

**Wesley, John** (1703–1791)
Anglican clergyman, energetic preacher and evangelist, who, with his brother Charles, founded the Methodist movement.

**Westcott, Brooke Foss** (1825–1901)
Bishop of Durham and theological scholar.

**William of Saint Thierry** (1085–1148)
Theologian, author of mystical writings and adversary of early medieval rationalistic philosophy.

**Williams, Dick** (b.1931)
Writer and compiler of collections of prayers; rector of Croft with Southworth in the Diocese of Liverpool. Diocesan newspaper editor.

**Williams, Rowland** (1818–1870)
Anglican divine, preacher and lecturer.

**Williams, Susan** (b.1932)
Teacher, photographer and poet, married to Dick Williams with three children.

**Wilson, Thomas** (1663–1755)
Bishop of Sudia and Manx; published first book in Manx, helped translate the New Testament into Manx.

**Winstone, Harold** (b.1917)
Theologian and eminent Roman Catholic liturgist, now retired; founder and former director of St Thomas More Centre for Pastoral Liturgy, London.

**Woolman, John** (1720–1772)
American Quaker leader and preacher who worked for the abolition of slavery.

**Wordsworth, Christopher** (1807–1885)
High Church Anglican, headmaster of Harrow School, later Bishop of Lincoln; best remembered for his hymns.

**Xavier, Francis** (1506–1552)
Greatest Roman Catholic missionary of modern times, as a Jesuit he brought Christianity to India, the Malay Archipelago and Japan. Honoured as a saint by the Roman Catholic Church.

For the following authors only their dates are available:

Charles J. Besson (1816–1861)
Herman Bezzel (1861–1917)
Walter Russell Bowie (1882–1943)
Henry W. Foote (1838–1889)
Abbot Grimald (ninth century)
Maria Hare (1798–1870)

S. C. Lowry (1855–1932)
Robert Nelson (1665–1715)
William Perin (d.1557)
John Suter (1890–1962)
Laurence R. Tuttiett (1825–1897)

Insufficient information was available to provide any biographical note for the following authors:
Lewis Bayley, Joost de Blank, G. C. Binyon, B. C. Boulter, George Dawson, William Hampson, Margaret H. Hancock, John Heuss, M. E. Procter, Melchior Ritter, W. E. Scudamore, J. Barrie Shepherd, Malcolm Spencer, Roger Tomes, Heinrich Tschokke.

# CHRONOLOGICAL LISTING OF AUTHORS

## FIRST MILLENNNIUM
(date of death only given)

Polycarp of Smyrna (156)
Clement of Rome
Irenaeus of Lyons (202)
Tertullian (220)
St Hippolytus of Rome (235)
Origen (254)
Cyprian of Carthage (258)
Afra of Augusta (302)
Severus of Thrace (304)
Serapion of Thmuis (after 339)
Eusebius of Caesarea (c.340)
St Hilary of Poitiers (367)
Ephrem Syrus (373)
St Athanasius (373)
St Basil the Great (379)
St Gregory of Nazianzus (390)
Macarius of Egypt (390)
St Ambrose of Milan (397)
St John Chrysostom (407)
St Jerome (420)
St Augustine of Hippo (430)
St Paulinus of Nola (431)
Rabbula of Edessa (436)
St Patrick (461)
Anatolius (5th cent)
Boethius (524)
St Fulgentius of Ruspe (533)
St Benedict of Nursia (547)
St Columba of Iona (597)
St Kentigern (612)

St Columbanus (615)
St Isidore (636)
Venantius Fortunatus (640)
Caedmon (680)
St Julian of Toledo (690)
The Venerable Bede (735)
Alcuin (804)
Emperor Charlemagne (814)
Dionysius Telmaharensis (845)
King Alfred (901)
King Robert I of France (923)
Simeon, the New Theologian
   (1022)

## SECOND MILLENNIUM

St Bernard of Clairvaux (1090)
St Margaret of Scotland (1093)
St Anselm (1109)
Peter Abelard (1144)
William of Saint-Thierry (1148)
St Aelred of Rievaulx (1167)
Baldwin of Canterbury (1190)
St Francis of Assisi (1226)
Stephen Langton (1228)
St Edmund of Abingdon (1240)
St Richard of Chichester (1253)
St Thomas Aquinas (1274)
St Bonaventure (1274)
Mechthild of Magdeburg (1297)
St Gertrude the Great (1302)

Jacopone Da Todi (1306)
Richard Rolle (1349)
Thomas Bradwardine (1349)
Johann Tauler (1361)
St Bridget of Sweden (1373)
St Catherine of Siena (1380)
Richard de Castre (1401)
Julian of Norwich (1416)
St Vincent Ferrar (1419)
St Bernardine of Siena (1444)
King Henry VI (1471)
Thomas à Kempis (1471)
Nicholas of Flue (1487)
Thomas More (1535)
John Fisher (1535)
Desiderius Erasmus (1536)
Johannes Ludovicus Vives
  (1540)
Martin Luther (1546)
Francis Xavier (1552)
Lady Jane Grey (1554)
Nicholas Ridley (1555)
Thomas Cranmer (1556)
Ignatius of Loyola (1556)
William Perin (1557)
Johannes Bugenhagen (1558)
Michael Coelius (1559)
Philip Melanchthon (1560)
John Calvin (1564)
Thomas Becon (1567)
Miles Coverdale (1569)
Vittoria Colonna (1572)
Mathew Parker (1575)
St Teresa of Avila (1582)
Thomas Tallis (1585)
Sir Philip Sidney (1586)
Mary Queen of Scots (1587)
Philip Howard (1595)
Philip Neri (1595)
Sir Francis Drake (1596)
Peter Canisius (1597)
Edmund Spenser (1599)
Queen Elizabeth I (1603)
William Shakespeare (1616)

Sir Walter Raleigh (1618)
Thomas Campion (1620)
Johann Arndt (1621)
Francis of Sales (1622)
Leonard Lessius (1623)
Jacob Boehme (1624)
Lancelot Andrewes (1626)
Lewis Bayley (1631)
John Donne (1631)
Naketenus (17th century)
George Herbert (1633)
Gertrude More (1633)
George Chapman (1634)
Jane de Chantal (1641)
William Laud (1645)
King Charles I (1649)
Joseph Hall (1656)
Jean-Jacques Olier (1657)
Thomas Fuller (1661)
Blaise Pascal (1662)
Christopher Harvey (1663)
Jeremy Taylor (1667)
William Bridge (1670)
John Cosin (1672)
Robert Herrick (1674)
John Milton (1674)
Thomas Traherne (1674)
Claude de la Colombiere (1682)
Horneck, Anthony (17th cent.)
Sir Thomas Browne (1682)
John H. Oldham (1683)
Robert Leighton (1684)
Richard Baxter (1691)
Brother Lawrence (1691)
Henry Vaughan (1695)
Thomas Ken (1711)
François Fénelon (1715)
George Hickes (1715)
Robert Nelson (1715)
Benjamin Jenks (1724)
Alexander Pope (1744)
John Cennick (1755)
Thomas Wilson (1755)
William Law (1761)

Rev. Samuel Johnson (1772)
John Woolman (1772)
Dr Samuel Johnson (1784)
John Wesley (1791)
Madame Elizabeth of France
   (1794)
William Cowper (1800)
John Nicholas Grov (1803)
Reginald Heber (1826)
Adolphe Monod (19th cent)
Ludwig van Beethoven
   (1827)
William Blake (1827)
Elizabeth, Countess of Craven
   (1828)
Samuel Taylor Coleridge
   (1834)
Mary L. Duncan (1840)
W. E. Channing (1842)
Dr Thomas Arnold (1842)
Robert Southey (1843)
Heinrich Tschokke (1848)
Thomas Moore (1852)
Søren Kierkegaard (1855)
Sir Henry Lawrence (1857)
Leigh Hunt (1859)
Christian C. J. Bunsen
   (1860)
Theodore Parker (1860)
Charles J. B. Besson (1861)
Elizabeth Barrett Browning
   (1861)
Arthur Hugh Clough (1861)
Frederick Faber (1863)
George Spencer (1864)
George Edward Cotton
   (1866)
John Keble (1866)
Charles Dickens (1870)
Maria Hare (1870)
Rowland Williams (1870)
Henry Alford (1871)
Charlotte Elliott (1871)
Charles Kingsley (1875)

George Dawson (1876)
Frances R. Havergal (1879)
Fydor Dostoevsky (1881)
Henry Longfellow (1882)
Edward Bouverie Pusey
   (1882)
Victor Hugo (1885)
General Charles George
   Gordon (1885)
Samuel Osgood (1885)
Seventh Earl of Shaftesbury
   (1885)
Christopher Wordsworth
   (1885)
Richard Chenevix Trench
   (1886)
Mary Carpenter (1887)
Edward Rowland Sill (1887)
Thomas Ashe (1889)
Eugène Bersier (1889)
Horatius Bonar (1889)
Robert Browning (1889)
W. Gray Elmslie (1889)
Henry Wilder Foote (1889)
Gerard Manley Hopkins
   (1889)
John Henry Newman (1890)
Ashton Oxenden (1892)
Charles H. Spurgeon (1892)
Phillips Brooks (1893)
Christina Rossetti (1894)
Robert Louis Stevenson
   (1894)
Edward White Benson (1896)
Paul Verlaine (1896)
W. Walsham How (1897)
Laurence R. Tuttiett (1897)
Charles J. Vaughan (1897)
Dwight L. Moody (1899)
James Martineau (1900)
William Bright (1901)
Brooke Foss Westcott (1901)

# TWENTIETH CENTURY

(date shown is date of birth)

Frederick Temple (1821)
Richard Meux Benson (1824)
George MacDonald (1824)
Walter James (1828)
John Dowden (1840)
W. Boyd Carpenter (1841)
Robert Williams Buchanan (1841)
Edward Rowland Sill (1841)
George Matheson (1842)
William Canton (1845)
James Whitcomb Riley (1849)
John Hunter (1849)
Francis Paget (1851)
Edwin Markham (1852)
Henry Van Dyke (1852)
John Oxenham (1852)
S. C. Lowry (1855)
Sir George Adam Smith (1856)
Sir Henry Lawrence (1857)
Charles de Foucauld (1858)
Columba Marmion (1858)
Hermann Bezzel (1861)
Walter Rauschenbusch (1861)
Charles H. Brent (1862)
Alexander Nairne (1863)
J. H. Jowett (1864)
H. G. Wells (1866)
Percy Dearmer (1867)
John Galsworthy (1867)
Amy Carmichael (1868)
A. Herbert Gray (1868)
Frederic Lawrence Knowles (1869)
Walter de la Mare (1873)
Frederick B. Macnutt (1873)
Evelyn Underhill (1875)
William E. Orchard (1877)
Harry Bisseker (1878)

Bede Jarrett (1881)
Pierre Teilhard de Chardin (1881)
William Temple (1881)
Pope John XXIII (1881)
Walter Russell Bowie (1882)
Hugh Stobart (1883)
Kahlil Gibran (1883)
Eric Milner-White (1884)
Romano Guardini (1885)
Chester W. Nimitz (1885)
Karl Barth (1886)
John Baillie (1886)
John S. Hoyland (1887)
T. S. Eliot (1888)
Katherine Mansfield (1888)
Karl Bernard Ritter (1890)
John W. Suter (1890)
Reinhold Niebuhr (1892)
Leslie D. Weatherhead (1893)
C. S. Lewis (1898)
Elizabeth Goudge (1900)
Caryll Houselander (1901)
George Appleton (1902)
Peter Marshall (1902)
Alan Paton (1903)
Karl Rahner (1904)
Dag Hammarskjöld (1905)
Hubert Van Zeller (1905)
Dietrich Bonhoeffer (1906)
William Barclay (1907)
Helder Camara (1909)
Frank Colquhoun (1909)
Louis Evely (1910)
Mother Teresa of Calcutta (1910)
Basil Naylor (1911)
Ralph W. Seager (1911)
F. W. Harvey (1912)
Trevor Huddleston (1913)
Anthony Bloom (1914)
Thomas Merton (1915)
Roger Schuetz (1915)
Carl Burke (1917)

Harold Winstone (1917)
Kenneth Greet (1918)
Alexander Solzhenitsyn (1918)
Leonard Barnett (1919).
Pope John Paul II (1920)
Michael Hollings (1921)
Michel Quoist (1921)
Robert Runcie (1921)
John R. W. Stott (1921)
Michael Botting (1925)
Michael Buckley (1924)
Timothy Dudley-Smith
   (1926)
F. B. Meyer (1927)

Jean Vanier (1928)
Jamie Wallace (1929)
Llewellyn Cumings (1929)
Monica Furlong (1930)
Bruce Prewer (1931)
Dick Williams (1931)
Susan Williams (1932)
Alan Warren (1932)
Henri Nouwen (1932)
Huub Oosterhuis (1933)
Richard Harries (1936)
David Silk (1936)
Christopher Idle (1938)
Rex Chapman (1938)

Some modern writers' dates of birth were not available and
therefore they are omitted from the above.